Praise for Just Be

Just Be is more than a memoir, it is manifested love through the thick fog of grief. Author Lindsay Gibson takes you on a journey through her life that leaves you inspired to reflect upon your own passions and pains, nightmares and memories. This is a memoir about learning to love yourself, and others, inspired by and despite the ups and downs, twists and turns of grief and life. Lindsay's raw and real style of writing grabs the reader by the hand, opens their heart, and breaks them wide open. If you are wondering if you should read this memoir of hope, love and redemption? As her husband, Jason Gibson often says, "Yes, love. Yes."

—Ginny Limer, founder of Scared SIdless, author of *When You Grieve from A to Z*

At times gut-wrenching, Lindsay takes us on an inspiring journey and an emotional rollercoaster of suspense, heartbreak and surrender. A raw and very real depiction of the power of faith, unending love, and the mother-child connection. You will walk away enlightened and encouraged, I know I did."

—Donna Palomba, Founder of Jane Doe No More & Author of *Jane Doe No More: My 15-Year Fight To Reclaim My Identity--A True Story Of Survival, Hope, And Redemption*

Lindsay Gibson's life has been a terribly dark but ultimately triumphant study of the meaning of human suffering. I have worked with thousands of women who have endured the life-threatening torment of a pregnancy plagued by hyperemesis gravidarum, and have witnessed first-hand its devastating effects upon their bodies and spirits. But like other women, there were also other traumas inflicted on Lindsay. She lost her childhood to rape; lost a child in a stillbirth; and lost her faith, for a time. Her haunting and fascinating account of the dreams and premonitions that brought her closer to God during her ordeals is a must-read for those who seek to view their own challenges in a greater perspective."

—Lyle Brooks, Volunteer Coordinator of The Hyperemesis Research and Education Foundation

INCREDIBLE......Lindsay Gibson's memoir, *Just Be*, is an incredible story of overcoming tragedy and finding hope again. Above all it is a story of unconditional love between Lindsay and her husband Jason who walks beside her every step of the way. In this heartfelt memoir, Lindsay describes the pain she endured as a result of her rape and how she was able to finally set herself free from memories that held her captive for so many years. Lindsay's description of her son's Joseph stillbirth and her resulting anguish will resonate with anyone who has suffered a pregnancy loss of their own. The intensity of Lindsay's emotions conveys the deep pain she experienced as a result of her postpartum depression and PTSD. I could just feel each emotion with every turn of the page. Just Be is an inspiring and powerful read for anyone who has suffered tremendous loss in their life and wondered how they would ever live again. Through her amazing book, Lindsay shows all of us that with unwavering bravery and loving support, you can conquer any tragedy and find yourself again.

—Sharon Ehlers, Award Winning Author of *Grief Diaries*

Lindsay Gibson's memoir *Just Be* shows the world what having real strength, courage and a heart full of love can do. What Lindsay has successfully done with her raw honesty and commitment to share her story is give others hope that there is more to their story than despair. My emotions ran high from the first page to the last while reading her and her families incredible journey. I highly recommend this book to not only those who have suffered the loss of a child but for anyone who wants to learn about living and growing through the darkness all the while keeping faith and hope.

—Lindsay Lipton Gerszt, Producer/Executive Producer of *When The Bough Breaks-a documentary about postpartum depression*

Each of us experiences dark nights of the soul. Situations and circumstances present that seem to overwhelm all sense of being. Yet in these darkest hours, there is an opportunity to learn and evolve into our authentic selves. So is the journey of Author Lindsay Gibson in her lovely memoir "Just Be." In it, she shares her story of loss, love and letting go to find a place of healing grace. Her memoir is a lovely reminder that light always follows the dark.

–Lillie Leonardi, Author *In The Shadow Of A Badge* and *The White Light of Grace just Be*

Copyright © 2018 Lindsay Gibson

All rights reserved. Some names and identifying details have been changed to protect the privacy of individuals. No part of this book may be reproduced, or transmitted in any form by any means, without permission in writing from the copyright holder, except for brief quotations in a review or on social media.

The author has tried to recreate events, locales and conversations from her memories of them. In order to maintain their anonymity in some instances some names of individuals and places may have been changed to include some identifying characteristics and details such as physical properties, occupations and places of residence.

This book is not intended as a substitute for the medical advice of physicians. The reader should regularly consult a physician in matters relating to his/her health and particularly with respect to any symptoms that may require diagnosis or medical attention.

Just Be is published by Kat Biggie Press.
www.katbiggiepress.com

Cover design by Michelle Fairbanks, Fresh Design
Author photograph by Melissa Mirabilio

ISBN-13: 9780986196935
Library of Congress Control Number: 2018932757

10 9 8 7 6 5 4 3 2 1

Soar High My Son -
Joseph Michael Gibson

Dedication

To my love, my sweet and gentle Jason...
Our love has no beginning and no end – it is infinite in time. It is limitless. It always has been and always will be.
When we pass into eternity, our love will carry us far beyond this lifetime – for when I look at you, forever is all I see.
I couldn't have written this memoir without you. This - sweetheart - is our story.

All my love,
- L

Note to the Reader

Even as I concluded writing this memoir, new discoveries and more lessons have come. Life never stops, and this is why, surrendering to what is and choosing joy is an ongoing process. It is also an ongoing opportunity to grow - as we move in different ways to get to that point of understanding- that healing begins when we let go.

How I experienced my grief and Post Traumatic Stress Disorder (PTSD), will not be the same for everyone. In fact, not everyone even experiences PTSD after trauma. There might be parts of my story you can relate to and others that you don't. That is the beauty of being human – that we are all unique and amazing within our differences.

For me, the death of my son prompted me to seek answers for the first time in my life over what had happened to me at sixteen-years-old. It became a spiritual awakening, full of opportunity for self-growth. This doesn't mean the death of loved ones will do the same for others. However, it is possible that it can lead you to a place of growth within your own journey. How you get there – will be individual to you – and that is a beautiful thing. My realization at the end of my story is shared with not the intention to tell you how to perceive life, but rather to help open doors for you to find your own conclusion and healing.

Sharing my dreams, especially in the beginning of this story was something I had to dig deep to find the courage to write. I always judged myself for having such intense dreams and as I wrote all of the dreams that I chose to share – I realized – that was a part of me that needed healing too. To not be ashamed of what had happened to me nor who I am. Today, I still work on this area of my healing.

My hope for all of you who are reading this memoir, is that it brings you to your own place of inner healing and power. To be able to find hope again, reconnect to love and rediscover the joy that is always in you.

To be able to take a deep breath and let it back out – and just be.

Love,

Lindsay Marie

HOW MY STILLBORN SON TAUGHT ME TO SURRENDER

LINDSAY GIBSON

Prologue

June 1995

The summer air was thick, sweat was pouring down my beet red face, but I kept running. I saw him running in front of me, turning to laugh with me and within seconds we jumped through the sprinkler, feeling the relief of the cold water against our skin. Andy was my best friend. He was more than a friend, he was a third brother to me in many ways, protecting me against the world.

It was June, in the summer of 1995 and we were eleven-years-old. We just finished fifth grade and we couldn't wait for the summer ahead: playing, exploring and getting lost within our imagination. Andy lived two doors down and we became fast friends from the first day we met. He was the youngest of three older brothers, as was I with two older brothers. That tied us together instantly, always running from our brothers or making up games to drive them crazy.

Andy and I grew up in Southbury, Connecticut, a quaint little suburban town in the northern tip of New Haven County. Our street was picture perfect. We lived on Holly Hill Lane which was tucked away behind Kettletown State Park. All around it was beautiful New England country scenery, filled with mountains and trees. You would often see lemonade stands on our street, kids playing basketball or riding their bikes and you would hear endless laughter echoing throughout the yards of all the homes. It was a dream neighborhood for any child. It was quiet and safe and we would spend from sun up to sun down playing all up and down it, often venturing into the woods and getting lost. We had other kids to play with us who lived near, but in those early days of my childhood, Andy was my first choice. We usually spent hours running through the sprinklers, but today I suddenly stopped dead in my tracks and felt my stomach tie up in knots. Was I getting sick? Something didn't feel right. Here we go again…

"I need to go home, I don't feel good!" I shouted to Andy and dashed off toward my house. As I raced home, flashes of a new home with my mother kept running through my mind. I started to get really sad because what was scaring me the most, was that I didn't see my dad with us in this new house.

I had always carried a gift as a child, an intuitive ability and was able to predict many scenarios before they were about to happen. I would see them play out in my mind exactly how they did. It wasn't fun, in fact it was often frightening to me. It didn't end there. Starting around age four, I began to have intense dreams and they would shock my mother with what I knew when I told her. I would literally see myself sleeping in many of them before the dream would take off in all kinds of directions. The most chilling part of it all, was how I would meet many people "on the other side," such as deceased family members and even strangers.

As I grew, my stomach became my next communicator along with these dreams. It was the sensation that I listened to first, even before the images in my eyes and the sounds in my ears. I would feel incredibly nauseated, to the point of nearly getting sick when I would get "a feeling" that something was about to happen and something always did. Mom always told me that we all have that ability to make decisions using our stomachs and to just listen to "our gut feeling." This helped me to relax a little, but I was still afraid of my dreams. Therefore, I stayed quiet about them. As a child, I wasn't sure how to organize it all in my mind or understand them.

Around seven-years-old, I didn't know what to else to do with the dreams, so I pulled out my first journal and began to write them all down. I would take the bad feelings I had about my dreams and open my journal for a release. I would write about my feelings, the dreams in detail or visions that I would see, which were usually out of nowhere. I would sit on the floor of my room, on my knees, bent over my bed and write, sometimes for hours. Writing has stuck with me ever since. It became the tool of God's grace for me.

As I ran home that day from playing with Andy, I knew when I opened my front door and went inside, something big was about to happen. I also knew that it wasn't going to be easy. Voices boomed out from the living room, next to the office my dad just remodeled. I walked by the office, pausing to listen to them. I ran my fingers along his skillfully crafted bookshelves he made that held all of mom's books. My hands were shaking as I slowly walked into the living room. Mom shifted in her seat, looking very uncomfortable. I looked over at dad, who was also uncomfortable with his arms crossed. My oldest brother, Matthew, came over and took my hand and put me on his lap. A strong smell of roses filled the air; my head started to spin and I put my head on Matthew's shoulder, in attempt to keep myself from getting sick. The rose flower was with me as far back as I could remember and I just never knew why, so I wasn't exactly surprised by the scent of them. My brother, Derek, got up and sat on the other side of Matthew. As the oldest of the three, Matthew was the rock for both Derek and me. Mom finally broke the silence.

"Okay, now that Lindsay is home, we can share it with her too. Lindsay," she turned to me and I noticed her eyes were red and wet from crying. "Before you came home, we were talking to your brothers about this," she took a big breath, "your father and I have some sad news to share, but we both want you to know that you'll be okay. Everything is going to be just fine." *No, it wasn't. It's never okay if you have to start the conversation like that,* I thought. She continued, "we have decided to separate. Your father and I love you three very much, but right now, we need to separate from each other. We're getting divorced." Divorced?

Derek stood up and ran upstairs, slamming the door to his bedroom so loud that the walls shook. Matthew tightened his grip on me, not knowing what to say yet. My mother went upstairs to talk to Derek. Dad, with his head low, stood up and slowly walked out of the room. Matthew hugged me tightly, telling me it was all okay. I felt my stomach start to knot up again. It was once again right with its prediction. No matter how many times it was right, I was always surprised, which was odd because it never failed me before. I pushed away from him and went upstairs to my room, wanting to just hide.

As quietly as I could, I shut my door and locked it. I sat on the edge of my bed, silently letting the tears fall as I listened to Derek's rage on the other side of the wall. Mom was desperately trying to reason with him. I held in my sobs because I knew Derek needed her right now. I heard Matthew quietly knock on my door but I stayed frozen with tears falling and pooling onto my legs. Leaning onto my bed, I began to push back a feeling of self-hatred that seemed to be overtaking my mind. Somehow, I felt like this was all my fault. I ignored Matthew's gentle, consistent knocking.

I reached under my bed and pulled out my journal to write, as I kneeled on the floor. I thought about something that my mother always told me, which was if we are troubled to talk to God and the Angels and ask them for help. As the words flowed from my heart through my pen and onto the pages, an aroma of roses surrounded me again. I began to relax into my writing.

Dear God and the Angels, my Mommy and Daddy are so sad that they cannot make up from their fight. They are going to separate and maybe you can help them be happy again so we don't have to all split up? I feel sad too and I don't know if it is okay to tell them.

I stopped writing and began to cry, hiding my face in my bed. I wanted to scream, as anger circled underneath the tears and dark thoughts began to play through my mind. At eleven-years-old, I didn't want to live anymore and I looked down at my journal one more time and wrote:

Can't I just come to heaven and live with you, God? I don't want to be here anymore...

I stared at my words, taken back by them. Standing up, I opened the closet door and hid my journal and covered it, so no one would find it. I didn't want anyone to see what I wrote. In the mess of my closet, I paused and picked up a musical jewelry box with a horse on it. Before I could stop myself, I smashed it on the floor in complete rage. Running back to my bed, I cried as quietly as I could, in my pillow. I didn't want my parents to split up or my daddy to not live with me anymore. I wanted more than anything, to grow closer with him and if they divorced, how would I accomplish that? The tears kept coming and I could still hear Derek on the other side of the wall, crying with our mom. After what felt like hours, I drifted off to sleep, praying that I would wake up and this would all just be a bad dream. As I started to doze off, my dreams became clearer and clearer and I heard an ethereal voice begin to sing.

I was in a trance-like sleep but I was still awake enough to question if I should wake up? Was it my mother singing to me? No, my mother's voice was different and I felt chills run up my back. This voice soothed me deeper into the rest I needed to recover from this shocking news. I noticed I was standing in my closet again, holding the broken jewelry box that I just smashed only minutes ago.

She continued to sing, but this time it was more of a humming. Like a mother does with her newborn baby in a rocking chair. I wanted to turn and see who this was, but I was afraid.

Finally, curiosity took over and I slowly turned around and my mouth dropped open in surprise at what I saw. A lady stood before me with skin so fair and beauty like none other, dressed in blue and white, with roses all around her. I inhaled sharply and the chills I felt turned into an intense warmth, rushing through my body. I stared at her with eyes wide in wonder and then everything went black.

Part One
The Awakening

"Mary, Mother of Jesus. Please be a Mother to me now."
-Mother Teresa

One

June 2016

The red cardinal flew by me, gliding his way to his spot on the fence. His vivid red color full of vitality and strength. Dancing her way through the water spraying about, my oldest daughter Lillian sang to the rhythm of her movements. The gentle melody she hummed, pierced through me, easing me into deeper relaxation. Nostalgia crept in as I watched her twirl, remembering a time of my own lazy summer days as a child, with Andy and other friends. I smiled in those memories as my heart filled with happiness watching Lillian. The cardinal began chirping, as if he was singing along with her movements. The water seemed to move with her every jump and I felt a burst of energy pulsing through my veins. This warm and vibrant feeling was exhilarating. I smiled again, in response. It felt so good to smile, enjoying inner peace and being in harmony with the beauty that surrounded me in that moment.

I looked up at the summer sky and breathed in fresh air as I thought about my younger daughter Layla, peacefully sleeping in her nursery inside. The tree limbs began to move as a slight wind, heavy in the summer's heat pushed through the air. I looked up at a big oak tree, so powerful in my view and so strong in its natural beauty. I never noticed before, how the trees looked when they sway in the wind, especially now as they danced alongside Lillian as she spun about. Or how it felt to feel my breath, as my chest moved up and down, filling my lungs with pure, sweet air. Being present is something that is new to me, a victory in my battle for the privilege to love life again.

I closed my eyes and felt a sting vibrate through me as I know it has taken so much for my soul to grow to this point. I felt time rewinding as my life raced through my mind: One horrific night of violence and stolen innocence. The dark, yet beautiful days of Boston. Finding true love with my husband, Jason, and fighting my way through severe Post Traumatic Stress Disorder. The births of our daughters Lillian and Layla, the death of our son Joseph and the gift of the powerful dreams that guide me. Life - such a courageous ride that we all must be on here on earth.

One dream in particular, of someone very special to me, is one that I forever hold dear to my heart. I thought about her first visit to me, the day my parents announced their divorce. Her skin glowing, her eyes warm with grace and her presence so incredibly robust with intense love. Her blue veil falling over her shoulders, with a smell of roses so strong. The special relationship I have had with this divine woman still brings me to my knees for all that she has shown and taught me. I opened my eyes and continued to watch Lillian at play in the sprinkler. I took a deep breath and let it out slowly, beaming within my thoughts. I smiled again and faced the warm sun. A feeling of complete joy overcame me and my biggest relief? The fact that I could feel absolutely everything again. It is miraculous to me.

I am still breathing. I am still standing. I am still alive. But damn, has it been nearly impossible to get here.

November 2013

The silence was almost deafening and darkness was all around me. My heart began to beat loudly, breaking the silence as fear pushed into my body with each pulse. Was I still in the hospital? Where was my son? I reached over to turn a light on, but I couldn't find it. I tried to call for help, but the words never left my throat. I sat in the stillness, hearing my heart race faster and beating into my ears. I knew I wasn't alone. But I was not in the company of my son or my husband. All I felt was complete terror.

I heard him whistling and laughing behind me. No, no please someone help me!

I opened my eyes and sat up in bed, with sweat pouring down my face. The horror from the nightmare still overwhelming me. I looked over at Jason who was sleeping on a cot next to me. Behind him, there was a beeping noise, from the monitor that was hooked up to my belly, recording my heartbeat and contractions, as I continued to labor. I felt my stomach churn as I looked at the screen. There was only my heartbeat and the other was measured in silence. Fresh tears sprang into my eyes and I put my hand over my belly, feeling his lifeless body. My son, my sweet boy.

No! Please, no! My mind screamed, but the room remained silent against my expressionless face. I felt numb and as dead as my son's body was inside of me. My heart seemed to stand still as I remembered his kicks only the day before, happily jerking against my womb. Our son, Joseph Michael, had passed away, at 26 weeks' gestation. What I did not understand though was that within this painful loss, how something else was opening a door in my dreams and consciousness for the first time in thirteen years. My past. Something I had worked very hard to keep locked shut behind that door. The nightmare I just woke from was one of many, that I had already experienced in the last twenty-four hours, since I lost my son. Fresh tears began to build up behind the old ones that were still wet on my face. I couldn't take much more and didn't know how to control it all.

My mouth was so dry, so I reached for water. A small laugh got caught in my throat as I took a sip and randomly thought about how I couldn't drink water during Joseph's pregnancy at all. Grape juice was the only beverage I was able to sip on while plagued with hyperemesis gravidarum. This juice would spark him into a kickboxing match with my stomach. The laughter instantly turned to sobs. I bent over in my hands, screaming as the pain of his loss sent merciless grief through my body.

It was day two and my body was shaking with fatigue from trying to labor and release him. There were many unexpected complications, so his labor was taking much longer than the doctor anticipated. Should I just go back to sleep? The reality of his loss was too intense to bear, but the horrors of what nightmares could come up, terrified me to fall back into the comfort of sleep again. I had nowhere to turn for relief. The nightmare I just had was a gruesome memory from my past and it was too much to handle. I began to cry even harder and the tears of both grief and frustration, spilled through my eyes. Jason woke up and slid into my bed behind me, pulling me back against his chest. I heard him stifle a cry as he leaned into my neck, whispering a prayer to help me find relief. It didn't.

I looked up at the ceiling and my mind was racing with thoughts and pure panic set in. How did I get here? Hadn't I been through enough already? The whistling from the nightmare echoed in my ears. I closed my eyes for a moment and begged it to stop. Just stop! A contraction hit me and I flinched in pain.

"Breathe, just breathe through the pain," Jason whispered, as he took big, deep breaths in and out for me to follow. The stable rhythm of his cleansing breaths began to steady my racing heart. I started to breathe in sync with him and felt my body shake out the anxiety. Jason knew that breathing exercises were the only thing that helped me handle my paralyzing attacks of anxiety that I have suffered with for many years. "Release him darling, let our Joseph go," he continued and held me tighter. "Let him work through you. You see my love, he has you now, you don't have him. Let him guide you out of this darkness. But first, you need to let his body go."

Taking a deeper breath in, I breathed out the shock of what was happening. Trying to birth my son, my dead son. *Our* dead son. I couldn't bear to look into Jason's eyes since we found out. I felt like my body failed and I was so ashamed. Each second that passed, took me further and further away from Joseph. I didn't want to deliver him and let him go. How could I? How the hell does a mother give birth and say goodbye to her baby? I sat up with another contraction and clenched my body, while bending over, burying my face into a pillow. I screamed into it against the contraction.

Paul McCartney's lyrics softly fell into my ears as my husband sang the sad and haunting words, *Let it Be*.

Jason continued to sing and I pushed my questions aside to listen. His voice was so beautiful, so soothing, even in a time like this. He began to rub my belly, pausing with each contraction as he felt my stomach tighten.

"He's safe," Jason whispered some more. "The angels have him already." He kept the silence filled as he hummed the remainder of Paul McCartney's song.

Within the comfort of his hands, rubbing the pain of the contractions away, I closed my eyes. The anxiety began to lift a little more and my breath went back into a stable tempo. With Jason's breath in rhythm with mine, I fell gently back into a lucid state of sleep. A voice started whispering to me and as it grew louder, shock pierced through me as I instantly recognized it. There was no mistaking, who was coming to me again. A voice that I never forgot, nor could forget. It was the same angelic voice that eased my sadness that summer day at eleven years old, the day my parents split.

She started singing softly and her voice was felt all around me; as if she was a part of me. The room began to fill with the aroma of roses and I knew then, that it was surely her. Gasping, I tried to move but was frozen.

I was aware that I was asleep, yet I could feel my husband's strong grip still holding me from behind. It was like being caught in-between worlds of consciousness, something I was used to with my years of lucid dreaming. The sweet melody of her beautiful voice continued to sing to me, but still couldn't see her. I looked around my hospital room, trying to find her.

Suddenly, a light began to brighten the room at the foot of my bed. I squinted my eyes and couldn't believe what I was seeing. What was this light? It was so startling, that for an instant, I wanted to wake up.

"Lindsay, wake up!" I heard my own voice in my mind.

Something pulled at me and I felt a strange, warm presence pulsing through my body. This sensation was incredibly soothing and I was instantly calm and tranquil. It felt like my whole body had a surge of heat pulsing through it. Then, within the bright light, I saw her. For the second time in my life, she was there to soothe my bleeding heart.

She was still as magnificent as ever, wrapped in blue and smiling at me. Except this time, she held her hands in front of her and an image of a rose was in the middle, glowing through its brilliant petals. It started opening all the way, to reveal the beauty it possessed. Laughing, with delight, she held it up, allowing its petals to glorify itself in the room. As the petals opened more and more, I saw myself flip through its layers. Images from my childhood, all the way until now kept racing through as the rose continued to blossom. Once it was fully open, she looked back down at me and laughed with such grace. I felt an intense love wash into my body. I stared at her holy presence with awe, allowing her glorious love to continue to fill me. I never wanted to leave this moment.

Jason's voice began to break through the dream and I woke up. I woke up this time feeling calm, so calm in fact, that it was almost unsettling. Rubbing my eyes to wake up a little more, I looked around my hospital room. Waking up in the exact same room that a dream took place was still so puzzling, even after years of experiencing it. Jason's voice continued behind me:

"Hail Mary, full of grace.
Our Lord is with thee.
Blessed art thou among women,
and blessed is the fruit of thy womb"

Another contraction came and I shifted to my side, with my heart beginning to pound against my chest, struggling through the pain. No! I didn't want anxiety to take away this feeling of peacefulness. Sweat began to trickle on my forehead as Jason held me tighter. I felt annoyed over the prayer I just heard him say. I don't want to hear that prayer or any prayer. I tried to speak, but my voice was so scratchy it felt like I swallowed glass. I cleared my throat to speak again.

"Jason, why did you just say that prayer?" I asked and he remained silent. "No, please explain to me right now! I'm confused, so why?" I shouted at him and leaned forward again, with my stomach hardening against my fury.

"Why are you confused?" Jason finally responded.

"I..." I struggled to find words but my mind was still distracted from the woman I just saw in my dream. Who was she? "I was just asleep, right?" I asked him.

I was starting to get more and more aggravated. The incredible feeling of warmth and love that I felt while asleep was slipping away and I didn't understand why I saw her in the middle of a stillbirth? Or why was she there after my parents announced their divorce? What was even more confusing was how much peace I felt. Perhaps, I was just so desperate for relief from this pain. I began to cry again, feeling so overwhelmed with sorrow. Jason stayed quiet, letting me release all the tears that I needed to, as I started rambling.

"Am I losing my mind? I must be. Were you really praying or did I make that up?" I asked, so frustrated now as another contraction hit and guilt rushed through me. How could I have felt so much love and peace at a time of despair, in the death of our son? I didn't deserve to feel any relief while he laid dead in my body – a body that totally failed him.

As my stomach tightened with another contraction, I closed my eyes and my mind flashed back to the first time I saw her at eleven years old. I saw the broken jewelry box and heard the singing. Opening my eyes, I let the contraction complete. What was happening to me? Anxiety increased and my heart picked up speed. I turned around and looked directly at Jason for the first time in nearly two days. He leaned down and kissed my forehead. The contraction went away but I began to cramp, with slicing pain all the way around to my back. Tears began to build again and I bent over my womb, holding it as though I could still protect my son somehow. I clenched with every ounce of my strength as the labor progressed.

Dreams had always been a huge part of my life, guiding and supporting me, but not now. Not today! I was not prepared for the one I just had. Here I was, giving birth to my dead son and I am having a déjà vu dream, filled with peace and love? It was like I was going in and out of insanity. I looked up at Jason again and he actually had a small, calm smile on his face. I wanted to smack that smile right off his face! How could he possibly be smiling? He pulled me back into his arms and despite my anger at him, I relented. He was the only person I wanted right now while my body continued to cramp, bleed and open to give birth to our son.

"Jason?" I finally said, in almost a whisper. I took a deep breath and sat up to face him better. Before I could say more, he held up his phone with a picture on it, still smiling.

"Lindsay…" he said softly, "was this the woman in your dream?" I gasped, as my mouth fell open.

Two

I continued to sit in silence, staring at the woman on his phone. It was a picture of Mother Mary, looking exactly like the woman in my dream. How did I not ever make this connection before? Even more, how did Jason possibly know?

"WHAT? HOW?" I nearly shouted at him. "And WHY are you smiling?"

"I don't know, I...." he paused, for he was just as surprised as me. "I'm smiling because she has such a beautiful presence. I can't really explain it, but while you were sleeping, I had this overwhelming urge to start reciting Hail Mary. I've never recited it before until now and felt so calm while saying it too. She's here. I feel it," he took another pause, "Baby, God's here. They're with us." I felt rage wash over me. Mother Mary? God? Is he serious right now? It was JUST A DREAM! How could God be with us when our son was dead? That isn't the God that I knew. I ignored his statement about Mother Mary and my dream for the remainder to the day. I just couldn't wrap my head around any of it.

The next day, day three, was the hardest of the entire five days that it took to birth Joseph. This was because the doctors were deciding between surgery to remove him or giving me one more day to keep laboring him. It was hard to wait. I was nervous with what they would ultimately decide because surgery would be an abrupt end to this and I was not prepared for that. Truthfully, I didn't want this to end. My body did not want to let him go, neither did my heart. I was like a wild animal protecting her young against predators. I didn't want to just hand him over to the nurses, never to have him again. I couldn't fathom the thought of that and therefore, my body continued to hold onto him, slowing down labor, despite the medication they gave me to speed it up. They decided to let me keep laboring for one more day.

Later that day, the room began to darken, as the sun set. Jason and I were laying in the silence together, both lost in our own thoughts as we continued to get through each contraction. Jason was first to break the silence.

"I think she's been trying to tell you something your whole life," he said softly.

"What?" I asked, feeling irritated.

"Mother Mary. I know you're confused about the dreams you've had of her, but I just want you to know, that I think she has been alongside of you since the rap…"

"STOP!" I screamed, cutting him off and was so loud, that the nurses buzzed the room to check on us.

My heart started to beat fast because of what he was about to say. Why would he bring up that night, especially now of all times? Also, again, Mother Mary? I still didn't believe it! I wouldn't allow myself to go there because if it was her, how could she take our baby boy? Worse yet, how could God do this? The Mother Mary I always read about was filled with love. She wouldn't take my innocent baby from me. Yet, no matter what angry thoughts passed through my mind, I couldn't fight the truth of what I the saw the day before in my dream and as a child. I also couldn't deny, that she always brought me comfort each time she appeared. I closed my eyes, breathing through more contraction pains. Each contraction only made me angrier, no matter how much love was trying to win this fight or who was there to show it to me.

Suddenly, I felt a warm sensation tickle me from the top of my head all the down to my toes. It was the same sensation that I experienced in the dream. It was almost like a softness cradling my sorrow and a gentleness that was embracing my pain, keeping me still and calm. What was this strange, new feeling? Pain was the only thing I knew and it controlled most of my life. I sat in awe. I couldn't quite explain what was happening to me again, but it was like my grief was joining together with serenity and this time I was awake. All I could do was let this warmth continue to fill me. An energy around me was keeping me motionless, despite all of the labor pain. Then, in one single thought, without any more resistance; I finally gave in. It was her.

Our blessed Mother Mary was here, standing by my side. I knew it deep in my soul and didn't question it any longer. She was here, poking at my doubt, but why? I had been unsure of my faith for so many years because of all that has happened to me. Yet, right now, feeling so much warmth, my faith was slowly reawakening. The rose flower in her hand, was the most interesting part of it all. It is in all the pictures that we see of her, so it must have been her way of making herself known to me all throughout the years. Roses always showed up during difficult times, especially in my darkest moments of PTSD. Pieces of the puzzle just came together. How did I miss this for so long – the beauty that was still within my bruised and battered soul? The biggest question I had right now: Was I willing to keep this love flowing through me and my faith alive? I wasn't sure.

The incredible feeling stayed with me a little longer. It felt like a great wind was blowing out old, pent up emotion that kept me in fear, for so many years. Despite my festering doubt, I felt anchored within this beautiful feeling. Centered in the midst of this storm of grief. Just like the rose flower, I was unfolding a new layer, awakening to the possibility of hope. Unconditional love was showing its first signs to me, slowly working its way through the cracks of my broken heart. I wasn't sure how long it would last, but I knew one thing: I could breathe, I was still alive and feeling peaceful. A powerful contraction slammed through my body, startling me out of the temporary bliss. I looked up at Jason and he was staring at me, calmly waiting on me to share my thoughts. He could sense this deep realization that just came over me.

I looked over at the monitor that was measuring the contractions and reality hit me again and hit me hard. Anger came bursting out, slamming any peace, I had, right back to the ground. Who gives a damn what kind of hope there is? My son is dead and he was not coming back! Grief sucked me right back into its funnel of chaos. Before Jason could say anything, I pushed away from him and sat up on the edge of the bed. I couldn't accept what just happened. It was just my longing for life instead of my son's death. It had to be, right? I fought to get air as more anxiety picked up speed.

"Baby, talk to me," Jason softly said.

"I'm such a bad person. I just convinced myself that my dream was Mother Mary and that she was showing me love. What the hell is wrong with me? It's just another one of my crazy dreams," I replied.

"Or you're still in denial," Jason said, almost in a whisper and I snapped.

"STOP! Denial? Really, Jason? I know our son is dead! What are you talking about?" I shouted. As I glared at him, a wave of pain, with another contraction nearly knocked me off the bed. He grabbed my arm to steady me. I waited until the pain passed and looked at him heatedly.

"If it really is someone so powerful, so divine, as Mother Mary, why would she do this to me? To us? Why would she take Joey from us? Answer me that Jason!" I said, through clenched teeth. "He was just a baby and so innocent! And why..." I was now shaking with fury, "why does she always 'show up' when I'm in complete misery? Why doesn't she just stop it all from happening in the first place?

That's not 'divine', it's cruel!" I shouted, bending over and holding my hardened stomach; willing the contractions to just end.

Jason stayed calm and let me run through the emotions that he knew were cycling over and over through me. He understood my thoughts and my questions more than I did and just sat still, witnessing this battle of my soul. He pressed on after a few silent minutes.

"I know you know, that Joe is dead. That's not what I mean. You can fight love all you want because it's all you know how to do. So, go ahead, keeping fighting it Lindsay. Aren't you exhausted yet? You can argue in your head back and forth why someone as significant as Mother Mary came to you, but eventually you just need to let it all be," he said. Shaking even more now, I turned and looked at him with vehemence. I wanted to hit him. I wanted to scream. I wanted to run. I glared at my him as if he were a stranger now.

"Love doesn't kill innocent babies! Love doesn't strip a young girl of her innocence, attacking her so violently and nearly leaving her for dead Jason!" I was nearly shouting at the top of my lungs at this point and surprised the nurses didn't buzz us again over the speakers or come in. I stopped yelling and paused. I couldn't believe I just said that. I never talk about that night. Jason continued to stay steady, eyeing me right back and not afraid to keep challenging me.

"No, sweetheart, it doesn't," he answered me, with tears filling his eyes, "but love is the reason we grieve and love is what is going to bring you back. Love has never left you. Don't you see?"

I gasped, replaying his words over and over in my mind. Anxiety was now in full force, pulling me down. I ripped the monitor off my belly, stood up, and went into the bathroom. I splashed cold water on my face, then held onto the sink to help steady my quivering legs. When I stood up and looked in the mirror, I caught my breath. There, I saw a young girl staring at me. I inched closer to the mirror, shocked that the image did not copy my movements. The young girl stayed still, gazing at me and I recognized her. It was me. I saw my sixteen-year-old self, staring back at me. I panicked and stepped away from the mirror.

For a moment, I feared I truly was going insane. I tripped over the step stool that was outside of the small shower and when I regained my balance, I looked back at the mirror and saw my distraught face in pain. The trauma I endured at sixteen, literally just haunted me and I had a sinking feeling, it wasn't over. Inside, the shadows of my past were only growing darker in contrast to the light of love, sparked by Joseph's death. The love I have for my son was too powerful for darkness to prevail. Walls of denial were shattering around me and I was absolutely numb with fear.

"No!" I screamed inside the tiny bathroom. A strong contraction sliced through me, almost in response to my fright. I could feel my son's perfect body making its way lower, so I could push him out and it seemed as though along with him, my past was sliding out too. Grief, with her pitiless ability to strike you over and over, overwhelmed me and I dropped to the floor, sobbing in complete anguish. Jason opened the door to the bathroom and with one swift movement, he scooped me up.

"Jason, I'm losing control! Get the nurse, I need medication NOW!" I yelled and looked at him with panic. He quickly walked me back to the bed. The pain of more contractions was ripping through my womb at a faster pace now, all the way around to my back. They matched the frightening memories in my mind as Joseph's body was pushing its way out. Jason laid me down and put a cool washcloth over my forehead and rang for the nurse and told her we needed something to calm me down and fast. Within minutes, a doctor came in and put anti-anxiety medication in my IV.

"You're my hero," Jason whispered, leaning over me with tears of helplessness washing down his face. The room spun from the medication, calming me down. I smiled at him in response, closed my eyes and surrendered his little body to earth and his spirit to heaven.

The labor was over and Joseph was out. There were no first cries, no pink, warm baby to hold in my arms. There was no baby to nurse at my aching breast. Only stillness. He was delivered back into eternity, yet his spirit was hovering close to me. I felt him all around. For the first time in four days, I watched my husband fall to his knees beside my bed and sobbed like I never heard him cry before. There are not many things that can break this man's strength, but there is also no pain in this world quite like the pain of losing your child. Jason's strength was swept from under him when we said goodbye to Joseph.

By the end of the day, I was ready to be discharged and as I was getting wheeled out, my arms never felt so empty. Holding my still large belly, I felt a sadness that was so heavy on my chest that I could hardly breathe. How would I face the world now? I wanted to stay in the protection of the hospital. I still felt like a failure, no matter how many times the doctors and nurses told me it wasn't my fault.

My daughter, Lillian came into my mind as we got closer to the entrance of the hospital. My amazing, seven-year-old, first-born daughter, who waited so long to have a sibling, was waiting patiently at home for us to return. In her innocent mind, she thought her brother was going to come home too. Jason and I had decided to wait until we were home to tell her. My mind raced with how I was possibly going to tell her the news that her brother was dead and continue being her mommy? I didn't know where to start with all of that and with each tear that fell, I silently begged God to take my life too. I just wanted to be in heaven with my Joseph. I was so angry, that the thought of ending my life, tore open my already fragile faith.

We waited at door, while valet was getting our car. Three nurses came down with us, all of them crying and when I saw their faces, I felt so grateful for the care they gave Jason and me. I realized that the entire week was full of caring people: hospital chaplains, including my own Pastor who had been with me the whole week offering prayer and support, along with family and friends. I was so lost in my thoughts, dreams and flashbacks all week, that I didn't notice how many people helped us.

I also wasn't conscious of what was spreading like wildfire through the very cells of my body. Love was pouring through my heartbreak, gently beckoning me to be whole, even in my grief. It would be awhile before I could do that. Our car pulled around and it was finally time to say goodbye to the nurses. They all had well-meaning last-minute words of advice and comfort:

"Just be the mother you have always been, you will find a way to do it."

"Just be thankful you have a daughter already."

"Just be aware of your grief but don't let it overcome you."

"Just let Joseph go…."

I struggled to respond and I turned around, looking desperately up at Jason. He came around to the front of me and bent down, so we were eye level with each other.

"Just be nothing, my darling. Just be." He whispered. *Just be.*

Three

The ride home was completely silent, as I thought about our daughter Lillian again, who was waiting on us with a heart full of anticipation. I fought violently against the tears. I did not want her to see my sadness and be scared by it. Walking inside our apartment building, I hung my head low. I heard her little excited voice, as her footsteps drew near on the other side of our front door. She opened the door and let out a squeal of happiness.

"Mommy! Daddy! You're home! Where's Joey? Was he born? I'm going to give him this teddy bear of mine." She ran out to the hallway past us, looking frantically for her brother, holding the teddy bear to her chest. I completely froze. Jason sensed my panic and moved quickly. He scooped her up and gave her a big hug.

"Yes, we're home! I hope you've been a good girl for your Nonni!" His voice was jolly despite the truth of the situation that was looming around us. He carried her inside and she looked over his shoulder at me, as we all went inside.

"Hi Mommy! Your belly is still big, so is he still in there? Silly doctors! They probably thought he was ready to come but he wasn't!" She laughed at her own reasoning as to why her brother was not here. I couldn't even bring myself to smile at her. My mother appeared from Lillian's room, her eyes swollen with her own tears of grief, yet she hid it well from my daughter while we were in the hospital. Lillian was so innocent and it my heart broke all over again thinking about how in minutes, the pieces of her small heart would fall to meet mine.

My mother bent down to hug her goodbye and we locked knowing eyes, sharing the sorrow.

After we settled in, I got Lillian ready for bed. She put her pajamas on and leaned over to kiss my belly. Tears burned in my eyes and a fire sank in my stomach.

"Why were you in the hospital all week mommy, if Joey is still in your belly?" I stuttered to find the right words. For seven years, I have never fumbled in discussion with her. We were extremely close and could always talk about anything. But not this. Telling her that her brother was dead, left me speechless.

"Because mommy needed help from the doctors." Jason's strong voice saved me, "Lilly, let's go sit on the couch and chat for a bit."

As we sat on the couch, Lillian climbed up onto Jason's lap and when her tender, young eyes stared back into ours, everything spun around me. I heard Jason begin to explain to Lillian, that her brother, whom she loved so very much, went back to heaven. Even though Jason was right next to me, his voice seemed miles away. It felt as though a knife stabbed my heart when I felt Lillian's body go limp, as she started to panic.

"What? What do you mean he went back to heaven? You mean, he died? A baby can die? I thought only old people died!" Her voice got louder and louder with each question and she was soon caught in an eruption of sobs. "Mommy, is Joey dead? Mommy!" Her voice was faint underneath my flood of tears. My mind was in compete disconnect. She began to wail even harder. She tried to reach for me and I still couldn't look at her face. Instead, I looked down at her hands, her white knuckles desperately clutching to Jason, as this shocking news sank deeper into her. I felt my body tense up with each shriek, but just as quickly as she started to cry, she stopped.

She looked up at me, studying my face and reaching deep for her own strength, as she stretched her arms out for me. This time I let her in and she gently wrapped her arms around me, sliding over to my lap. Her words will forever be etched in my mind. It was as if for that one moment in time, she aged well beyond her years to bring me comfort. The bond of love emerged, holding our hearts together.

"Mommy, I love you. I'm here. You just need Daddy and me. We'll take care of you. Don't worry about anything." I couldn't believe the maturity in her profound words, which helped ease me into the aura of love that she had protecting her. She pulled back and slid off of my lap. With her knees on the floor, she bent over me and laid her head against my empty womb.

"Goodbye Joey. I love you so much." I saw tears silently slide down her face, even though she tried to hide them from me. Not even after the violence I faced at sixteen, did I ever feel so frail, falling deeper into hopelessness. Watching my daughter's heart break with grief, was enough to push me far away from all of the beauty and warmth I experienced in the hospital.

A week later, we said our final goodbyes to Joseph in a memorial service. November 23, 2013 was a chilly, windy day. Lillian worked very hard to write a letter to her brother. She wanted to release it to the heavens, tied to a white balloon. The week was a blur; the idea of leaving the house frightened me and the medication that helped me sleep made my dreams blank. I knew it was time to put the medicine aside and begin to face the world somehow.

Jason opened the door to our bedroom on the morning of the service, holding a plate of breakfast he so lovingly made. I forced myself to smile and took the plate, staring at its contents. My stomach rolled as I thought back to the days of my pregnancy with Joseph and the sickness that I battled each day with him with hyperemesis gravidarum. In that moment, I would have given anything to still be fighting that battle. Hyperemesis gravidarum is severe nausea and vomiting in pregnancy and for me, it lasted the entire time with Joseph, gaining strength as each week passed. I had never heard of the term 'hyperemesis gravidarum' before I got pregnant with Joseph or the kind of hell it is to live through it. Even when I first looked it up, spellcheck didn't even recognize it.

It was all so new to me because it was nothing like my first pregnancy with Lillian, which, for a young woman of twenty-one, had its own challenges. I was sick with her, on and off throughout her pregnancy, but it was manageable. I was able to keep myself hydrated and out of the hospital. However, with Joseph, it was an ongoing fight, which I lost in the end. It felt as though I was a soldier, losing a battle in a big war. A random strength suddenly arose, against my dark thoughts about hyperemesis because I realized, that though I lost the battle with Joseph's death, I did not lose the war. Where did that thought come from? It was not a physical strength, but more like an inner stirring in my soul, showing me again, that while I had fallen into grief, good things will be coming. I felt confused, just as I had been during that magical moment in the hospital, feeling Mother Mary's love during my suffering. I shook it off and thought: What does that ultimately do for my aching heart? It won't bring my son back.

I could still feel the area on my arm where they inserted the needle for the PICC line. I closed my eyes, remembering all the details, as I traced my fingers along the scars that were all over my arms, where the nurses poked my collapsed veins, over and over for months.

Four days after I officially found out I was pregnant with him, I found myself on the bathroom floor, unable to move from the relentless nausea and vomiting. I had been nauseated on and off for few weeks leading up to testing, but now I couldn't eat or drink. I literally lived on the bathroom floor and Jason and my mother were beginning to get concerned. This was not normal and none of us knew what to do.

Then things shifted rather fast. I began to vomit blood, bursting the blood vessels in my eyes and passing out, so we headed to the emergency room. I was very weak and nearly unconscious. Doctors moved fast to start an IV and rehydrate me. They were eager to get some nutrition back into my body from days of not eating. I was scared. No, I was absolutely terrified. Was I losing the baby? What was happening to me? I heard Jason tell the doctor that yes, I was pregnant and it was still early and we hadn't seen our own OB doctor yet.

Within minutes, a nurse rolled in an ultrasound machine and an internal ultrasound was done. I heard Joseph's loud heartbeat fill the room and realized he was still alive despite how poorly felt. Everyone went in a super-fast mode at that point. I heard a lot of talking around me, concerned nurses, doctors and mom advocating for me, asking them to get things under control. I felt the tight grip of Jason's hand that kept me reassured. What was this? It can't be morning sickness. Was it a flu? I closed my eyes to shut out the chaos, listening to the gentle rhythm of my baby's heartbeat as exhaustion overcame me and I dropped into unconsciousness.

The stallion was so magnificent. Galloping all around me in his striking beauty. The consistent pounding of his hooves hitting the ground, rearing up every now and then to take his stance with the anxiety, frustration or pressure he felt near me. It was almost as if he was desperately trying to connect with me. My voice was silent and my heart and body felt frozen. The stallion finally turned and dashed off into the darkness, his hooves loud, thudding in the distance.

My eyes shot open. It was so bright in the room and so silent. Jason leaned over and was smiling at me and confusion set in. What happened? Was I just asleep? I looked down at my arm where the IV was in. My body was soaking in the IV hydration like a sponge.

My stomach felt settled enough from the anti-nausea medication they gave me before I passed out. A few minutes later, the doctor came back into the room with another doctor. I felt Jason's hand squeeze mine.

"I'm happy to see you awake again. You passed out from such bad dehydration!" The ER doctor said and turned toward the other doctor. "This is Dr. Lee. He's one of the obstetricians who is from Labor and Delivery. He was able to come down to check things out. We're going to do another ultrasound, ok?" I managed to nod my head.

The two doctors then performed another internal ultrasound and Joseph's heartbeat echoed in the room again, matching the thudding of the stallion's hooves in the dream I just had. The obstetrician sat down in front of the screen this time and studied it for a minute. He finally was done and as he took off his gloves, he smiled at me.

"The baby looks great so far. You're measuring about 8 ½ weeks and the baby has a strong heartbeat at 144 bpm. I will call your regular OB after I leave here and get you scheduled in to see her tomorrow. I know you have your first appointment in a few days, but I don't want you to wait that long," he said and then he paused as he saw the confusion on my face. Why did I need to see my regular OB right away if he just checked me? Was something wrong and he wasn't telling me? I still didn't understand why I was so sick?

"Okay, but why the hurry to get to my OB? Why have I been throwing up so much?" I asked him.

He took a deep breath before he began to explain to me what was wrong with me and he became the first doctor to introduce me to the term: Hyperemesis Gravidarum.

"I know that you're nervous, especially coming into the ER this sick and weak. It's not common to be this ill. Your husband asked me while you were asleep, was it morning sickness? Essentially, yes, this is a form of "morning sickness" but it's really not the same at all. You have Hyperemesis Gravidarum or HG, which is, for lack of better words, morning sickness on steroids. It usually doesn't end from my experience or ends much later in the pregnancy than what's usual for morning sickness. There's no way to really tell how long it will last, though, because it is different for everyone. We also don't know the actual cause either. Most of the patients I see that are this bad, are on bed rest until further notice, usually the entire pregnancy. Movement is very difficult, as you know. You just need to stay hydrated. I'm going to also order home hydration or we will admit you here fully if we can't get it under control at home. Your husband explained to me that you can work from home and have your own company, so being on bedrest is no problem. I'm relieved to know that because I've seen many of my own patients with HG lose jobs. It's so rough to go through this. But the good news is, the baby looks really good so far," he explained.

What? So far? My mind went into complete overdrive. *Did I just hear him correctly? IV hydration…at home?* They kept me for another 24 hours and the next day, with fluids on board, I was sent home, but the nausea raged on. I kept telling myself: It will end. It must end. *Nobody gets sick this long during pregnancy, right?* But it never ended and as the first trimester came and went, the sickness gained strength. A PICC line was ordered to replace the IV, weekly home care with nurses turned into daily, a Zofran pump inserted directly into my stomach and endless mixtures of medications were being pumped into my body in hopes to control it. I eventually just put myself into fight mode and the only thing that kept me going was dreaming of holding my baby.

As a seasoned mom, I knew how intoxicating that moment is when you are handed your newborn for the first time. I laid on my couch day after day, and prayed while I kept that picture in my mind. I fought the good fight, waiting to finally give birth and meet my sweet baby. However, the horrors of what I faced each day was nearly impossible. I was so weak that most of the time, I would doze in and out of sleep. When I was awake, all I could do was just listen to the voices around me. I listened as Jason and Lilly talked and ate meals together or hugged and laughed. I couldn't join in and I felt like an outsider looking in, as my family continued their lives around me. All I could do was just lay there, completely helpless and suffer.

My stomach was so raw with nausea that even if I took a deep breath, I started dry heaving so violently, that I couldn't breathe. Therefore, I stayed as still as I could, caught in hell. I missed Jason and Lillian so much that my heart hurt. Unlike the guilt I felt, Jason wasn't even phased by it as he took care of Lillian and me. He just wanted me comfortable and was happy to do whatever was needed around the house. He was so nurturing through this time and a new part of him emerged. His thoughtful words always kept me from giving up completely. He became my knight in shining armor with a broom, bucket and Clorox!

One afternoon, he bent over the side of the couch, kissing my forehead as I was waking up and I heard him start to sing. It was our wedding song and my heart burst with love. I opened my eyes and he was fast to wet my lips with a washcloth that he kept near me. He smiled and before I tried to talk, he shushed me to stay quiet.

"You're so beautiful. So very brave and so strong. And there is nowhere else I would rather be, nothing else I would rather be doing and no other wish I would rather have than to be right here, experiencing this with you. I promise that when this is over, when you are well and strong enough to move again, I will show you the world. In sickness and in health my love. Forever on our journey through time together, loving each other more each day. This, my darling, is love." I burst out crying from his loving words.

My spirits lifted after he said that, giving me the will to keep fighting. Yet, the fight would continue to test me further. By eighteen weeks, the sickness grew even worse and a feeding tube was being ordered by the doctors. Concerns of organ failure were discussed and while that scared me, I stayed present as much as I could and continued the fight. At twenty weeks, the hell I was in was momentarily halted, when my obstetrician said, "It's a boy!" A little boy! I could hardly contain the excitement. I felt so blessed and Jason was ecstatic.

We named him Joseph Michael and as I envisioned holding him in my arms, sitting in a baby blue nursery, I continued to push through my battle with HG. Days later, I felt his little kicks begin and they grew stronger every day. I hung on to each and every kick as they were proof that he was doing well. They inspired me to get through this nightmare together with him.

One morning, I woke up to Lillian rustling in the kitchen. Beside me was a plate with my medications and a note from my husband: Call me when you wake up. It was our routine over the months to call him when I woke up and he would check in. He would love home immediately to help me. Luckily, at the time, he worked as a Property Manager in the apartment complex that we lived in and so this made it very easy to check on me, all day long. I saw a text on my phone from my mom, asking me to call her as well, once I woke up. She and Jason had teamed up to provide me with round-the-clock care, alongside the home care nurses.

Before I picked up the phone, I unhooked my PICC line port and forced myself to get up to see what Lillian was doing. Getting her ready for school while I was so sick became a new routine too. Jason would lay out her clothes, pack her bookbag, lunch, and have her breakfast ready to go. Lillian would handle the rest with getting herself ready. Jason would then come help me get my PICC line going with hydration and medications and then take Lillian to the bus stop. While we had the routine down solid, I continued to feel guilty for all the trouble this sickness was causing everyone.

I felt the nausea intensify as I sat up and grabbed the garbage can next to me. Gagging for what seemed like hours, I finally gathered enough strength to stand up. Walking into the kitchen, I saw Lillian spreading butter on a piece of toast with tears falling down her face.

"Lillian, baby, what's wrong?" I approached her and grabbed her arm. I fought against the nauseating smells of the kitchen and forced myself to hug her.

She pushed me away and began to cry harder as she dropped the butter knife and fell to the floor sobbing. I reached for her and by the grace of God, the puking paused in this one moment.

"Mommy, I'm making you toast. You always make me toast when I have a bellyache. Toast is supposed to be help bellyaches, right? Why isn't your bellyache going away Mommy? I don't want you to die!" She collapsed in my arms and we cried, releasing all of the fears we both had, with our arms around each other.

I couldn't believe I had the ability to hold her, something I couldn't do for months now because being this close to anyone made me vomit. Call it the strength of a mother, call it God, call it whatever, but I was able to hold my little girl and soothe her. It was the best feeling in the world. Rocking her back and forth, I began to sing *Twinkle, Twinkle Little Star* and Lillian relaxed into my arms. Even though she was not a baby anymore, this was her favorite song that I sang to her, while nursing her as an infant.

After the tears began to slow, I took a deep breath and fought the anger bubbling up inside of me. *I hate you HG!* It would have been really easy to just let myself get angry and fall into complete victim mode, but that would have pulled my daughter down with me. Before I could say anything more to her or fall apart, more strength washed over me and I was able keep holding her. I didn't know how much longer I would be able to keep it together like this, but I was granted the ability to hold my daughter who needed me so much after months of no physical contact. I couldn't have been more thankful. I looked up to the ceiling, smiling and mouthing the words, "thank you." Despite my weakened faith, I knew something bigger than me was giving me this time with her.

With a renewed sense of control and a few quiet minutes of much needed hugging, I finally spoke to her. "I know this is so scary seeing me this sick. I know that you want to make me all better and I love you dearly for that. Thank you for loving me so much that you would make me toast. Toast will make me feel so much better." Lillian pulled out of my grip, looked up and stared at me for a second. I gave her an encouraging smile.

"Really?" Her frown instantly turned into a smile and she jumped up, pulling me up with her. "Here, Mommy, here!" She excitedly handed me her toast.

"Wonderful Lillian! Thank you!" I hugged her again, helping her get her shoes on so she could catch the bus. I called Jason and after he settled me on the couch, with the IV fluids and medicine flowing, he left with her.

After they were gone, I hugged the garbage can, retching and crying with each upheaval. I wanted to curl up into a ball and cry for the rest of the day. Hyperemesis gravidarum was now impacting my daughter and seemed to rule both of our lives right now. My little girl was so scared and there was nothing I could do to make this all stop.

Defeat washed over me, but I stopped crying and forced myself to soak in the miracle that just took place. I was able to thank my daughter for her efforts, which was exactly what she needed to hear. I was able to hold her and sing to her. She needed to know that all was okay and to feel as though she contributed to that. Laying back down, I closed my eyes and sat with gratitude, smiling through the tears. The toast remained un-eaten on the table beside me and while I knew that one day this would be all over, what I didn't know was that it would end the way it did. I felt Joseph kick me and I put my hands on my stomach and laughed. He must have enjoyed that moment with his sister too.

"Everything will be all right, my baby." I rubbed my belly and closed my eyes to try and rest. Sleep was the only relief from the relentless nausea and vomiting, so I tried to sleep as much as I could to get through each hour of the day. Joseph continued to kick and weeks later, he would kick for the last time.

As the memories of the hyperemesis faded and I returned back to the present, I looked up from the plate of food and into Jason's eyes. I put the food down and tried not to cry. I didn't want to seem ungrateful for Jason's loving gesture, similar to Lillian's toast. I trembled as I tried to hold my tears back. I realized, as I stared into his eyes and he stared back into mine, that fighting the pain inside of me only amplified it and that it wasn't helping anything. Sobs choked my throat and I couldn't hold it in anymore.

"I know sweetheart, I know." Jason reached for me, wrapping his strong arms around me to let me cry. The last time he kicked was all I could think about as the tears fell. I could almost still feel his little kicks and I instinctively put my hand to my stomach, remembering that sad November morning.

Four

It was dawn on November 12, 2013 and as I prepared to face another day of intense nausea, Joseph was kicking me harder than he ever had. I laughed, despite the sickness that was also waking up with me. Joseph was determined to make himself known with those strong kicks! It was as if he knew I needed them. I looked over at the latest ultrasound picture from only a few days before. I was twenty-six weeks along. Almost in the third trimester!

The morning carried on as usual, as I waited for the nurse to arrive. By late morning, I knew she would be at my house soon, so I mustered up the strength to take a shower and I didn't notice that he hadn't kicked in several hours, since those first morning kicks. Later that afternoon, after the nurse left, I decided to take a nap, but something didn't feel right. I tossed and turned and could not get comfortable. A strange surge of panic suddenly rose in me. I also noticed that my underwear was really wet and I feared my water had broken. I had a slow leak with Lillian, but that had started in the last couple weeks of my pregnancy with her, before it finally burst at the end. It would be entirely too early to have water leaking now!

An icy chill ran up my spine. My mother's intuition was keen. I just knew something was terribly wrong. Jason must have had a bad feeling too because just as I picked up the phone to call him, he called me first.

"Is everything alright? I don't know why, but I don't feel like it is," I heard the worry in his voice and instead of matching it, I changed my tone to try and ease his concern.

"Yes, all is okay," I said to him. Both of us were quiet for a second. I couldn't fool him. I sighed. "Actually, I'm not sure because I think I'm leaking fluids or maybe just urine? I'm going to call the doctor to be on the safe side."

He wasn't convinced it was just urine leaking and within the hour, we were on the way to the doctor. The drive over was in complete silence. I tried poking and rubbing my belly to get Joseph to respond and kick back, but my continuous pushing was met with an eerie stillness. I felt a chill run up my spine and my heart responded with a quickening beat full of rising panic.

"Jason," I leaned forward, feeling dizzy with fear. "Jason, he isn't kicking me back. I'm really starting to worry. I can't even remember the last time he kicked today, other than when I first woke up."

I opened the window, trying to take some deep breaths and calm down. Jason didn't respond, his face stayed glued to the road, with his jaw clenched. He knew too, but neither one of us was willing to say it, so we stayed in hopeful silence for the remainder of the drive. We arrived at the doctor's office and while I sat in the waiting room, I saw a mother staring at me. She looked to be about nine months pregnant and uncomfortable sitting in the chair. I gripped the puke bag they gave me to wait with. She spoke up first.

"I remember seeing you months ago, holding onto a puke bag. I don't mean to pry but are you still this sick?" I looked at her without responding, trying to remember her, but I couldn't. I nodded.

"Well, I'm not sure why," she continued, "but I feel compelled to pray for you right now, if that's all right with you?" I nodded again, thinking that was a bold statement to say, but I didn't have the strength to say anything.

"I'm Lindsay. What's your name by the way?" I asked. The smell of roses whiffed by me and I turned my head to follow the smell, wondering what might come next?

"Mary. My name is Mary," she said and I froze. I looked back at her and she had a smile on her face. Mary? This name brought butterflies to my stomach, coupled with the waves of nausea. The smell of roses came back and seemed to just settle heavily around my head. Mother Mary's face came to my mind as I continued to look at this mother across from me.

"Lindsay! We are ready for you!" The nurse's voice boomed loudly into the waiting room, snapping me out of my thoughts and Jason helped me up.

The nurse was smiling at the door as we walked toward her. I turned one last time to look at Mary again, and smiled, but she wasn't smiling anymore. Another chill came over me. It was as if she knew something was about to happen too. This made me feel unsteady on my feet as I walked down the hallway to the exam room. Mary's intuition was about to be proven correct. So was my own.

I felt the nausea turning worse and I started to gag as I walked into the room. I wasn't sure if it was because of the encounter with Mary in the waiting room or my own nerves, but all I wanted to do was check on Joseph and go back home. My doctor came in, grinning from ear to ear. Why was the staff so smiley in this place?

"Let's just cut right to it, shall we?" She said, lifting my gown and the ice-cold gel poured all over my stomach and in seconds, Joseph's body was displayed on the screen. "Let's check on our little guy here."

For a moment, my nerves settled as I looked at Joseph, so little and safe inside my womb. He was so perfect. The doctor grew quiet as she stared at the screen. I felt my body begin to shake again. Her silence made me more anxious because she was never this quiet. Was I overreacting?

"Okay," she finally said, "his fluids look really good actually. So, let me just see…" her voice trailed off. I waited.

"See what?" I prompted her.

Instead of responding, she held the wand against my stomach for another few seconds, leaning forward, carefully examining him. The panic that was brewing since the car ride began to kick up a notch. What was she looking at? I was so focused on her, that I failed to notice that there was no heartbeat coming from the speakers. A flash in the corner of my eye caught my attention and I turned to see what it was. For a second, I thought the fluorescent lights above our heads flickered off and on. I didn't see anyone by the door where the light switch was and I glanced at Jason. His eyes met mine and he gave me a reassuring nod, gripping my hand harder in his best efforts to protect me for what was about to come next. What was the flash in the room? Before I would contemplate it any further, I looked back at the doctor.

"What's wrong? Please tell me what you see. I'm getting a little scared here." Jason and I were both tense and holding our breath. There was nothing we could do but wait.

The doctor paused the screen and I looked at Joseph and noticed his back was facing me. I could see his beautiful spinal cord, starting from his head all the way to his bottom. His flawless little body. God's perfect image created in this tiny little human being and he was all mine. My love for him swelled in my heart and through my entire chest. I turned and smiled at Jason, but he didn't look at me. He was staring directly at the doctor, with fire red eyes from tears that were building. What he feared as we drove here was confirmed to him as he looked knowingly at the doctor, but I was still in denial. I followed his gaze and looked at the doctor too. She looked directly into my eyes and took my hand from Jason's grip.

"Lindsay, look at the screen," and she turned the screen to face me better. I looked where she pointed, right to a circle she drew around something. "That is his heart in the middle of the circle," she continued, "and right now the screen is paused. I'm going to unpause it and I want you to see what happens."

Before I could even begin to think about what was happening, she un-paused the screen and his heart so little yet so full of love, stayed still. As the horror of this moment became a new reality, my world as I knew it began to unravel. The flash from before, seared across my vision again and my ears began to ring. Panic rose up in my throat.

"Did you un-freeze the screen?" I asked, hoping she would say no. She nodded her head and her own eyes were now brimming with tears.

Panic turned into confusion, then quickly back to panic and I looked at Jason, whose face was now drenched with fallen tears. His hands were clutching his head, as if he was trying to steady himself. He began to cry harder and I looked back at the doctor.

"Is his heart okay?" I still didn't accept, that my precious baby was gone.

"No. No, it's not okay. Lindsay..." the doctor choked up, looking down on the floor and took a big breath. She could barely get the words out. After a few seconds, she looked back up, squeezing my hand and tried again. "Lindsay, he has no heartbeat. I'm so very sorry. But Joseph has died." Tears were now spilling onto her cheeks.

The room began to spin and I nearly passed out. Panic erupted into a blood curdling scream. I felt Jason's body lean over to hold me from falling off the table. In that moment of complete misery, I began to beg. I begged to give my Joey back. I couldn't even feel my own heart beating. I was completely broken. Our son was gone. Gone. Those kicks I felt in the early morning hours, were his last. The doctor stood up and told us she would give us a minute. I continued to sob and scream into Jason's chest, clutching his shirt with both of my hands, as a new and profound grief was slicing through my heart. My body physically hurt and I couldn't stop shaking. Jason stood strong and still, holding me tight and keeping his own cries of despair from escaping. His mind went into protection mode and he knew he needed to somehow get me off that exam table and onto a chair.

"We'll get through this. Lindsay, listen to me, I'm going to get you through this." He cupped my face, forcing me to look up. "Look at me sweetheart." I could hardly look into his eyes, the eyes that have loved me through so much, and the eyes that were going to love me through this tragedy that has struck us both.

I felt so ashamed and instantly blamed myself. Another flash erupted behind him and I shut my eyes in response. The ringing in my ears grew louder and louder and I held my hands up to my ears to cover them. I yelled loudly above the ringing, "Jason! What's that..." I didn't finish because suddenly, I heard it, loud above the ringing. A voice that nearly brought me to my knees. A voice that I wanted to forever chase after and find. A voice that I wanted to leave this earth and be with. A voice that simply said, "Mommy." It was him. Our Joseph was with us.

I leaned over and vomited all over the floor.

"Lindsay? Are you with me here? Hello? Look at me," Jason's voice broke through my flashback and he was standing next to me. I looked at him with a confused and hazy look. Jason continued, "I lost you there again! We really need to get ready to leave. I'm going to check on Lillian and make sure she's ready." I nodded in response, still feeling foggy from the memory of that awful day.

My stomach was churning from the intensity of recalling both the months of sickness and the day we lost him. It was all just too much to handle. I felt queasy as I tried to push all of these memories away so my stomach could settle. That was the very last thing I needed right now, was to get sick again. I was still nauseated during the day, which I blamed mostly on my grief. Learning to eat again after twenty-six weeks of surviving on IV's alone was hard enough because the simple act of chewing still sent me into dry heaves. Mix that together with grief and it was truly a living nightmare. However, the thought of walking out the door to say my final goodbyes to Joseph felt even worse and sent me running to the bathroom to vomit.

After cleaning up at the sink, I stood up and stared at my reflection, squinting at myself. All I saw was a shell of a young woman with swollen eyes and pale skin. Who is this woman? This frightened, sick, and traumatized woman couldn't be me. I splashed my face, trying to get some color to my cheeks and hurried out of the bathroom, feeling very shaky. I couldn't take anymore memories, so all I could do was hope no more came. However, I had a very uneasy they weren't done. It was like having PTSD all over again, with these constant flashbacks.

The bedroom was empty because Jason was still in Lillian's room, getting her ready for the service. My body felt very heavy all of a sudden, like someone had put fifty pounds weights on my back. I sat on the bed and laid down, not wanting to leave. I was doing everything in my power not to face Joseph's service. All I could do was lay there with tears sliding down my face and wait for whatever was going to happen next. I felt so helpless, with no reason for life anymore. My body felt cold and all I wanted was to hold my son. The ache I had to hold him again was excruciatingly strong and my heart literally felt as though a hole was in it. Birthing your dead baby and handing him over to the nurses, never to have him again is something no mother should ever have to do. I remembered hearing his tiny voice in those first few minutes after I knew he was gone. All week, I begged him to talk to me again or to visit me in my dreams, but he stayed silent and distant.

Jason was calling me from the living room. It was time to leave. I looked over at my anxiety medication across my room on my dresser, feeling like I needed to take some to get through the service. I stood up to go get it, but something stopped me. That's when I fell to floor and prayed. I wasn't sure if there was even anyone there to hear me, but I felt so desperate.

"Can anyone hear me? God? Are you even there? If so, please take me. Just take me too. I can't do this anymore. I'm on my knees, begging for relief."

A chill ran down my spine and what felt like fire burned up my arms. I grabbed my arms in response. I laid all the way down on the floor and curled into fetal position. Thoughts were swirling in my head, but none of them made sense. Jason came in the room and had me standing and leaning against him, in his strong arms within seconds. He began to sway with me into a slow dance, humming as we moved back and forth.

"Jason, please make this all go away," I pleaded with him, as if he could change what happened. We paused, he stopped humming and I felt his body tremble, as he started to cry.

I wanted to comfort him back, but my heart was too numb. I didn't know how to reach him in this moment, especially because he just suffered another blow the day before. We found out that his beloved grandmother, Agnes, was in the hospital in Ireland and we knew she was not going to make it. His grandmother, was an incredibly strong mother figure for my husband, as well as the rest of his family. She was truly a remarkable woman and taught Jason so much. The idea of losing her, too, brought even more agonizing pain. He began to sing now, through his tears and it was bringing us momentary comfort. I held onto him with as much force as I could. I didn't recognize the song, an old Irish tune, but it sounded so good as we held onto each other.

I drifted as he sang, imagining Agnes laying in her hospital room. I felt a few moments of peace wash over me, realizing that if she passed away, my son would have her with him up there. This thought surprised me because I haven't given this much thought to heaven until now, even after my own grandparents died. I turned away from

God after that fateful night in the summer of 2000 and wasn't sure I would ever come back, especially now that Joseph was gone. Even though my Christian upbringing had always led me to believe in an afterlife, Joseph's untimely death made me wonder now: Is heaven real?

Losing Agnes would be hard, but having a grandparent pass was not the same as a baby passing. Therefore, I really hoped that what I was taught to believe in was, indeed, real. I was so afraid that if it wasn't, Joseph was nowhere safe. It was like I needed God to confirm where he was because right now, I just didn't know.

"Where's my son?" I asked, without thinking, as Jason held me tighter. "Please God, show me a sign!" Jason stopped singing and swaying and we stayed still, holding each other up under grief's grip. I needed a sign and I needed it now, to know that our son was okay.

Looking past his shoulder, I noticed a pink scarf on the floor, that had belonged to my grandmother, Oma. It seemed to have fallen from the drawer of the dresser. She loved to wear that scarf so much. I remembered how she used to sing to me too, just like Jason was just doing, whenever I looked troubled. Singing also kept her calm, when her world was nothing but horror for so many years. Nostalgia washed over me as I thought about her, longing to have her next to me now, telling me to be strong and singing to lighten my mood. Jason knows the comfort singing brings me because of my Oma, which is why he does it often.

Oma was the bravest woman I've ever known. She was a World War II survivor from Germany. She had seen the worst of the worst and never recovered. A part of herself remained hidden after the war because she was part Jewish and never told anyone. Even as a child, my mother worked hard to take care of her and keep her comfortable after they came to the United States.

Like me, she suffered severe Post Traumatic Stress Disorder, but for her, it eventually manifested into schizophrenia. Her suffering was not in vain because the lessons I eventually learned from her life, have been profound. She knew what had happened to me at sixteen and as I stood there, staring at her scarf, I remembered the day I told her.

It was the summer after I graduated from high school and I was just about to leave for college. Oma was over our house for dinner and she was sitting on the couch in the living room, staring at our fireplace. Her eyes were always so glazed over. It was like her mind was in overdrive and her body was stiff.

"Oma?" I came over and sat next to her and like always, she did not turn her head to look at me. It was rare she would have any conversation with me, however, that night would be one of those infrequent times. "Oma, I'm leaving for college in a couple weeks. I'll sure miss you." I expected her to continue to stay staring at the fireplace, but to my surprise, she didn't. She turned and looked at me.

"College?" she asked and I nodded my head. I reached for her hand and kissed it. She smiled at me. "Be safe always." Even after all these years here in America, her English was still very broken.

"Oh Oma, don't worry. I will be perfectly safe," I responded and squeezed her hand. She stared at me some more and I could tell she was trying to find the correct words to tell me something, as was I, so I jumped in first.

"Oma, something happened to me a couple years ago. Something very bad. A man hurt me," I blurted out. I don't know what provoked me to tell her, but it came out. I told her what happened from that night and while I couldn't bring the word "rape" to my lips, she understood. She cut me off before I could finish by waving her hand repeatedly in my face to silence me, looking away with tears. After a few minutes, she looked at me again.

"Lindsay, let me share with you a story, about when your mother was very small," she said, pausing for a second. I held my breath. Her German accent was so thick, so she always had to talk slowly for people. She proceeded to share with me how much she suffered after arriving here in the United States with my grandfather and mother, after the war ended. She was not liked very much as a German and had a terrible time adjusting to her new life in a new country. What she told me next shook me to my core.

One night, while my grandfather was out and living on an army force base, violence found her again. As if World War II wasn't enough in one lifetime. My mother was only four and her brother was two and they were just finishing dinner. Suddenly, two soldiers who were very drunk broke into her home. My Oma, being the strong survivor that she was, heard them busting through her kitchen door and was quick to hide her two small children in a closet. The men proceeded to rape and beat her. For my Oma, that was the last straw; she was never able to heal after that night.

This was the last real conversation we ever had and I deeply cherish it. It was like my soul was blending with hers and we needed this moment to connect in a unique and special way. After our conversation, I buried her story with mine. I closed my eyes at the painful memory of that day and felt her around me. However, the pain was not only for her. It was also for me. Both of our stories were still lost and that is how I wanted it to be. She did manage to express to me right before she died years later, how scared she was that I would end up like her - forever, lost and forever frozen in fear. Her last words to me before she passed came into my mind next:

"End this Lindsay. End this for our family. Love. That is all you need…and just dance. Dance like no one is watching," she reached for me, struggling to get the words out. I laid her back down, not knowing what to say in response and kissed her forehead. She died that night.

While she was never able to be the grandmother that she wanted to be while she was alive, hearing her voice in my head brought comfort to me. As I stood on shaking legs, trying to endure my grief, she was able to fill that role. My dear Oma was there, I just knew it and was singing as she always did. Her spirit holding onto Jason and me in love.

My husband reached for my hand and we began to dance again. Dancing away, just like Oma told me to do so long ago. A small laugh erupted as I thought about her advice and how confused I was then. Not anymore. Now in my despair, it held such strong power. It was just what I needed to remember to get through this hard moment. I needed her strength and wisdom to hold me, to help me get to Joseph's service and say goodbye. Just as she had to say goodbye so many times in her life.

The room grew warmer and an amazing realization came over me: This was the second time since that day in the hospital after Mother Mary's dream, that I was being shown this powerful unity. It was the sign that I just asked for. I was in awe. Grief and love were swaying side by side as Jason and I danced, showing me just how linked they really were. Crying over my son and smiling at my Oma's wise words, all blending together in this beautiful, messy mourning. Jason must have sensed her spirit in the room with us too.

"We aren't alone in here," he whispered, smiling and twirling me. I nodded as I spun around, feeling stronger. I managed a smile back to him, even in my tears. Then I paused, stopping our dance and spoke out loud.

"Oma, where's our little boy?" I asked. I heard Jason take a sharp breath in.

"She has him, darling. He's safe in the arms of love," Jason answered, kissing my forehead. "Feeling ready now?" I nodded.

"Thank you, Oma," I whispered over my shoulder as we left the bedroom, putting my arm around Lillian who was watching all of this take place from the doorway. Her own curiosity was ready to burst out of her, with dozens of questions. However, she didn't say a word, as I lead her out with us. One day, I will talk to her about what was happening, but for now, no explanation felt right.

As Jason held the door open, I looked up at him and his blue eyes seemed to shine brighter through his tears. Once again, I found myself lost in them. I felt a longing wash over me, as I remembered the first time I met him; his eyes piercing my soul. Together, the three of us finally walked out, hand in hand to say goodbye to our Joseph.

My Oma, so full of love now, stayed in our bedroom, dancing away; with light radiating all around her joy. Waiting patiently, for me to find that joy too.

Five

Joseph's service had ended and I don't think I took one single breath the entire time. If I did, I was afraid I would lose control. The strength that my Oma brought me seemed to vanish, once the service began. Here I was again, questioning all the good that I felt from her memory, just like I did in Joseph's birth. I just couldn't believe I was sitting in a church, saying goodbye to my son and was no longer pregnant. The entire experienced tested my faith all over again and felt like it shoved me ten steps backwards. Grief waxes and wanes like that. I picked up a rose that was from his service and smelled it, letting its beautiful aroma comfort me.

As we drove home, I thought about all of the things that my mother, who is a minister, had taught me about God. More specifically, what she taught me about heaven and death. I was so desperate to find relief and wanted so badly for that relief to come from God. More importantly, for God to stay with me. I was so tired of going back and forth.

It always made me feel good learning about the Bible stories as a child. Now I had to make sense of them as an adult and I was angry. I was riding along these devastating waves of grief and pain, repeatedly washing up to shore over and over. Dancing with Jason in the bedroom was a beautiful moment, only to be interrupted by the next wave, knocking me down. How do I stand back up and stay up?

I started to question if I was too weak to actually heal from this.

Would I ever get to know what truly feeling peaceful was like? Peace was nonexistent prior to Joseph's loss for me and I certainly felt it would never happen now. I wondered if I could "end the fear and sorrow for our family," like Oma demanded? Looking over at Jason, as he drove, he was just as quiet as me. I looked out the window, watching the scenery move past me at a fast speed. Fast like my life had been for so many years.

Anxiety kept me from slowing down and in an odd way, this is what I often preferred. Chaos kept my mind busy and away from remembering that horrible night at sixteen years old. Being alone and slowing down was scary because this was when sadness and fear devoured me. Now, grief over losing Joseph halted me in my tracks. Everything was coming to the surface no matter how much I wanted to stuff it back down. My pastor told me after the service, to go home and take time for myself and just grieve. I didn't like that statement. Time to myself? I hope she didn't mean be alone with my thoughts because I just couldn't do that.

I had been that way from the beginning of my relationship with Jason. After Lillian was born, I would literally cling to him if he was going to leave the house, which he often did to work his second job in the evenings. While his patience with me all these years has been steady, I knew he needed me to wake up. During those nights alone, after Lillian went to bed, I buried myself in studying, social media, phone calls, having my friends over or my mom to come to my rescue when my anxiety was out of control. Quiet spaces scared me.

This eventually brought trouble to our relationship, forcing us to take a break. We both knew we wanted and needed more from each other. Spiritual growth, is necessary to grow as a couple and I was stuck. We had been through a lot together in the past seven years, but the separation we had from each other years ago, was the ultimate test. We split for a year and it was the hardest for me because it meant being alone. Jason had already begun his own inner healing by that point. He allowed himself to let go of the things that hurt him from his past and even more, he did it without ever leaving God's side. His faith was so strong. I admired him for this quality, yet I never understood how I could be free too. I was afraid to let go of the past. It was unknown territory for me.

During the year that we were apart, I learned many things, including *how* to be alone, but I still remained unconscious within. I grew, but not enough. Fear and anxiety still haunted me, as emotions rose that I didn't want to face. Therefore, I kept myself busy doing more. Doing more as a mother for Lillian. Doing more for Jason. Doing more with my career. I was never happy with things and certainly never saw what I already had, which is that "more" is *within* me. I didn't realize yet, that years of anxiety and anger, desperately trying to get more in order to be happy, wasn't sustaining true happiness. PTSD kept me from understanding this.

The love between Jason and I was too strong and after that much-needed time apart, we reconciled. Despite the areas of myself that I was still hiding from, we were both much stronger as a couple, once we were back together from the progress that I did manage to make. However, it wasn't enough, but the truth is, I just didn't want to test myself any further. While separated, I only put a toe in the water, testing its temperature. No way was I ready to jump in all the way and find true joy. Now Joseph's death pushed me right into an ocean whose depth I had never known. The real me was reappearing through the broken pieces of my heart. Love was reaching for my soul, but I wouldn't surrender fully without one hell of a fight. And that fight was still lingering on as we drove home from the service.

As Jason pulled up to a stop light, I shuddered. He reached for me, but this time I couldn't stop trembling.

"I'm so angry Jason!" I burst out. He kept his eyes on the road as he merged back into traffic.

"I know. I am too," was all he said and that was enough. I needed to know that I wasn't the only one who was angry over Joseph's death, but there was more underneath my anger. Anger that goes back thirteen years - after the rape - feeling like it was my fault and that I had failed somehow.

I wanted to scream, but I didn't. I wanted to run, but I couldn't. I sat helplessly in the car, letting my roller coaster emotions ride with me as we drove. This is why I avoided feelings at all costs. I never knew what to do with them. What I did know, was that it felt good to be angry instead of numb. This was because the one thing I thought gave me meaning and purpose, was being a mother. Now Joseph is gone and I felt like a failure again. I just wanted my son back. Why was I being punished? The bigger question is: Who was really punishing me?

I looked in the side mirror of the car at myself and stared, ashamed of my reflection. I hated who I saw and felt like I would never get over this guilt. I felt worthless. The fact of the matter was, I felt unworthy of love and now that Joseph died, any hope of feeling like I mattered after the rape, was slipping away.

Suddenly, my ears were ringing again and I leaned forward, holding them. Not this again. My head began to pound with a dull ache, along with the beat of my heart. Was it a migraine?

"Are your ears ringing again?" Jason asked.

"Yes! I can't handle it right now!" I bent forward some more, cracked the car window for air and tried to breathe it away. Knowingly, Jason reached for my hand again.

"Just stay calm, love," he said. How was he so put together when I was just falling apart?

I closed my eyes, keeping my slow breathes going and Jason squeezed my hand. Dizziness hit me out of nowhere and for a minute, the world spun. My ears rang louder, but that was not all I heard. A faint whistling was also there and it sounded as if it was coming from the seat directly behind me. The hair on my neck stood up and I squeezed my eyes shut, in hopes this would all end. As the whistling continued, I heard tapping next, like someone was tapping against the side of the car door. Tap. Tap. Tap. *Oh my god!* I screamed in my head.

I leaned forward once more, holding my head as if it would protect me against these sounds. I wanted to just open the car door and fall out. PTSD was getting the best of me and suddenly the words of my Oma jumped into me again: *End this Lindsay. End this for our family.*

Maybe trauma in our family wouldn't heal with me after all because right now, I didn't have the strength to fight. I began to cry, begging someone to make it all stop. The flashbacks were so intense and so frequent now, that all I could think to do, was pray. Just like I did in the bedroom before we left for the service. Prayer was something I fought diligently not to ever do again, yet, it was God for the second time that day, who I immediately turned to.

The dreams, the flashbacks, the ringing in my ear, the never-ending smell of roses, my daughter's sadness, the sound of my son's voice the day he passed; was too much for me to handle. Bowing my head, the power of prayer moved through my lips as my heart humbly submitted. I was lost in the spirit of divine stillness.

"Mommy?" I heard my daughter, Lillian in the back seat and I wanted so desperately to gain control so I could comfort her. But I couldn't.

"Mommy!" Lillian grew louder, but she seemed far away.

"Lindsay, just breathe. Look at me," Jason said as he tried to comfort me but my body and mind were frozen, locked in between the horrors of PTSD and the quietness of prayer. I kept praying. *Dear God, please help me!* I heard myself crying. I felt a shiver from my head shoot down my back and while I knew I was awake, my soul was coming out of a deep slumber. Another flash and more came out.

I saw the carpeted steps leading up to his apartment as I followed my friend inside. I felt my nerves begin to poke at my stomach, telling me to just turn around and go wait in the car. I paused for a few seconds, standing alone on the stairs. I heard the door open from the top of the stairs, as my friend went inside. I continued up, while my stomach rolled with urgency. I heard voices on the other side of the door and I slowly pushed it open. Once inside, I heard everyone in another room so I walked toward them, looking for my friend. It was the kitchen and as I walked in, I saw the back of him. He was facing my friend and her eyes were gazing past him right at me.

Jason's voice in the distance was desperately trying to get me to come back to the present. Coughing and choking, I felt like I was suffocating. Jason pulled the car over and was patting my back, telling me to relax. The stairs and demonic face of the man in the kitchen is something that I had not remembered in that much detail for years. I caught a faint whiff of the rose again, and it seemed to ground me.

"Lindsay, just keep breathing. Relax," Jason kept saying and I looked up at him. He took a deep breath of relief that I was awake. "Maybe you need to take more medication? I hate to see you suffering like this," he suggested. I was so frustrated that I couldn't turn this off and felt bad for Jason and Lillian who were witnessing it all.

Holding Jason's hand to reassure him, it felt sweaty. This was really beginning to shake him up. It made me appreciate just how strong he really is and how deep his commitment to me in this sickness called PTSD was. Something in me snapped.

"Why can't I control these flashbacks anymore dammit!" I cried in desperation, "I can't take it! Why is this happening to me?" I continued to cry. While the flashbacks paralyzed me, they also had a purpose that I didn't recognize. They served to purge the layers and layers of pain as love slowly put me back together. I was so upset, that I didn't hear Lillian crying too.

My nails were digging into the flesh of my hand, as I held tightly to the rose. Jason turned to give Lillian a reassuring smile and then continued the drive home. He just wanted to get me home and out of this car. I sat up straight and opened my window wider to soak in more of the fresh, cool November air. The silence in the car was suffocating. Lillian was shocked from what she saw and began to whimper. I finally turned around to face her.

"Lilly, baby, do you want to talk about it?" I asked her. Lillian shook her head and choked back a sob. "It's okay sweetheart, it's okay to cry...."

"Why Mommy? Why is Joey dead?" She cried out, before I could say anything more.

I had no words. The hum of the car brought somewhat relief to the silence and instead of even trying to console her, I closed my eyes, allowing myself to fall into a deep sleep. The intensity of grief exhausted me and my dreams welcomed me. It was the day Jason and I found out we were pregnant with Joseph and I was jumping on him with joy and excitement. I could hear myself giggling.

"I love you so much!" I laughed.

Jason hugged me tight, "We are pregnant! WAHOOOOO!" He picked me up and twirled me around and around and I couldn't stop laughing. "No WONDER, you have been so on and off nauseas for the past few weeks!"

Jason took me out to dinner that same night we found out and we blissfully toasted each other and talked excitedly about having a baby again. We even went into Barnes and Nobles and bought the newest editions of a few pregnancy books. We were excited to read about all the newest findings. I was so happy to be pregnant that I wanted to read everything while I waited for the next nine long months to pass.

Jason was looking at music books in another section while I scanned through the latest editions of pregnancy diet books. After picking out a few books to get, I went to find Jason and I saw him looking through a guitar book.

"Do you want to get that book, too?" I asked. He looked up and when our eyes met, butterflies filled my stomach. When he looked at me like that, I felt comforted, trusting, and safe. I could truly say after all these years together, I still fall in love with him over and over again each day.

"Yes, I want to get this book too. I want to learn some new songs to play for the baby," he said and my heart melted. We walked out of the bookstore, hand in hand, feeling so lucky and so excited for the future.

When we got home, I awakened, but this time with no panic, only happiness as I thought about that beautiful night. All I wanted to do was keep sleeping in that dream.

Six

Lillian jumped out of the car first and I sensed her frustration as neither Jason nor I could find the right words to comfort her during the car ride. The shock of losing her brother and being introduced to death at such a young age overwhelmed her sad heart, but I couldn't bring her any peace. Instead I went to bed and fell asleep, but this time a familiar nightmare revisited.

It was dark as the curtain opened. And then I heard it again. The whistling started, moving through the darkened stage floor. I was holding a rose in my hand as tears spilled down my face. I started to call out for my son. Wait, I don't have a son; I have a daughter named Lillian. I started to panic: why am I on a stage? So many questions swirled in my mind. The seats in the auditorium began to slowly light up.

One by one, in many sections of the room, I saw the people in my life light up and fade back out into the dark. I saw my mom crying under the soft light in her seat. I wanted to run to her but I couldn't move.

My hand was gripping the rose so hard, the thorns pierced my skin. Blood was dripping down my arm and for some reason, down my leg. I was horrified. Why was there blood dripping down my leg? I heard my pastor's voice reciting a prayer in honor of my son. Where was she and why was she reciting a prayer for my son? I don't have a son.

"Mom!" a male voice broke through the darkness from the back row of the audience. I heard him. I heard his voice calling for me, but I couldn't see him. Why was he calling me Mom? When did I have a son?

"Mom," this time his voice was behind me, softer now and I gasped. "Don't fight anymore, let me go. I am here to help you but you need to let

me go," he said. I turned to face him but no one was there and I felt myself spinning and spinning, my body began floating, like I was being carried by an angry tornado.

"My name is Jason, nice to finally meet you Lindsay." Suddenly, the scene from the day I met my husband was inside this tunnel I was spinning in. I wanted to scream for him to help me. I reached to grab his hand, but he spun away.

Then the room became still again and I was sitting in a seat in the front row of the audience. I heard a little girl giggling. I looked up to the stage that was dimly lit and saw a young girl, blonde like my Lillian, running toward me but disappearing as she got closer. I looked down in my lap and realized I was still holding the rose. Then I heard a man's hard breath behind me and I turned around. It was still very dark around him, but I saw his eyes and they locked with mine.

He glared at me with a smirk on his face, and as the lights went up, I saw who he was. I felt as though my body is collapsing within. I heard myself screaming but no noise came out. Suddenly, the lights went out completely. Darkness was all around me and I felt like I was drifting away. I dropped the rose into the darkness. It landed on the ground, its petals staying intact, glowing against the dark. The tiny light from the red petals, began to glow a little brighter in the darkness. Light always pierces darkness and I felt my heart welcome this light like a slowly blooming rose welcomes the sun after the night.

His whistling began again, echoing in the large auditorium and the lights went out. Complete darkness surrounded me and I didn't know how to get out.

"I guess you win this time, little girl," his voice broke the silence, deep and ugly.

The whistling faded away.

My eyes shot open. Sweat was dripping down my face, neck and off my nose. I felt Jason pushing back my hair off my clammy face.

"You okay sweetheart? You're shivering and sweating, are you feeling sick?" Nausea rolled within me from the nightmare and I blinked back the fog that remained in my brain and in my eyes.

"I don't know. What happened? Weren't we just in the car?" I asked.

"Here, drink this water," Jason said and I gulped it down. I handed him the glass and sat up, wiping my eyes, hurting from the contacts I forgot to take out. I looked at him confused. "You fell asleep the minute we got back here."

"He's here. He's here in the auditorium…he found me," was all that I managed to say, making no sense to Jason. "Where's our son?" I was not fully awake yet and so overtired that it was hard to get my bearings.

"What do you mean? We're home from the church and Joseph's memorial service," Jason answered, trying to orient me. My muddled brain, barely remembered where I was. The dream was oddly familiar, like Deja vu? When did I have that dream before?

Then it came to me. I jumped out of bed and ran to the closet. Underneath a giant mess of fallen clothes, I found it. Without even opening it, I held the journal from my pregnancy with Joseph. I felt tears sting my eyes. Jason stood up from bed and went into the bathroom.

"I think a nice bath will help you to relax again to go back to sleep," he called out and I ignored him. Taking a deep breath, I opened the journal and something fell out.

I looked down and saw a piece of my Oma's pink scarf that fell onto my lap. It was a piece from the same scarf I saw earlier that day. July 3rd, 2013, Jason and I finally had our dream wedding, so I had cut out pieces of her scarf and my mother's wedding dress and had them sewn underneath my train. There was so much insanity in the month leading up to the wedding, that I didn't realize I missed my period. I was battling continuous nausea during the wedding prep, but I chalked that up to stress, not knowing this was the beginning of my HG battle. Getting through the wedding was the only thing I was focused on. I missed her again as I looked at the scarf, but instead of wallowing in her memory again, I continued with what I was doing. I looked at my journal and it was dated, July 6th, 2013. The title read:

'I AM THREE WEEKS LATE. WE ARE PREGNANT!

Hot tears were building in my eyes as I read it. I flipped back one more page, to July 5th, 2013. There it was. It was entitled:

"The Stage"

With shaking hands, I read on. The nightmare I just had, lined up exactly with how I dreamed it the first time. The stage, the rose, the blood, my family and friends lighting up in the seats, the little blonde girl, and Joseph's voice. Oh, my sweet boy. Tears were now falling as my thoughts were flying through my head as I kept reading. I gasped in horror as I read the ending at the bottom of the page and I felt my stomach roll:

Please, please somebody. ANYBODY! Erase him from my dreams and my memory. I cannot handle seeing him and who was that little girl? Was she Lillian when she was younger? It didn't look exactly like her. And who was the man calling me "Mom"? I don't have a son.

My questions were so scattered, which was exactly how my brain felt at that moment trying to figure out why this dream came to me twice. I heard the bath water running and went into the bathroom. Handing Jason my journal, I slid in and the hot water felt so good against my aching body.

"Jason, read the July 5th entry." When he was done, he looked at me with tears.

"I've had this dream twice and I think Joseph was trying to tell me something," I said. Jason bent down and sat next to the bathtub, not saying anything. In the silence, it dawned on both of us. His presence in that horrible dream had a greater message. He was trying to help me to stop fighting.

Once I began to feel better, I decided it was time to get out and try to get some more sleep. After I got dressed, we hugged for a long time. I noticed the clock behind him and saw that it was nearly 2 am. Lillian!

"Jason, Lillian!" I pulled back from him and started toward the door to check on her, but he pulled me back.

"She's sound asleep. I got her ready for bed and read her three books. We also talked for a long time about Joey, while eating ice cream. We even prayed together. I held her until she was nearly asleep. She's okay." He is my hero.

I relaxed after that and got into bed. We were both silent, staring at the ceiling and I thought about his prayers with her. I wasn't upset, I was envious. I was still so unsettled about God and wished that I wasn't. I looked over at Jason who was staring at the ceiling too, deep in his own thoughts.

"Do you ever think that God doesn't exist now that Joey is gone?" I asked him. He was very quiet for a long time before he answered.

"No. But I know you do." We both shifted and faced each other. "Let me ask you," he paused and pushed my hair back behind my ear, "where do you think that nightmare about the stage came from?"

"I don't understand," I said.

"Let me explain. You had a nightmare about a son you didn't know you were pregnant with yet, telling you to let him, go six months before he died." I felt chills from the truth of his words. While we laid there, staring at each other face to face, his blue eyes stood out against the darkened room. "There is not a real clear explanation of the intuition we have as humans. Even those dreams you have had your whole life, including this nightmare with Joseph, are confusing, yes? But it is those unexplainable mysteries, that takes our breath away and increases our faith. Which keeps our hope alive and how we stay connected to love. A love that starts with you, right here" he explained to me and pointed to my heart. "That is God. God is in the mystery. And that is love because God is love. And that is where our son is now. So, do I believe in God now that Joey is gone? More than ever," he said and I closed my eyes, soaking in his words. He kissed my forehead. "Let go of trying to control the mystery of it all, Lindsay. Think back and go through the memories, the dreams, the flashbacks, the feelings and whatever comes up...just, let go." He leaned in and pulled me close to him.

*Think back and go through the memories...*his words were replaying in my head. Where do I even start? The skyline of Boston came into my thoughts. A city we both loved very much and held so many beautiful memories, along with painful ones that I needed discern. Was I *really* ready to do this? I wasn't sure yet but as I started to drift off to sleep, the first day of my freshman year of college greeted me in my dreams.

Seven

August 2002

Boston, my beloved "City on the Hill," was the darkest time of my life, with one of my brightest outcomes. Living in a big city was both frightening and exhilarating to my scared and intimidated soul. The day I moved into my freshman dorm is a day that I'll never forget. It was a day that initiated independence and new strength for me. I was a young woman who was so lost, unconsciously reliving a trauma that was buried deep in her soul, striking whenever it felt like it. There is no control with Post Traumatic Stress Disorder. All I knew how to do was stuff the symptoms back in.

My freshman year was spent at an all girl's school, Pine Manor College and for me, it was a perfect transition into city life from my quaint upbringing in Connecticut. It was also what sold my mom to letting me live in a big city like Boston, so we agreed I would go there first and see how I liked the city. She secretly hoped I would stay at that school all four years, but I knew I wouldn't last. I was planning on transferring to my first school of choice as soon as I could, Northeastern University where my brother Matthew went. On the ride up, I had a brand-new journal out and was already recording how I was feeling about starting college. Mom was driving and laughed when she saw me bent over writing in it.

"Geez already? I just bought that one yesterday!" she said. "I wonder how many journals you will collect by the end of these next four years!"

"Hmm," I responded. "I don't know, but I bet I can beat the amount that I already have!"

"Oh goodness, I hope not. I don't even know what to do with

all the boxes of journals in the basement. Like, why are we keeping them?" she asked. She loved cleaning out closets and basements.

"Mom! Don't you dare touch them. Those are sacred!" She laughed, knowing I was already reading her mind.

Mom and I were absolute best friends. She was so sad that I was leaving and trying her best to hide it, although, she didn't do a very good job. I was her last baby leaving the nest and she made sure to tell me that about a hundred times over the summer, with tears spilling down her cheeks.

"You're officially making me an empty nester, Lindsay!" She would say.

Two hours later, we were pulling into my new school. It was a gorgeous campus, with gardens set off by perfect trees lining the driveway. It was also a very quiet environment, just outside of the city and mom had a smile stretched from ear to ear.

"Look at how clean and safe it is Linds!"

I rolled my eyes. Mom was so OCD with cleanliness that it was almost scary sometimes. There were upperclassmen waving us in and we pulled up next to one with a clipboard.

"Hey there! My name is Jessica. What's your name?" She asked as she leaned down to look at me.

"Lindsay Mirabilio," I answered. She looked through her list until she found my name. "Okay, you're in West Village. Go straight and then take your first right and you'll see the parking lot for that building."

"Thanks!" Mom chimed in and rolled up her window. "Wow, I like it here! It's so small, that they can have a check list with everyone's name on it for housing! I like that!" I rolled my eyes again.

"Oh Mom, don't get too excited. It might be a little too small, quiet and clean. I'll be out of here after this first year," I said laughing.

Mom was silent as she pulled into the parking lot. I knew she was anxious, but I didn't realize just how worried she actually was about leaving me. She had been through a lot after the rape and became very protective of me.

"Ok, here we are," she said, taking a deep breath, as she put the car in park. When we got out, we both groaned when we saw how much stuff we had to unload. Then Mom's cell phone rang.

"Oh, it's Derek. Let's see where he is?" She answered the phone. My brother Derek attended school back home in Connecticut and he was driving up with the rest of my stuff.

"Okay, Derek, we'll see you soon. When you pull in, tell the girls at check in that Lindsay is in the West Village," she told him. "And no, there's not time to chat up the girls here. Just get here and help your sister move in." I laughed as she hung up the phone. *Oh, Derek.*

I arrived before my new roommate, Karen, who had already spoken to me many times over the summer. She lived close by, about forty-five minutes south of Boston and I was excited to finally meet her in person. Mom was pulling stuff out of the car to pile up next to the curb and told me to go open the room. Once inside, I opened the door and took the whole space in at once. It was rather large for a freshman dormitory and we were blessed with a bathroom that would only be shared by one other room. Definitely a perk of attending a small, private all-girls school.

I chose the bed on the left and placed the first of my bags down next to it. Mom came running in, carrying a huge load in her arms. For the next hour, we unloaded the car and once we got it all out, we stood staring at the unorganized mess. This was where mom shined! She was a master at organizing and cleaning up rooms, and had most of it put together in no time.

"Oh! I forgot the bag of new sheets we just bought you. They were in the front with you remember? I washed them all, so I want to get your bed made," she said.

"Of course, you do," I teased her. Mom loved making beds. I just didn't get her sometimes. She dashed out the door to go get the sheets and came back in with my brother, Derek close on her heels.

He had my microwave balanced on his shoulder and was laughing about my new college diet, which would consist of many heated up soups in that microwave. In fact, it was his microwave he used his freshman year. I started to feel my first wave of homesickness rush through my stomach, thinking of all the delicious meals my mom always made us growing up, that I would sure miss. I cringed at the thought of cafeteria food and my eyes began to well up with tears. Derek caught the look on my face, as I stared at the microwave he placed on the table behind my bed.

"Don't be so sad Linds, Raman Noodles aren't THAT bad!" He smiled at me and I wanted to smack him. After all, he attended school only twenty minutes away from home and could eat Mom's cooking whenever he wanted. I squinted my eyes and him.

"*Ha. Ha. Ha.* You're just full of endless humor," I said sarcastically.

Mom began to make my bed and I chuckled again watching her. This was always my mom's first "go to" in any new place. She got anxiety if our beds were not set up and made, so we could go to sleep. Just as I bent over to help her pull my sheets on, I heard a small knock and in walked Karen with her parents. She put her stuff down and we ran to each other and hugged. The feelings of homesickness and worry faded, and were replaced with excitement once I saw her. We giggled with anticipation for the new year ahead of us. Derek mocked our giggles by giggling behind us. I turned and glared at him before looking happily back at Karen. Over the summer, we chatted about all the different things we wanted to do in Boston, and couldn't wait to get the year started! Meeting her in person made it all finally feel real and lessened my fears.

"So, I take it, this is your brother Derek?" Karen looked at him.

"Yes, that's what they all call me!" Derek winked at her.

"Ignore him Karen, he'll be gone soon. I'm so happy to finally meet you in person!" I said to her and we hugged again. Mom and Karen's parents were chatting, as we continued to put our room together.

A few hours later, the new students, with their parents and families, all said their final goodbyes at an outdoor barbeque in the center of the campus. Derek was in heaven, mingling with all the girls. He was absolutely thrilled I was in an all-girls school.

"Hey Lindsay, I second Mom, with wanting you to stay here," he said as he came over with yet another refill of food.

"Why are you even still here?" I glared at him and he laughed, running off to go flirt with some more girls.

Karen and I spent the afternoon meeting other students at the barbeque and exchanging numbers. Then mom gave me her final tearful goodbye and I felt my throat catch, as tears stung my eyes again. I was going to miss her so much. She is the most incredible mom, but I was ready for this new adventure! I hesitated for a second, hugging her a little longer, standing on the threshold of new independence and wanting to go home with her. She must have felt my hesitation. Unlike me, she knew I still had so much healing to do, but supported me leaving for school anyway. That's what made her so amazing, her continuous love and support for my brothers and me. We finally pulled back from each other and just smiled, laughing at the tears that kept falling down our cheeks. Suddenly, I thought about my room at home, my comfortable bed and all the nights on the couch watching our favorite shows. I pushed these thoughts away because I knew one thing, homesick or not, I did not want to be in Connecticut any longer.

I felt safe in Boston. I thought once I left Connecticut, I could leave the horror of that night behind, but wasn't going to happen. I instinctively reached for my left shoulder, looking tearfully at mom.

This shoulder held the memory of his ugly hands slamming me onto the wooden floor. My heart was pounding now and I took a big breath.

I looked over at Karen, who was hugging her parents and then she turned, smiling at me with a thumbs up. She was so excited, so I wiped my tears and smiled back, giving her a thumbs up too. As we walked back to our dorm after everyone left, we were both quiet. She must have been thinking about what she was leaving at home too. We walked inside our room and both paused, staring at some of our stuff that still needed to be sorted out. My life in Boston had begun. Karen reached her arms up and cheered with excitement, laughing and twirling around the room.

"Hello Freshman year! Let the fun begin!" I smiled at her, feeling calmer and joined in with her happiness, as she turned on some music. We began to dance, laughing together. The phone to our room rang and Karen answered it, turning down the music.

"Hello! No, this is Karen her roommate. Who's this?" she paused, "*Ohhhhh*, checking in her already?" Karen laughed and handed me the phone. "It's your lover boy!" Will! I jumped over to grab the phone.

Will and I had been dating since the fall of my Junior year in high school. For two young adults, two years was quite a while to be dating, but we formed a pretty hot and heavy "puppy-type" love for each other. I wasn't sure where the relationship would go, but he was safe and that was all that mattered to me. The idea of so many men to choose from in such a large city like Boston scared me, so I felt secure with a boyfriend from back home. We both understood though, that there would be a time we would need to separate and explore the world on our own; but neither of us were ready to make the first move yet. So, for now, he was still in my life which I liked.

"Hi Will!" I said to him, with a little too much enthusiasm.

"Hey babe! Having fun, are we?" Will laughed at the tone in my voice.

"Yes! Only been here one day and I'm in love with college!" I replied.

"Well, that's great hun. I'm already bored of my classes," Will said, snickering a bit.

Will was one year ahead of me, a sophomore at Wheaton College, which was about an hour south of Boston. He had started classes a few days earlier and we knew that we wouldn't be seeing each other as much. We were already used to the distance anyway, since he left for college the year before. We chatted for a few more minutes and then hung up. I was so used to the privacy of my own bedroom, that it felt weird to have someone else in the room, listening to my phone call. It made me feel homesick again. When I turned to look at Karen, she had headphones on, bopping to the music and wiping her eye make-up off to get ready for bed.

"I'm off the phone now," I pulled one of the speakers out of her ear.

Karen jumped a bit and laughed. "Got it chief! Don't worry, I'm used to having sisters, so whenever one of us would be on the phone with a boy, we knew to put our headphones on to give the other one privacy. Sound like a plan?" She smiled and I felt relieved. The homesickness faded instantly as I agreed with her. I opened my journal and wrote:

Freshman year was going to be a blast!

My dream faded away, as I woke up. I heard Lillian's voice getting louder and louder in the background.

"Mommy?" She said again and I opened my eyes. My beautiful little girl was standing next to my bed with her favorite bunny.

My heart melted and I reached my arms up, as she climbed into the bed next to us. I snuggled into her, smelling her and feeling so especially grateful to have her right now. I looked over at the clock and saw that it was only 6 a.m. She never gets up this early, but I knew she must not be able to sleep very well either.

"Mommy, I miss Joey so much," she said against the darkness. The morning sun had not begun to rise yet to welcome the new day.

"I know sweet girl. I do too." It was so hard to explain death to a seven-year-old.

"Daddy says that all I have to do is think of him or pray for him, and he will come to me," she said and I could hear it in her voice that this made her feel better, so I didn't dare question it.

"Yes baby, Daddy's right. Joey will always be with you and he is always going to be right here, watching you grow," I responded, trying to convince myself the same. She grabbed my hand to hold it and heard her begin to cry.

"I'm just so sad Mommy. I didn't get to hold him or show him all my toys," she said through her tears, and it felt like the pieces to my broken heart just got stomped on. I didn't know what to say or do and fought my tears.

"No, you didn't, but he can see all of your toys sweetie, even if you can't see him." Jason's voice broke in behind us and saved me once again.

Lillian climbed over me and snuggled with her daddy. I didn't blame her. Jason's strong arms felt safe and secure during this horrible time. Within minutes she fell asleep right in our bed and for the next five months, that is where she slept. She was afraid to be alone and even more scared one of us would die too.

"How did I get so lucky to find you Jason?" I whispered.

"Luck is not the word to describe us darling. Fate is. Did you forget already?" He turned to look over his shoulder at me, smiling.

"Never," I replied.

He turned onto his back, so he could hold both of us and he whispered, "my wild Irish rose." I felt butterflies in the pit of my stomach, which was a familiar feeling, since the day I met him. The love we had felt new every single day. I sat up and looked down at him, kissing him. I stared deeper at his face, etched with all of our memories together.

I thought about the dream I just had of my first day of college, which was one of my favorite days in Boston. There were also good memories there, with Jason, in the city we love. When we first moved to Connecticut, we loved to sit and recall the beautiful moments of our time there. I realized it had been so long since I thought about all those wonderful experiences in Boston. Jason's words from earlier that night came to me again: *Let go, Lindsay. Let the memories come.* My first day of college was a nice place to start, but there was a lot of about Boston that I pushed myself to forget, both good and bad. I breathed in a long deep breath and let it out slowly.

In the stillness of the morning, more scenes of Boston started to come. I thought about all the friends I have there, that got me through college. The earliest memories of my love story with Jason and the challenge of being away from my mom with severe PTSD. What I experienced in the past couple weeks with re-emerging symptoms and the flashbacks, were terrorizing, but perhaps it was time to start facing it all.

There was so much I needed to remember and while I was not ready to face that one terrible night yet, I wanted to recall my college days. Joseph's death was the beginning of reaching into my soul to see the past thirteen years differently. Within my grief, the light was continuing to grow brighter with these realizations. My journey back to joy was unfolding and while I fully didn't know how to heal yet, I wanted to try. It wasn't going to be easy, with a lot of ups and downs and so I began, starting with Boston.

"I'm ready now," I whispered out-loud.

Part Two
Boston

"It takes an exceptional person to love a warrior, especially a warrior whose war will never cease."
-Welby O'Brian

Eight

August 2003

Karen and I stood hugging in the parking lot, just outside of the dorms at Pine Manor College. When she pulled back, she looked so sad. I was too. It was now our sophomore year, but things were going to be different with us. I had officially transferred to Northeastern University, just as I had originally planned.

"I wish you weren't leaving us here." She gave me a sad face.

"I won't be far. You can come stay with me anytime you want!" I tried to reassure her.

Karen and I had become so close since that first day of freshman year. We spent countless nights talking and getting to know each other, and had such a good time exploring Boston the year before. I was finally feeling comfortable in this large city and knew my way around pretty well. The feeling of homesickness had vanished, replaced with that of a strong young adult, ready to see what would come next. I was growing more and more independent. Yet at the time, what I failed to understand was that under the young, confident college woman, was a girl with a deeply tortured soul. I still had not acknowledged the pain I was in. I figured that was what alcohol was for - to cover it all up.

"Let's get together very soon and have some wine," I said to her.

I shifted my mind back to the positives and my stomach churned with eagerness about not only starting at Northeastern, but living in my very first apartment with new friends. Karen did not want to live off campus with me and commute all the way back to Pine Manor, so she chose to room with a mutual friend of ours on campus. While my freshman year was fun and she was the best roommate, I was so ready to try the apartment life. Even though she was still at Pine Manor and not too far, I had a funny feeling that we would not be seeing each other much more. No matter what happened though, she would always be a big part of my transition into Boston and I would forever be thankful to her for that.

"Okay, yes, let's do that! God, I'll miss you! But I know you're happy with starting at Northeastern and I'm happy I have a place to come stay, when I head into the city to party with you! That will make things a lot easier," Karen said and we both laughed. I hugged her one last time and turned to get into the car to start my sophomore year and new adventures.

Before I pulled out of my parking spot, I had to think through the directions to get to my apartment. Boston is such a poorly laid out city, with no clear way to get anywhere and having a car there was nerve-wracking, but I was also very glad to have it. It would make getting around so much easier. Since our apartment included parking, which in Boston was a rarity, mom let me have my car. I also had friends from childhood, who lived just outside the city and I was happy to easily be able to drive over to hang out with them much more. I had felt kind of isolated at Pine Manor, despite how often we headed downtown. Feeling so much more settled in the new school year here, Boston was rapidly becoming my favorite place to be.

As I drove along, my phone rang and I saw it was one of my new roommates calling again. They had been calling me all day, as I had told them I was leaving Connecticut early that morning, but I just had to stop and see Karen first.

Before I could even say hello, I heard Hannah's voice. "Where the heck are you?" I laughed.

"I'm coming! Be there in about twenty minutes," I said and hung up.

Hannah was a very social and fun girl to be around and I couldn't wait to party this year with her and the other three girls I would live with. They were all in their senior year at Simmons College, which was near Northeastern. All of my friends at Pine Manor still lived on campus, but I still had a city of people to choose from to live with, and felt so lucky to have found Hannah, Rachel, Jordan and Tara over the summer. I laughed at the idea of five young girls all crammed into an apartment, but with the price of rentals in the city, it was not uncommon for college kids to pack in together to afford it. *Job. I need to get a job immediately*, I thought as I drove along. That would be easy as Boston was filled with all kinds of opportunities. I turned up the radio, cheering with anticipation, as I sang along to the music. Life seemed perfect in that moment.

I pulled into the street my new apartment was on and parked. A group of young men walked by, loudly laughing at something, which startled me. I froze and put my hand to my chest to calm myself.

"Lindsay, get it together," I told myself. My phone rang and I jumped again. "Ok Lindsay, now you REALLY need to get it together. What's wrong with you?" I asked myself and answered the phone, "Hello?" It was Will.

"Hey, how's the move going? I'm sorry I couldn't get up there to help you with it. Preparing to go to Spain these past few days has me so busy." Everything in his life seemed to be more and more busy lately.

The year prior, we were still good, but things were shifting and we both felt it. As we both progressed through college, we talked that maybe it was time to try life without each other. We even discussed splitting up a couple times, but didn't do it yet. Just like I did with most things in my life, I continued to ignore the sobering fact that we were drifting away from each other. I was so scared to see life without him, even though I did not have any true love feelings for him anymore like I once thought I did. He was just safe.

"That's okay. But hey listen, let me call you later. I just pulled up and parked and need to get my stuff in." We hung up and before I got out, I sat and thought about the upcoming semester and my relationship with him. He was going to be so far away, studying abroad in Spain. Perhaps this was a good practice run of getting used to him being out of my life. I sighed. It just made me too sad to think about.

Snapping out of my thoughts, I got out of the car and put Will out of my mind. Right now, I needed to move into my first new apartment! The thought of that eased the anxiety, that was beginning to fester in me. It was the same anxiety that I battled down all day, every day, but at least this move was a good distraction from it. I got out and as I shut the driver's side door, I felt like I just stepped in a pile of something. Looking down, at what appeared to be rose petals on the street. Beautiful red petals, still fresh and scattered all around my feet.

"Gee, shocking," I said sarcastically to myself, however to see them like this, all dumped on the street was still odd. Roses literally followed me and I never understood why. I noticed that there was one rose stem still intact in the pile of loose petals. I bent down to pick it up and just then, my roommate Rachel came running out with a big smile.

"You're here! You're here!" She shouted and we hugged. For only knowing her for such a short period of time, we were already close. She helped me bring some stuff in and the rest of the girls were standing in the hallway. I couldn't believe I was in my first apartment!

Hannah began to blast music, cheering for the new school year ahead. I laughed as it reminded me of Karen on the first day of our freshman year, dancing around like that. I missed Karen thinking about her. Karen and Hannah weren't the only students in Boston that were most likely jumping and cheering, getting all excited for the wild night life that this city held. The new year had students all over eagerly awaiting all the fun to be had, as they came pouring back in after summer break. The term "mature adult," quickly vanished from my thoughts as I laughed at Hannah jumping around to the music. Rachel rolled her eyes and smiled at me.

"Goodness, Hannah would you calm down? You'll scare Lindsay away!" She said to her, before looking back at me. "Ignore her Linds, she's kind of nuts."

"Oh, believe me, so am I!" We all laughed.

Tara came out from the kitchen with some wine, popped it open and poured us all a celebratory drink.

"To us!" we shouted.

I walked into my new bedroom and put my stuff down, placing the rose on the ground in the corner and stared at it. It was so gorgeous. How could anyone throw such a beautiful bouquet of flowers onto the street like that? Must have been a bad breakup or something I figured. I finished getting all of my stuff out of the car and smiled when I saw one of the bags with my sheets and a note attached:

Don't lose these! I will make your bed tomorrow when I'm there!

-Mom

"Of course, she will" I said to myself and laughed.

My brother, Matt, was picking up the new bed that was waiting for me at a mattress store nearby, and was bringing it over with a truck he was borrowing from a friend the next day. He and his girlfriend, Melissa, lived in Quincy, MA which was north of Boston, so he was close by to help with my move, but also, if I ever needed anything. Last year, I hardly called him as I was tucked safely away on the mellow campus of Pine Manor College, but this year might be a bit different.

His girlfriend, Melissa, was a childhood friend of ours. In fact, they were among the rare of the rare and had been happily dating each other since high school. Unlike Will and me, they had only grown closer through their time in college. Melissa's sister Gina was another very close friend and she attended Northeastern like my brother Matt had and now me. Melissa and Gina were not only childhood friends, but also our neighbors growing up and I found it funny how we all landed in Boston together, minus my brother Derek. Gina lived in the city with her friends from Northeastern, about fifteen minutes away. I also had even more childhood friends, Christian and his sister, Kelly, who lived west of the city in Waltham, MA, about thirty minutes away. I absolutely loved that my closest friends growing up, were all in Boston with me.

I had a blow-up mattress that I would use for the first night and began to pump air into it. After I got it all set up, I pulled my journal out from my purse and began to write down the day's events. When I was just writing how awesome my new roommates were, I heard a knock at my door and Hannah and Rachel peeked in.

"Hey, how is the room coming along?" Rachel asked.

"Good so far. Got this thing blown up, which is good. I'm exhausted," I answered her.

"We're going to order some food and we're thinking pizza? Sound good?" She asked and I felt my stomach growl at the word, pizza.

"Sounds great! I'm starving!" Rachel left to go order the food and Hannah came and sat next to me on the blow-up mattress.

"Are you sure you can sleep on this thing? It feels so uncomfortable," she said and laid down. I smiled at her.

"Yeah, I'm good. It's only one night. I'll live."

After the pizza came and we all talked for a lot longer than I anticipated, I finally stood up and was ready to go to sleep. It was after midnight by that point, but we had so much catching up to do.

I really liked them and was so happy to be there. It felt cool to be in my first apartment too and was so much better than campus living.

The next day was a Saturday, so mom was able to drive up with the rest of my stuff. Matt and Melissa arrived with my new bed and, of course, mom got it all set up. The two of them were headed off to go run some errands, but told me to call if I needed anything else. After unpacking and organizing my room during the morning, mom and I decided to head to lunch and pick up some more things I needed. Before turning the lights off in my room, I spotted the rose I had saved from the day before, still sitting safely in the corner where I left it. I picked it up and tied a rubber band around it and hung it upside down on the doorknob to dry out. It was still so vibrant and full of red color.

We decided to take the "T," which is Boston's public transit system, since it is just easier to get into the stores we were planning on going. Parking in Boston, or any city for that matter, is nearly impossible. We stopped to eat in Coolidge Corner, which was in the town of Brookline and one of this town's biggest commercial hubs. The September air was still very warm as we walked back outside after lunch. Summer was holding on tight and I put my sunglasses on, facing the sun. Smiling, as I took a deep breath and soaking in its rays. I looked back down and saw the hustle and bustle around me on the street.

Boston had been such an amazing college experience so far. I thought about all great people I had met and even enjoyed all the studying I had to do for school. The friends that I had there were creating memories that would last a lifetime for me. However, I felt the faint flutters of anxiety, in my heart and frustration followed. I could never understand why I suffered from so much anxiety? Didn't I have enough to distract me? The distraction of college life kept my mind off the fact that I was stuck in darkness, but my heart and soul were not fooled.

"Come on Lindsay, we have to get moving. We have lots to get!

Let's take a cab the rest of the way to the stores, to make it faster." Mom walked past me, pulling me out of my thoughts. Besides making beds, shopping was her favorite activity and being in Boston to shop was like a kid in a candy shop to her.

I fell in step behind her as I laughed at how fast she was walking to the curb to hail a cab. I needed to stay focused with her for the rest of the day and not drift off in thought or let my anxiety take over too much. I got lost in my negative thoughts so often, although I did a great job of hiding it from others through my sense of humor. No one truly knew what was going on inside of me. I wasn't sure I did either. Frequently, when I was alone, I would start crying and not even know where the tears even came from. Drying my face, I would forget about it, which was usually when I turned to alcohol to drown my sorrows. It was exhausting to fight back the tears everyday. I didn't realize yet, that by not letting them flow freely, this was feeding my anxiety.

Just when we were about to hail a cab, the delightful smell of apple and orange all mixed together, caught my attention. Looking up, I saw what it was, The Body Shop, a skin care store, and I knew the smell could only be coming from there.

"Hey, mom, wait! I want to go in this store," I called out to mom, who was ten steps ahead of me.

We walked into the glorious smell that had now caught my mom's attention and inside there were beautiful displays of all the fall items. I began to browse their body butters, opening all the samples to inhale. Grabbing a basket, I began to put some of them into it, when one of the associates came up behind me.

"Hi there! Doesn't that mandarin and cranberry smell so amazing?" I turned and was greeted by a girl about my age, wearing an apron and holding some samples in her hand. She smiled at me as I nodded. She opened a small vile. "Here, smell it in the fragrance oil. That's what we are burning right now in an oil burner." She placed it under my nose.

"Yeah, that is a really yummy smell. Cranberry! I couldn't pinpoint exactly what it was outside. I want an oil burner for my new bedroom, for the new apartment I just moved into!" I proudly exclaimed.

"Oh awesome!" She smiled. "My name is Prisha. I live up the road and go to Northeastern. I'm in my Sophomore year."

"Me too!" I said excitedly. "I just transferred in from an all-girls school in Newton, called Pine Manor College. I'm so excited to be at Northeastern, but nervous too. They're two totally different schools."

"Oh, don't be nervous. Classes start Monday, so what time is your first class?" She asked.

"8 a.m. sharp!"

"Me too! I can meet you on campus, outside of the student center after our first class. Around 9:30 work? I can show you the campus. I'll give you my number." I gratefully accepted her offer. Prisha pulled out a pen and I handed her my journal.

"Here, write your number on this," I said.

"Hi, girls!" Another voice broke in behind us. I turned and saw another associate standing there, with her basket of samples too.

"Hi, Sam, this is…I didn't catch your name," Prisha said to me.

"My name is Lindsay." I shook the other associate's hand. "Prisha and I have just been chatting about the fact that we both go to Northeastern. I just transferred into there and I live right up the street on University Road."

"Wonderful! I'm Sam and I'm the store manager. Want a job?" She smiled at me and laughed a little.

Mom appeared behind us all and before I could respond, she jumped in. "Yes! She does!" We all laughed and I looked at Sam to confirm.

"Really? If you aren't kidding, then yes, I would love to work here!"

"Great! And yes, I'm serious. I need another part-time associate, especially with the holidays approaching. Let me give you the application to fill out now and then we can have you start next week. I only need you for about eight to twelve hours a week and the pay is $7.00 an hour. Does that work?" Sam asked, as she walked me over to the cash register to get an application.

"Yes, it does!" I said happily.

As I began to fill out the application, I heard my cell phone beep and saw a text from Christian.

Heyyyyy. What's happening?

I laughed as I read it and we texted each other for a minute:

I just got a job!

Awesome! Where?

The Body Shop near my apartment as a sales associate.

Cool. Kelly and I want to come over later and check out your new place.

Yes! I should be back around like 7 or 8 tonight. I'm out with my mom and we all know how that goes.

Yup, sounds like a plan. Be good.

I laughed to myself because "be good" was Christian's signature phrase. I couldn't wait to see them later because they always kept my anxiety down. My life seemed to revolve around my damn anxiety. I finished filling out the application and handed it to Sam.

"I'm really happy to have you on board! How about if you start next Tuesday at 11 a.m.? Does that work with your schedule?"

I pulled out my class schedule and glanced at it and then looked back up at Sam. "That would be perfect!"

As mom and I walked back out onto the street, with a bag full of fragrant oils and a new burner, I felt very motivated.

"Wow, what a day already! A new friend at my new school and a new job!" I said to mom, as we hailed a cab and got in.

"Yes, what a day is right! That will be a great little gig to have while in school for some extra cash," mom said.

The rest of the day was spent shopping for what we needed and browsing at things we didn't need as well, something my mom and I do best together. As we walked up and down the streets of Boston, it was really feeling more and more like home. This year was going to be different and I felt really confident. As mom was checking out of the last store of the day, I decided to wait outside on the sidewalk.

We were in Downtown Crossing, which was a shopping district right near the Boston Commons, where many professionals ventured down to shop during their lunch breaks or after work, so it was always busy. I opened the door and walked out to the sidewalk, pausing as a sign caught my attention:

"*Every two minutes someone is Sexually Assaulted. Out of every 1,000 Rapes, 994 Perpetrators will walk free. Speak Up and Break the Silence!*"

I felt a wave of dizziness wash over me and my stomach turned to knots. Everything around seemed to go into slow motion as I stared at it. I heard a whistling noise behind me and I started to panic, as I backed away from the sign. *No, not that noise! Anything but that noise!* The whistling stopped.

"Whoa, lady, watch out!" A man's voice was behind me. I turned to see a homeless man holding his sign.

"Sorry, I didn't see you," I managed to say.

"It's quite all right, pretty lady," He smiled at me and began to whistle again. I put my hands over my ears to block out the noise. It was a noise from my past, that couldn't bear to hear. Trembling now, I felt sick to my stomach with dizziness. My heart started pounding more and I wanted to run as if I was being chased. *Get a damn grip Lindsay!* my mind screamed as my mom came out of the store. She was carrying yet another bag for us to have to bring back to my apartment. She saw me and ran over.

"What's wrong, Linds?" She asked, putting the bags down and took my hands off my ears. "Why are you covering your ears?" She had concern all over her face.

"Oh. Um. Nothing, just this loud group of people walked by that's all," I stuttered.

"You sure?" She knew I was lying, but didn't want to press me too much in the middle of the street. I nodded my head. When she turned away to start walking, my eyes teared up with frustration. Why do I go into such hysterics so fast?

Mom looked at me oddly, but then glanced down at all the bags we needed to carry the long distance back to my apartment.

"We better get moving before everyone is out of work and this place becomes even more crazy with people," She turned to go hail a cab.

One pulled up and the ride home was silent. Mom was checking her voicemails and I was mesmerized with looking out the window, as the cab driver maneuvered his way through the city. I love to people watch. I always wondered what they did that day or where they are going? Boston was full of so many interesting people. As we slowed to a street light right before my street, a man, tall with blondish hair was walking alongside our cab. It looked as though he was heading the same direction as we were going because he paused, and turned to cross the road toward my street. Our eyes met through the window of the cab and I marveled at how blue his eyes were. The cab driver stopped and waved at him to go ahead and cross. He hesitated one more time and a small smile spread across his face and I quickly looked down, but those eyes were something I would never forget.

Mom decided to hit the road after we unloaded everything, since she had a long drive ahead of her. She hugged me and left. A short while later, Christian and Kelly buzzed the door and they came in carrying a bag of food and beer. Rachel came out of her room, excited to see new faces. Hannah and Tara weren't home yet, but they could meet them another time. The four of us sat down in the living room and Christian took to Rachel very well, and was having so much fun asking her all kinds of questions. Kelly and I talked about classes starting next week and she was giving me some last-minute pointers. She, too, had attended Northeastern but graduated when my brother Matt did. We ate and drank some beers until late and then Christian and Kelly headed back to their place. As I watched everyone interact, I felt so secure. It helped ease my anxiety to have them all in my life.

As I went into my room, I saw my new bed all perfectly made and thought about my mom. I called and checked in to see if she made it to Connecticut okay. After we hung up, I laid in my bed which was so much more comfortable than the air mattress the previous night. For some reason, a sinking feeling came over me in my stomach. Must be anxiety. It irritated me to no end feel this way all the time and in order to make it go away, I turned over and fell asleep. I knew I would wake up and it would be gone, only to return again at some point tomorrow. Battling anxiety was such a daily struggle.

Monday morning, classes began and while I waited for the T to get to school, I put my headphones on as I studied my schedule. For some reason, the man with the bright blue eyes popped into my head again. I looked up from my schedule and stared at the street sign to our road and the memory of seeing him walk by our car jarred me a bit. He was so handsome, his tall stature and those stunning blue eyes, like stars glowing right through me.

I shook my head and resumed studying my schedule. Northeastern University was like a night and day difference from Pine Manor College. I was so relieved I had met Prisha and even more happy I got a part time job. Things seemed to be falling into place and I smiled as the T pulled up and stopped. I got on, still smiling, yet my heart began to beat fast, nearly skipping a beat. I put my hand to my chest as I held onto the rope because there were no seats available to sit. Anxiety. It literally overcame my body and I could never predict when it would strike. Like a venomous snake, it would slither in and turn into a full-blown panic within seconds sometimes. It would also take hours to recover from some attacks.

As the T made its way down the tracks, it got noisier with each stop, but my mind was somewhere else. I felt my heart racing faster and I took big, slow breaths to stay calm. I just needed to get to campus and Prisha would be there to greet me after my first class. The T went underground and the anxiety grew worse as it slowed to a stop, in-between stations. I felt my head spin with dizziness and I bent over to get some more air.

"Hey, you ok?" I heard a woman's voice next to me. I felt my knees shaking and now my heart was racing so fast, that I thought it would drop out of my chest.

"I...I'm sorry, I just..." I couldn't find the right words nor could I get much air in my lungs.

"Are you claustrophobic? I am too, so this scares me a bit too every time we stop like this. But it's okay, we're probably just waiting our turn to get to the next stop. Breathe. Just breathe," she said and patted my back. Claustrophobia was the last thing I was thinking about, but maybe she was right? After all, I didn't like elevators and tried to avoid them at all costs, so maybe the subway scared me now too. I was close to hyperventilating and I looked up, noticing that a few other people were staring at me in concern. The lady who was helping me told them I was all right, just a little nervous.

"I can't breathe," I told her and she smiled at me.

"Yes, you can, because you are breathing. Let's do some big breaths together," she said and together we took a few big breaths. It felt good to get the air in. We did that a few more times and she kept rubbing my back. The train began to slowly move again and I felt my heart finally begin to return to its normal pace. We pulled up next to Park Street Station and both got off. I was still shaky, but much better than before.

"Thank you so much," I said to her. She turned to me, nodded her head in response and smiled. We waved at each other as she walked off to her next destination.

I felt a lot calmer as I waited for the next train to pull up that would bring me to campus. When it did, I got on and put my headphones on. A short while later, we were back above ground and pulling up to the stop at my school. I got off and looked around. Students were everywhere and the buildings were so much bigger than the tiny ones at Pine Manor College Excitement replaced the intense nerves that I just experienced underground and I walked across the street with the rest of the Northeastern students onto campus to begin my new adventure! Life seemed good and for that, I was glad. At least, that is what I told myself.

Nine

The tapping on the door behind me was very loud. His voice, barely above a whisper, could be heard on the other side.

"Lindsay..."

He said my name a few times. My heart was pounding with sheer terror so hard that I felt it pulsating through my ears. My body was shaking uncontrollably, almost convulsing and sweat was pouring down my face.

"Lindsay..."

His voice again behind the door. Tap. Tap. Tap.

"Okay, little girl, you win this time."

Darkness now. I looked behind me and there was no door. I started to panic. There was no light. I felt a hand reach for mine and I jerked my hand away.

"Darling...."

Was that an Irish accent?

"Don't be afraid. I will find you." *Who said that?*

My alarm on my phone rang loudly and I sat up fast. I was sweating and felt really dizzy. The dizziness continued as I drank the entire glass of water by my bed to try and stop the head spins. I felt chills run up and down my back and kept one question in my mind:

Who was the man in the dark with an Irish accent?

My shades were still drawn, so the room was still dark, but I heard a faint notification that someone sent me an IM. I got out of bed to go see who was sending me an instant message and tripped over something on my floor, as I tried to stay steady on my feet. I saw that it was Christian and his words helped to pull me out of this trance from the nightmare. I laughed a little when I saw what he wrote:

HAPPY FIRST DAY OF WORK! Call me after! Be good.

"This is your first day, right?" I heard Rachel say and saw her smiling in the doorway. I didn't even notice she had opened the door and I nodded. She stared intently at me. Maybe it was her Psychology background speaking or simply the fact that she has a heart bigger than Texas in her small body, but I could tell she felt my hesitation.

She continued, "What's wrong? Are you nervous?" I nodded again.

"Yeah, just nerves." I said to her.

Without saying anything, she turned and went into her room and found a song that she knew would make me smile and turned the volume way up, giggling as she came back into my room. I laughed and then grabbed my towel to take a shower. Rachel believed everyone could cheer up with a good song playing. I could still hear her music from the shower and it made me laugh again. I finished getting dressed, ate some scrambled eggs and dashed out the door.

"Bye! Good luck!" Rachel called to me as I sped by her room.

I left my building and immediately put on my headphones to drown the noises from both outside and inside my head. I put on my favorite playlist and went to wait for the T, as I stared at a nice couple, walking up hand-in-hand, both dressed for work. So sweet, I thought. Then I thought about Will. He left for Spain and I missed him, but not as much as I should have. The night before he left, he was so weird on the phone. He didn't seem like he cared about anything I had to say, which really bothered me. As I watched this couple, it made me realize I deserved so much better. I wanted what that couple had.

The train pulled up and just as I was about to get on, I was blocked by a man that jumped off last second. We collided and our eyes locked. I stared into his familiar blue eyes and felt my heart leap. I looked away and went in to sit and glanced out the window. He was walking away from the train and just as we were beginning to pull away, he turned and our eyes met again. How ironic that I was just thinking about how I deserved a better man for myself and that blue-eyed man showed up out of nowhere. I was lost in thought after that, wondering who he was? A tap on my shoulder snapped me out of my thoughts and when I turned, a woman was pointing to the floor.

"Are those yours?" My eyes followed to where she was pointing to and look down. What I saw next nearly knocked me out of my seat.

A perfectly put together bouquet of red roses sat abandoned on the seat just behind me. Again? My dried up rose collection was starting to get really big from all these roses I keep finding everywhere! I looked back up at the woman and shrugged. When she turned away, I reached behind me pulled one out to keep and took a big inhale of its heavenly fragrance. It smelled so good and was so gorgeous. Without even knowing why, tears began to slide down my face as I thought: *I wish I was this beautiful.* An unsettled feeling from this thought sank into the pit of my stomach, reaching a deep sadness that was dormant inside of me. Doing what I did best, I ignored it in favor of looking out the window and noticed we were approaching my stop. The train slowed and as I got off, I saw Prisha waving at me from across the street, near the store. I wiped my face and took a deep breath. Forgetting all that just happened on the train, I waved back at Prisha. Time to begin a new job!

Later when I was home again, I fell into exhausted sleep around 7 p.m. My first day at my new job went so well, however rushing to class afterwards made me so much more tired at the end of the day. Such is life living in a big city. Getting from one place to the next by foot will tire anyone out. I had to write a paper that was due the next day but I just needed a little nap first. As my mind rolled into my dreams, the blue eyes were staring at me again. I heard his voice, soft with a faint accent whispering.

"I love you..."

I woke up sweating around 3 a.m., with my heart pounding through my chest. It's him! The random man with the Irish accent from the nightmare the night before, is the same man with the blue eyes! I didn't know who this mysterious man was or why he was now in my dreams, but the comfort and connection I felt from him was powerful. I sat for a while, with my thoughts rolling through my head. Finally, I looked at the clock again. It was 3:30 a.m. *Oh boy, time to stop fantasizing about a total stranger and get started on that paper!* I stood up to go get coffee and shook my head, almost laughing at myself and my intense dreams.

When I got back from the kitchen, I turned on my computer and saw all of the instant messages that were left for me while I was asleep. Two other messages were from Christian wanting to know where I was and why I did not call him. That made me laugh again. I looked down at my phone and saw a missed call from his sister, Kelly. A new message from Gina popped up just then:

Hey girl!! Where did you disappear to? I'm doing an overnight at work and saw you came out of idle. How was your first day of your new job? I must come in and stock up on those body butters. I miss you! When are you coming over for chicken and mac and cheese? Why are you even awake?

I laughed out loud as I rubbed the sleep away from my eyes and quickly shot back:

I fell asleep earlier and need to write my paper that is due today! I will call you later!

I knew my paper was waiting to be written but for a moment, I thought about my childhood days with Gina. I felt a strong nostalgia rush over me. I will never forget that first day she and Melissa moved onto our street. Like Andy, she became one of my closest childhood friends and I smiled at the sweet memory of those days together. We used to have a blast together growing up and her friendship was extremely special to me. I looked back up at my computer, with tears pouring down my face now. How I wished so much to be that innocent again. I shook the longing that was rising from my heart, shoving back down the happiness and love that these memories were pointing me to.

Winter of 2004 had major ups and downs. My job at The Body Shop was still going strong and Prisha and I became even closer friends since that first day we met. We spent the whole fall and winter getting to know each other more, hanging out at work, on campus, attending parties and out in Boston with its magical nightlife. Boston seemed to be one giant crowd of friends and parties and I loved it. There was one friend that faded from my life just as I had predicted she would. Karen soon became a long-lost friend because I didn't see her as much as I had hoped. She slept over my apartment once, but that was it. She was planning on leaving Pine Manor once the spring semester was over and go back home for a while. She wasn't feeling happy anymore where she was.

The biggest fall out that winter, however, was not with Karen but with Will. To make matters worse, the winter itself was a doozy with blizzard after blizzard blanketing the city. We were stuck inside much more than we liked and cabin fever set in, intensifying my already chronic anxiety. Mix in a break up and the ingredients made for a setback emotionally.

Even though it had been a long time coming, I was still upset those first few months after the split. I wasn't surprised when he ended it with me during the very first time we spoke after his return from Spain. He had only contacted me once through email while he was there. His email was also very distant and I knew by that point, he was interested in seeing other people. However, I still appreciated the time we spent together. I was happier when we broke up, but I was also feeling very vulnerable and I wasn't sure what to do about it.

Will was and had been a "safety net" for me from the very beginning of our relationship. He was a big reason that I was able to hide easier, all the years we were together. He was my excuse to stay far away from meeting and dating other men. Without even realizing it, I lived in complete fear, but it was the only way I knew how to live since I was sixteen. Kelly would even call me the "two-week wonder" after the breakup because every poor guy I met, who had interest in dating me, I would disappear after two weeks. I was great at the disappearing act. I just couldn't handle it and felt such sadness inside that my life had to be this way. Or did it? Why couldn't I just be normal?

To cope, I mastered the art of humor. Making people laugh, partying and acting silly was how I pushed through my anxiety, nightmares and depression. I figured, as long as I was laughing, I could make it through. Prisha was the one friend who saw right through it or at least she was the boldest in addressing it with me. During the months, we spent growing our friendship, she was able to feel my pain underneath my comedian act, especially after Will and I broke up.

There were many nights, after a fun night out on the town, where we laid next to each other on my bed, talking and laughing until we fell asleep. Sometimes that would be how it ended, with laughter and girl talk, but many nights, our talks grew more serious. She would ask me why I grew quiet when we were out at bars or parties? That question was always so hard to answer. She was very good at observation. Alcohol helped me to express myself, but not enough to let me pain out. Sometimes, I would not respond at all and simply let my tears soak the pillow, after she fell asleep.

While my roommates and I got along famously, I didn't share my private life with them. It made me feel uncomfortable to let my raw feelings out to the people I lived with. What if they judged me? What if they thought I was crazy and kicked me out? What if they didn't believe me? I battled these questions daily in my mind.

That May, our roommate, Jordan, moved out and this put Rachel, Hannah and Tara and me into a down mood. We were sad that she was gone, so we decided to attend a party in Rachel's hometown one night, which was not too far outside of the city. Since it was late spring, the days were getting longer and warmer. This one particular night was hot for that time of year, so I put on a jean skirt and tank top and while I was putting on my makeup, Hannah came bouncing into the room. She always seemed to dance everywhere she went and I absolutely loved her for it. The two of us loved to make everyone howl with laughter. We were a lot alike. She set down a mixed drink and sat on my bed.

"Come on, drink up! No time to waste tonight!" She demanded and fell back on my bed.

I laughed and took a sip, nearly choking on the intense, spicy flavor of it.

"Hannah, are you trying to kill me?" I said, still coughing. "What on earth is that?"

"Gin and tonic!" She said and burst out laughing at the look of disgust on my face. Rachel appeared in the doorway, scrunching up her nose.

"No. Hannah, just no. Gross," she said. Hannah got up and walked out of the room.

"Babies! You all are giant babies! L-kid, drink it. No excuses from you!" She called over her shoulder on her way out. I laughed at the nickname they had all given me which was "L-Kid." I was the youngest of the group so to them, I was just a kid. I heard Tara laughing from the living room. She emerged from her bedroom to see what craziness we were up to now and was watching me from the hallway.

"Are you going to make a rare appearance with us tonight?" I asked her.

Tara didn't come out with us often. She was in a serious relationship with her boyfriend, John, and preferred to stay back with him most of the time. We didn't mind because she usually hung out with us well into the early morning hours after we got back.

"No, not tonight," She answered.

"I figured!" I winked at her.

Rachel came hopping into the hallway, music blasting out as she opened her bedroom door.

"L-Kiiiiiid!" She sang to me.

"Cominggg!" I called back, laughing. I loved my roommates so much. Finishing up my makeup, I went into her room to hang out and waited for Hannah to finish getting ready.

A short while later, we all piled into Hannah's car. Hannah was blasting music and Rachel was arguing her on her song selection choice as usual. Some country music song was blaring through the speakers. The night was starting off just like any other night.

"Seriously, Hannah, what the heck are we listening to?" Rachel said and tried to turn it off.

"Rachel, this is called good music," she replied and they both grew silent. Meanwhile, I was cracking up in the backseat because I wasn't even sure Hannah like country. She just loved to annoy Rachel.

"Ok, Hannah, you win," Rachel finally said after a few minutes and they began to giggle and chat together.

I grew quiet in the back, lost in thought, with anxiety creeping in. Sometimes when my anxiety was hovering, I tried to drown out everything around me and stop it from getting worse. Just keep breathing, I said to myself, In and out. In and out. I closed my eyes. I heard my mother's voice in my head from the very first panic attack I ever had, "Lindsay, what you are experiencing is something called anxiety."

All of a sudden, before I could stop it, my thoughts flashed…the bathtub, the bloody water and Derek on the other side of the door, telling me it was okay to talk to him. I leaned forward, heart pounding through my chest. Lindsay, pull yourself together! Hannah's laughter broke my thoughts and I looked up at them. My body was still shaking as Rachel turned and looking at me.

"What's up?" I asked.

"We were wondering if you were going to date again. It has been months since Will got out of the picture. Pretty much all of my friends from home would be interested," Rachel said, laughing to herself. Just answer her, Lindsay, and stay calm. My mind raced as I tried to answer her calmly.

"Oh goodness, I don't know. There aren't any I'm interested in really." Liar. Tell her the truth, Lindsay. Rachel smiled at me, not answering and grew quiet. I swear that girl can read my thoughts sometimes.

We arrived at the party and the rest of the night carried on without any more flashbacks or anxiety. The drinking, the people and the many conversations easily lulled me away from what I experienced in the car. What I realized that night, was how much better I was becoming at pushing every negative thought or emotion aside, through parties and drinking. Denial had become my best friend and I welcomed it more and more as the days passed. As the night carried on, I drank much more than usual and soon blacked out, in hopes to erase it all. Just the way I liked it.

Ten

Spring rolled right into summer and my hours at the store increased to full time. I had decided to take a couple summer classes to get ahead, with the extra time, I was able to work a lot more. I hadn't experienced another flashback since that night in the car with Hannah and Rachel. In fact, things seemed to be easier without a heavy school load. My roommates and I were planning on moving into a better apartment a little further out in Watertown, MA. We all had cars, so we needed better parking and the apartment we were looking at had a driveway but also had public transportation nearby as well. It was perfect.

We were planning to move in at the end of the summer and we were excited. Plus, this new apartment would be closer to Kelly and Christian! I had been enjoying my summer nights with them as well. Prisha had taken to them, too, and we were often at their apartment in Waltham, hanging out after we closed the store. Life that summer was fun and easy, just how it should be in your college days.

The day before the Fourth of July, I was at home and packing my bag to head to Christian and Kelly's apartment to spend the holiday weekend with them. My roommates were not there as they had their own holiday plans and being alone was something I hated. After my usual closing shift at work. I needed to hand in the final papers for my summer courses before work. Packing as much in one bag, I grabbed the binder with all my papers, and opened it to double check. One of my papers was missing and a quick glance at the clock told me that I only had about five minutes left before I needed to leave, so I turned it on the computer to print it. Opening my email to find the email that had my paper attached to it, I noticed a new email from the Boston State House. Weeks prior, I had applied to do my first co-op there in the fall. Curiosity got the best of me, so I opened it. It read:

Dear Lindsay,

We are pleased to offer you one of the co-op positions in the Press Room for the Fall 2004 semester. This is a very competitive position, so please see the attached job description, salary offer and then sign and mail to our offices by August 1, 2004. The position will run September to February of 2005 at 32 hours a week. The pay offered will be $12.00 an hour.

I couldn't believe it. I got my first co-op! This was going to be my very first "real" job experience and I was so excited, I could hardly stand it.

"Wahooo!" I cheered.

I turned on my instant messenger and in my "away message" I put:

"Hello weekend and soon to be HELLO MIDDLER YEAR! This girl has her very first co-op in the press room at the BOSTON STATE HOUSE!"

I shot Christian a quick IM, letting him know that I would be at his place around 9:30 that night, then went to my email where my paper was and printed it out. As it was printing, I thought about the upcoming semester and how much fun the job will be. It was such a good opportunity, especially as a Communications major, with a concentration in Public Relations. I was also a double major in Psychology, but I wanted my co-ops to be in PR. For a long time in college, this was where I wanted my career path to go. I was stoked and grabbed my paper, put it in the binder with the others, picked up my overnight bag and dashed out the door. It felt good to feel so accomplished. Maybe things were turning around for me and my anxiety and my past was becoming just a distant memory. One can only hope.

The store was buzzing when I got there a couple hours later. Prisha was restocking the shelves with all of the men's products on it. She looked up when I came in and held out one of the shaving creams.

"Smell this. It smells like a sexy man. I just love it," she said and I leaned in and took a whiff.

"Yeah, sure does," I said and went to the back to put my bag down.

"What a big bag that is! Where are you going? Christian's?" She followed me to the backroom.

"Yeah, my roommates are gone all weekend because of the holiday and you know how it goes with me being alone," I said to her.

"What are you two up to tomorrow night? There's a party on the hill that Natalie and I are going to. Want to come?"

"I'll ask Christian, but you know how he is about getting dressed and going into the city," I laughed and she nodded her head. It took a lot to get Christian out of Waltham and downtown for parties.

"True! Well, just let me know," she said.

Just then the front door swung open and Gina and her roommate, Kristen came waltzing in, laughing at something.

"Hey girlllllll!" Gina called to me laughing. Her greeting always made me laugh since we were young.

"Hey!" I called back and walked over to them.

"What are you up to this weekend?" She asked me. I told her I was heading over to Christian's and she told me she and Kristen were going to get some dinner and then she had an overnight shift at work. Gina worked at a home nearby that helped children from all kinds of traumatized backgrounds. She was a psychology major at Northeastern, where Kristen had also attended and they both recently graduated.

"Did you get your dress fitted for the wedding?" Gina asked. Matt and Melissa were finally tying the knot the following month in

Bermuda and we were so excited for them and the upcoming trip. We were both bridesmaids in the wedding and I couldn't wait for a week of fun in the sun. So many great things were coming up and it had been a great distraction from so much of the agony that was still festering within. Anxiety had stayed quiet during the summer days – at least so far.

We continued to talk for a little bit longer and made plans for me to come sleepover at her place the following week on the night she was off. I was not twenty-one yet, so it made going downtown limited, but Gina didn't mind. We had more fun hanging out at our apartments anyway.

After they left, Prisha and I finished our shift at the store. I called Christian to let him know that I was done and that I would be at the station stop near him in about an hour. I got on the train and rode a few stops to the junction with the Red line, where I transferred trains. From there, it was a straight shot to Christian's apartment. Once I was there, I saw Christian and his roommate Allen waiting for me in their car parked outside the station. They saw me and Christian leaned out the window.

"Hey there, good looking. Want a ride?" I laughed and got in the back seat. Christian turned up the music and the two of them started to sing along and dance. They helped me relax and laugh and I sighed in relief to be there. I always felt safe when I was with Christian and Kelly. Kelly especially took care of me so well and had been like an older sister, guiding me since the first day of transferring to Northeastern. She was also the one who helped me craft my application to the State House. She was going to be so happy when she heard the good news. We pulled into their apartment complex and parked. Kelly was sitting outside on their patio with their other roommate Mike. They were both having a drink and chatting.

"Hey, CJ & Allen. Hey, Linds!" Kelly called with excitement as we approached the house. "So, Linds, I was thinking. Tomorrow, let's head to The Home Depot and get some plants. CJ brought home this gardening kit from the bank with knee pads and all. Let's make this place prize winning with flowers!"

I burst out laughing when she showed me the kit that Christian had brought home. Christian had an internship that summer at a bank in the city and he had brought home a few of the gardening kits that they were giving away when people opened new accounts there that summer.

"Gardening, Kel? Me? This will be interesting," I said to her. The guys erupted in a fit of laughter at the thought of us gardening, but I was up for the challenge! No matter what I did with Kelly, we had a blast.

"Guess what?" I asked. "I got the co-op position at the State House this fall!"

"What? Yes!" She cheered for me. "Grab a bevvy and let's celebrate!"

The rest of the night was filled with nonstop laughing, drinking and talking until early morning. Basically, I became a fifth roommate to them and I absolutely loved being at their apartment. We shared a family-like bond for a long time. It was yet another escape from the past because of the comfort that their friendship brought me. It was times like this that I could feel something good inside versus constant unhappiness or anxiety. Even though I felt silly and jovial around them, there were still shadows and darkness around my true feelings. Most of the time I didn't recognize the enjoyment in those moments, they were just - moments.

My mind and emotions were totally disconnected, making being present nearly impossible. It had become so trained at pushing away the horrors of the past, that it was like I lived in two worlds: One world was a young woman trying to make a new future for herself and the other world, a young girl tortured by the violence in her past - battling down waves of uncontrollable anxiety as emotions tried to surface. Instead of trying to face the emotions, I was content living in the two worlds - stuck at sixteen-years-old.

The next few weeks were somewhat boring, besides preparing for the wedding that was in August and the move to our new apartment. My anxiety continued to stay at a dull roar and I was putting in as many hours as I could at the store with Prisha. My earlier suspicion about my weakening anxiety was all about to change and very abruptly. Post-Traumatic Stress Disorder has no timeline. There is no prediction of when it will return. Flashbacks can strike out of nowhere, even after they lay dormant for weeks, months or even years. When things seemed good during my time in Boston, I always knew that it wouldn't last. In reality, my pain was just cycling deep inside, only to rise up again to try to get me to awaken - but I didn't.

One Saturday night, just after we locked up, Prisha told me she had to get home in a hurry because she had to get changed and meet one of her sisters somewhere. The nice thing about the store we worked at, it that it was a "street side" store, versus one in an indoor shopping mall. Therefore, the hours were really good. We were done with our shifts by 8 p.m. and this still gave us plenty of time to go out and have fun. Prisha ran off to catch a train and I was hungry, so I decided to grab a burrito at a little Mexican food place that was right down the street. Everyone there greeted me with a smile as they knew I was a regular customer. The lady behind the cash register waved at me.

"The usual?" I smiled and nodded.

I sat down to wait for my food and saw that Hannah and Rachel had texted me to see if I was going to come to the bar with them. They told me it was 18 plus for that night, so I could come. I sighed. I couldn't wait until my 21st birthday, but that would not be until the following March. Therefore, we always looked out for when bars opened their doors for 18 plus nights or stuck to the bars that my fake I.D. worked in, which was not too many places. They called my name for my food and I texted my roommates back, then walked out to catch the T. As I stood there, a group of men behind me were loudly laughing at something and I turned to see who they were. One of them caught eyes with me and I quickly tried to look away, but he already zeroed in on me.

"Well, hello there, beautiful," he said to me. "Where're you headed to?" I stared down at the ground instead of answering him.

At that moment, in the two years I had lived in Boston, I realized I had never had a man flirt with me without one of my friends nearby. I choked as my heart pounded in my throat and my ears began to ring. Everything whirled around me in panic and my face felt hot with embarrassment. *Why am I so frightened?* They were just a group of college guys and besides, there were a lot of other people nearby waiting for the train. Words stayed stuck in my throat as I continued to stare at the ground.

"What's wrong?" He asked and I finally looked up at him. He was a good-looking, nicely dressed nicely man, but he could have been 'Godzilla' as far as I was concerned. I still couldn't talk. One of the others in his group noticed my nervousness.

"Hey man, leave her alone. She obviously doesn't want to talk to you. Dude, this happens to you a lot, so you're used to this," he teased. They moved away from me and continued to laugh loudly amongst themselves.

How could I be such a baby? Anger began to rise as I realized how dumb I must have looked. It wasn't like I was under a bridge by myself with him. I was in the safety of a public place and some cute guy wanted to talk to me. *What do I do? I completely shut down!* Hot tears of frustration and growing anger found me boarding the train, as a panic attack gripped me. With knees shaking, I sat down as far away from that group of men as I could, resting my head in my hands. Everyone's voices sounded like they were a million miles away. *Breathe Lindsay, just breathe!*

"Are you all right, young lady?" I looked up and saw an elderly and kind looking man staring at me with concern. He was sitting directly in front of me.

"Yes, I just have a really bad migraine brewing," I responded quickly. That was partially true because sometimes my panic attacks created monster migraines. My head started to pound. My eyes lost focus on the elderly man and trailed past him, toward someone that was behind him. I rubbed my eyes and blinked, nearly screaming. I saw a face that I never thought I would never see again. A face that was locked so deep within my subconscious, where I thought it was sealed away for good. The face of my rapist. He was glaring directly through me, in a satanic kind of way and when he saw me look at him, a smile spread across his face. I jumped up, wanting to open the doors to the moving train and leap out. The elderly man stood up with me, holding his hands up as if he was going to catch me before I jumped.

"Miss, please sit down. If you have a migraine, you need to sit down," he said and tried to touch my hand to help me sit back down, but I jerked it away.

I looked down the train aisle and the group of guys from the previous station stop, were now all silent and staring at me. My eyes shot behind the elderly man again to see if the man I saw was coming after me, but he wasn't. It wasn't the face I thought it was. He was a stranger who was now staring at me confused. *Oh my god! I'm losing my mind and imagined the entire thing.* I sat back down in complete shock at what had just happened.

A few minutes later, the train pulled up to my stop and I ran off, leaving my dinner on my seat and running as fast as I could to my apartment. Safely inside, my roommates were in the kitchen, laughing and eating. All I wanted to do was change my clothes and slip into my bed with my lights off. Rachel walked by my room a little while later and noticed I was in bed.

"Hey, Linds? Are you okay?" She came in to sit on my bed.

"Oh, hi, Rachel. Yeah, I got hit with a nasty migraine and I'm going to pass for going out tonight," I said. "In fact, I want to just head over to Christian's because I don't want to be alone."

"Oh, migraines are the worst! Do you need anything while you wait for him to come get you?" She asked. I shook my head and when she walked out, I quickly texted Christian, begging him to come and get me because I didn't feel well. A half-hour later, he was at my door. I never told him or anyone what happened to me earlier. How does one even begin to explain that you might be losing your mind?

July turned into August of that summer and it was time for the big wedding! Matt and Melissa tied the knot in a gorgeous ceremony right on the beach of the resort in Bermuda. It was a wonderful party, with lots of laughter and dancing. Derek and I and the rest of the younger gang made sure to keep the party going all night. Bermuda was a wonderful escape for everyone and such a beautiful island. It made the wedding feel so much longer because many family members stayed a few days after too. Matt and Melissa were heading over to Jamaica for their honeymoon and everyone was so happy for them. They were among the small percentage who stayed together after high school and married, so we were all proud of their love story. Gina and I had been "planning" their wedding since we were kids, as were much of the family, so it was a long awaited and glorious celebration that finally came true.

The flight home found me rested, sun-kissed, and relaxed. While away, I easily erased out of my head, what had happened on the train in Boston from the month before. The rest of the summer was spent packing up our old apartment and getting ready to move. When moving day came, my roommates and I looked around the empty apartment and I felt a little sad. It was my first apartment and held some good memories, but we were ready to make new ones somewhere else. Plus, we were excited to leave the constant scratching of mice in our walls behind. The day we moved into the new place, we all got to work unpacking and of course, Rachel, started to blast the music, while Hannah was hopping around the place like normal. I laughed as I put my clothes away in the closet. It already felt like home.

Eleven

Summer turned into the fall semester of 2004 and the school year was underway. It was my "middler" year and my first position for my school's infamous cooperative education program also known as "co-op". Northeastern was unique with its co-op education system, which graduated students after five years with one year as a co-op. I was expected to complete at least three, six-month paid positions in my field. The good news was that during the co-op, you didn't have to take any classes, so I was looking forward to a year of study break. I just needed to find another one to do starting in February, but I still had time to send out applications. Very few of my friends at Northeastern liked this extra year, but I was really looking forward to it and eager to get started with my first co-op job at the State House. The two classes I took over the summer would knock down some of the load I would have to do the in my junior year, so I was feeling ahead of the game.

The day before I began the job, I got up early and headed to the Cambridge Side Galleria to get some new professional clothes for it. I didn't go with anyone, as I liked to shop for clothes on my own usually. To make things easier, I decided to drive there and park in the garage. The day was filled with lots of shopping and I forgot to eat lunch. It was late afternoon when I finally stopped and made my way to the car with a handful of bags. Good thing I drove as the bags would have been cumbersome on the T!

On the way home, I called Kelly and she invited me over for dinner. I got to my apartment to drop off all of my new clothes and get them out of the bags. Throwing in a load in the washing machine, I went back to my room and turned on my computer. While I waited for my stuff to finish washing, I clicked on the State House's website and read up on all the current news with the present government leaders. Mitt Romney was the governor and I googled some of the things he was doing. After catching up on as much of the government affairs that I could, I put my clothes in the dryer and went into the kitchen to leave my roommates a note. Grabbed a bottle of wine and headed out.

My mind was mulling over all of the things I just researched and made mental notes so that I would be up to date on anything important. The news was not my favorite past-time, keeping me behind on a lot of political stuff. I also made a mental note to ask Christian and Allen everything they knew because they were always up to speed on political news. When I arrived, Kelly had music going that I could actually hear from the street as I walked up. She had candles lit on the patio outside and plates out for everyone. She was such the "group mom".

"Hello!" I called out when I went inside.

"Hey! In here!" Kelly answered. "How does chicken marsala sound? It'll be ready soon! CG is upstairs."

"Cool. I brought some wine," I said and opened the bottle, poured a glass for myself and everyone else then went up to see Christian. Like in my own apartment, music played everywhere and Christian had his on too. I knocked on the door and went in.

"Hey! Party is here!" I said. Christian swiveled around on his desk chair and smiled.

"What's happening?" He asked and I handed him a glass of wine. Laying down on his bed, I stared at the ceiling.

"Well, my co-op starts tomorrow and I'm actually very nervous. I did some research today on all the politics and realized I know absolutely nothing," I said.

"Well, don't worry. You're a smart girl! You'll learn," he said. We talked a little more until we heard Kelly call us down for dinner. The rest of their roommates joined us at the table on their patio and we all sat down to eat. Kelly raised her glass of wine and glasses clinked for my new job.

The next day, 5 a.m. came and I couldn't sleep. Lying in bed, I stared at the ceiling and waited for my alarm to go off. Once it did, I was up, showered and out the door to make sure I caught the bus in time. The commute was going to be at least a good hour, as I had to get all the way downtown every morning by 9 a.m. sharp. That involved a bus ride, boarding the right train and finding a seat among many professionals and students rushing to get where they needed to go. Some students were laughing near me once I got on the T and for a moment, I wished I was one of them, dressed in casual clothes, just heading to class. My nerves were on edge as I got off the train and back outside near the Boston Common. There in front of me, just across the park was the gold arch of the State House. I took a deep breath and began to head toward it.

A sign in the lobby, pointed the students to where they check in. I wasn't the only one starting a co-op or an internship, which made me feel better. Wandering down a hallway on the first floor, a friendly lady greeted me, smiling broadly. She was an executive assistant for the human resource director and handled the student workers every semester. After taking my driver's license and social security card to make copies she gave me some paperwork to fill out. After that was done, she gave me directions to head upstairs to the Press Room on the second floor. That was where I would be spending the next six months.

Once I opened the door, my nerves instantly turned to excitement. Phones were ringing nonstop; employees and other students were bustling about the room. It was easy for me to get caught up in the buzz and within a few minutes, the person who headed the students each year came right over to me. I was wearing a lanyard around my neck, so it was pretty obvious I was a student. He was a short guy and even in flats, I was looking down at him.

"Hi there. Name?" He asked, looking down at his checklist.

"Lindsay Mirabilio." I answered him. He studied his list and then found me.

"Got it! Okay, so this is the Press Room. See?" He turned and gestured towards the room. "So now that the "tour" is out of the way. Let's get you started on your first list of things to do. There's no slow warm up in this office. News doesn't stop! Never forget that! Come with me and I'll show you where you'll sit." He dashed off, with his short legs picking up pace quickly. We walked across the room where two other girls about my age were sitting. After a brief introduction, our instructor continued.

"You'll be working with them this morning on organizing these press kits for the press conference tomorrow. That should take you into the better portion of the morning, then come find me after lunch. Lunch is always at noon sharp for the students. It's an hour and that's it! Don't dilly around outside shopping or anything. I assume you gals know how to introduce yourselves? Great! Get to work you three," he ordered us, as a peculiar noise erupted from him. It took me a second to realize he was laughing, so I laughed with him and looked at the other two girls who covered their faces laughing at my reaction to his odd noise.

"What the heck was all of that?" I asked them as I sat down. They all laughed again and then got to work. I jumped in fast and noticed that my heart was racing along with the high buzz in the room. The fast-paced energy, made my anxiety feel right at home. I was ready for the challenge!

A few weeks into the job, my tasks got bigger and bigger and pretty soon, I was writing press releases, editing a lot of documents, attending press conferences and other events. I wasn't sure if Public Relations would be my final path in life, but for now it was something I enjoyed and was good at. The press conferences bored me to tears, but the other events were fun. However, there was one major event that really made this co-op worth it. The Boston Red Sox were in their final game of the playoffs that season and if they won, it would be the first World Series win in eighty-six years! The press room was all over this event.

My roommates and I ventured down to The Boston Beer Works the night of the game, to watch the big event. With my fake I.D. in hand, I was able to get into this particular bar. I was never a baseball fan until I moved to Boston. Boston Red Sox fans have a bad rap back in Connecticut with the New York Yankee fans, but I loved it. Before we walked inside, I smelled a whiff of the infamous Sausage Guy and turned my head towards the delicious aroma. With this game happening, he sure would be busy tonight! As he cooked away, I couldn't wait to get a sweet Italian sausage roll later after we left the bar. Turning around to go inside, I bumped into someone and looked up into the blue-eyed man, which stopped me dead in my tracks. He met my gaze and was just as surprised as I was. This guy, again? I wondered if he had a twin running around town since I was always bumping into him. Before I could say anything, he winked at me and kept walking. I stood there mesmerized and watched him walk down the street, until Hannah pulled at my arm.

"L-Kid lets go," she said.

Later that night, Red Sox won and Boston erupted into complete chaos. My phone was vibrating non-stop and when I glanced down at it, I saw that it was Kelly frantically texting me:

Lindsay, get out of Landsdowne! The city is going WILD! I'm watching it on the news!

I couldn't blame the Boston fans; after all, it had been so long since we last won the World Series, but they were out of control. The curse of the Boston Red Sox was finally over! My roommates and I made a run for it to get out of the rapidly forming rioting crowds. I watched all around me in amazement as cars were looted, sidewalk trees were lit on fire, and the Boston Police were swarming in like bees. We made it out of the crowd just in time and began walking towards Beacon Street to get away from it. We eventually found a cab and went home.

The months went by quickly and finally it was Christmas. I only had a month left at the State House after I returned from the holidays and I was feeling a little sad. My anxiety had picked up again during the three weeks that I went home for Christmas. The slow, quiet pace at mom's house in contrast to my life in Boston made my anxiety obvious. Instead of enjoying my time off and resting, I counted the minutes until I was back in Boston. The times I slowed down were the times when my past would creep up on me the most and I couldn't wait to get back to the city and drown in the noise. Another new co-op was coming up and though it seemed great, the State House work was fantastic and I didn't want to switch. Reality that these were temporary jobs hit me once I was fully back in my apartment after Christmas.

My new co-op position was with a large media company that hosted many major trade shows throughout the world in addition to other big events, and handled a lot of digital and content marketing. I was given a position as a Public Relations assistant, so I was going to be handling a lot of the same things that I did at the State House. They were headquartered in Newton, MA near Boston College, so the commute would be a little easier. I could drive there which made all the difference in the world. However, I was still bummed to leave the State House because it was my first job working in the real world and I would never forget all that I learned. As I got up one morning to get ready during my final week there, I was certainly not expecting anything bad to happen.

It was the middle of January 2005 and the air sliced through my lungs. Boston winters are brutal, especially downtown when you get caught in the wind tunnels from the breeze off the ocean. On this very cold morning, I was walking across the Common to get to work and the air stung at my legs. *Why did I wear a dress today?* I picked up my pace in my high heels to get to work faster. I was so relieved to be back inside the warm Press Room. The high-level activity in there actually made the room hot, no matter what time of the year it was.

The day went by fast, as it always did, and my manager asked me to do one last thing before I headed out. He wanted me to bring some mail down to the mail room in the basement that needed to be sent out that day. I grabbed a mail cart and began to fill it up with what needed to be sent out. Just then, a new intern came and stood beside me. He was a tall, handsome guy wearing a lanyard that said "Sophomore, Boston College." His striking looks quickly faded against his rude personality that soon presented itself. I smiled and introduced myself, stretching out my hand for him to shake. He glared at me and rolled his eyes, ignoring my hand.

"Whatever. Once they see how insanely smart I am, they'll probably offer me a job here after I graduate," he said and began to help me fill the cart. I didn't understand where his cocky attitude came from, so I decided to ignore it and keep making small talk anyway.

"So, Boston College? That's a great school!" I tried to smile at him, but my pounding heart made it hard. No matter how hard I tried to be nice, he was making me really nervous with the way he continued to glare at me. I silently cursed my anxious mind as my hands began to shake. I dropped all the mail I had been holding.

"Dammit!" He nearly shouted and bent down to pick it up, "What school do you go to anyway?" He asked as he stood up and practically threw the fallen mail onto the cart. I felt like an ant as he looked me up and down.

"North…. Northeastern," I barely managed to get the words out. My eyes stung with tears.

"Well, that figures. Let's get this mail downstairs so I can go back over there and do something with important people," he pointed to the other side of the room, where the Editor-in-Chief was standing and talking with our manager. I tried to fight back my nerves and the tears that were still building behind my eyes.

As he continued to growl at me, it was too late to stop them. The tears began to pour and my anxiety turned into a full fledge panic attack. I turned away from him and quickly wiped them away. I was determined to finish the task and get the mail downstairs so I could be done with this guy. I told him I would be right back and went out to the hall and ran into the bathroom. I splashed water on my face and tried to stop shaking. *What was wrong with me? He's just a dumb, cocky guy!* After a couple minutes, I held my head up high, marched into the room, pushed the cart out towards the elevator, ignoring him. Looking at the golden doors of this ancient elevator, made my anxiety go into overdrive. I realized that I would be alone with him on this old, slow-moving elevator. The doors opened and he held them open so I could push the cart through. I felt myself begin to hyperventilate, wanting to run, but it was too late and the doors shut. I bent down, in a panic trying to breathe. He turned to me, nearly laughing at how I was acting.

"What's the matter, little girl, afraid of elevators?" *Little girl? Where have I heard that before?*

"Yes...I...I just don't like them. Is it moving? I feel like it's stopped," I said, my voice shaking.

Fully laughing now, I saw him push the stop button. "You mean stop like this?"

No, he did not just do that to me. NO! My knees buckled as I fell to the floor, crying and trying to breathe in every ounce of air I could manage.

"Chill the hell out, girl." He pushed another button and I felt the elevator jolt as the world went black.

A female voice was talking in the distance as water dripped on my face. My eyes fluttered open and I saw the same jerk staring over me. The other voice I heard was a woman who was holding me and keeping a cool, wet paper towel on my forehead. We were on the floor right outside the elevator door. *Oh my god, please, get me out of here!* The words screamed in my head.

"You ok?" The woman asked and smiled at me.

"Yes, I just need to go home. Are there stairs?" My whole body was shaking.

"Yes, there are, right there," she pointed. I pushed myself up, steadied my quivering knees and bolted toward the door to the stairs. I heard the guy I just met open the door to the stairwell behind me.

"Hey! Don't trip! And listen, I didn't mean to cause you to pass out! You're hot anyway, like most Northeastern chicks! But you're nothing, remember that. Go home and don't bother with this job here, it's not for women like you!" I heard him laughing and I froze on the stairs. "Dumb bitch," I heard him say more quietly.

But you're nothing, remember that! His words stuck to my heart like glue. They were so familiar. My ears rang and my nerves were on fire as the scene of what just happened repeated over and over, all too familiar. All of a sudden, I heard his voice, not the voice of the elevator asshole, but a voice I had not heard since that fateful night.

The voice of my rapist.

You win this time, little girl!

By now, my face was hot. burning from anxiety and anger penetrating me, as I forced myself up the last section of the three flights of stairs, slowing to a walk once I got to the Press Room. Grabbing my purse, I told my manager I was sick and nearly ran out of the State House toward the T. Standing outside the subway, I couldn't bring myself to go down the stairs to get on. Everything around me felt like slow motion, so instead I sat down on a bench nearby to collect myself as the biting cold air helped me to calm down.

I sat there for a long time, watching all kinds of people walk past me. It was late afternoon and many working professionals were starting to trickle out of the surrounding buildings. A mother, holding her young daughter's hand, smiled brightly at me as she passed. I couldn't smile back. The girl let go of her mother's hand and paused to look at me, smiling some more, but I was too annoyed to be comforted by her innocence.

"Hi." Her smile seemed to explode on her face as she tried again to get me to smile back.

"Hello." I glared at her.

"Come on, honey, let's not bother this woman. Sorry," she looked at me apologetically. As they continued walking, the little girl turned one last time.

"Don't be sad. There's always a reason to smile. That's what my Grampa always tells me," she called out to me, smiled at me again and this time, I gave her a small smile in return. What a brave, sweet little girl, I thought as she walked away. She had a point, but not for me. I had too many reasons not to smile most of the time, especially now. The intern's vicious comments were still echoing in my head when another flashback sparked and my rapist was now louder in my head:

Shhhh. It will all be over soon.

No! Make it stop! I wanted to scream his voice away. His ugly face flashed before me and I bent over, holding my head, desperately pushing the image out of my mind. *My rapist.* Like a cancer, the word grew and spread all over my being. It was a term I fought daily to keep out of my mind, refusing to ever say that word aloud. Sitting up tall, I took some long, deep breaths and pulled out my headphones and put them on. Reaching for my journal in my purse, I began to write frantically. Words of hatred and everything I wanted to say both to the guy in the State House and my rapist flew across the page. My mind drifted off and the noise of the city faded to the music. The sun set and it was dark and bitter cold, but I hardly noticed. When I was done the same words written over and over at the end: You are a nobody. My hands were frozen from the cold.

I began to cry, silently begging God, if he was there, to just end my misery. I couldn't filter the intense amount of pain that was bubbling to the surface and instead of getting on the T, I started to walk. I walked across the Common and onto Newbury Street and just kept walking in my high heels for miles. With each step, I pushed those feelings back down, hiding them deeper than they were before. When I finally stopped walking, I paused to see how far I had gone and gasped when I saw that I had made it to the store in Coolidge Corner. I must have walked for close to two hours and I could feel the blisters forming on my frozen feet. A homeless man with roses, began to walk toward me.

"Hey, pretty lady, looks like you need a pretty flower tonight." He wobbled over to me, stumbling on himself. Drunk, I figured. "This rose is calling you!" He handed me a rose.

Its petals were still closed tight, matching the tightness in my shoes and in my chest. Instead of keeping it, like I usually did with roses, anger busted out and I threw it on the ground. I decided to take the train for the last couple stops. Too upset to watch where I was going, I tripped over a bag on the ground. Voices around me asked if I was okay. Standing, I pushed everyone away from me, nodding that I was fine. The train pulled up and this time I got on, still shaking from head to toe from all that had happened that day.

After we pulled away from the stop, my breathing began to slow a bit, but I could feel chills run down my back as if someone was watching me. Turning around to look, my mouth dropped open. I saw him. Seriously? I was starting this think that this man was either following me or not even real. His blue eyes were staring at me, so intensely that they seemed to pierce right through my heart. For some reason, his stare calmed me, which was strange for me. We locked eyes longer than we ever did before. I wanted to say something, but nothing came out.

Eventually, I turned back around and waited for the few minutes until we reached my stop. When I stood up to get off, I noticed he was standing too. We both got off and I began to walk to where I needed to go next. He followed in the same direction I was going. Each time I glanced back, he kept looking at me, a small smile on his face. Finally, I turned around one last time, to finally question him, but he was standing in the doorway to City Side, a local restaurant. His unbroken gaze caused butterflies in the pit of my stomach, but finally, he turned and went inside. This shook me somewhat, so I ran to my bus stop. I just wanted to get home and end this bizarre and frightening day. My curiosity over the blue-eyed man was now at its height. Who was this man that I have been seeing everywhere for over a year now? Do I have a reason to be afraid of him?

Once I got on my bus, the blue-eyed man faded as the day went through my mind. Shaking with anger, I wanted to scream, but it stayed stuck in my throat, along with the rest of my past. Tears fell instead. When I got off the bus and walked up the quiet street toward my apartment, my eyes stayed focused and the fighter in me emerged.

"Nothing will hurt me. Nothing will break me down." I said and stuffed the events of day away, hiding in my heart, along with everything else I hid from.

Twelve

I never went back to the State House, to finish out my last week. Instead, I pretended to be sick with the flu. The nurse at my school, helped me get a waiver so I wouldn't get in trouble and lose nearly six months of hard work. I just couldn't face that guy again. I had a few weeks off before the next co-op started in mid-February. This one was shorter, just under four months but I was able to get it approved from my academic advisor.

A few weeks later, my new co-op began and I was a lot less nervous this time around. Since I was able to drive, I overestimated how long it would take to get there and arrived early. When I pulled into the lot and found a parking spot, I paused before getting out of the car since I had time. This was a huge company and even larger building than I imagined, but considering they handled some of the world's largest trade shows, I wasn't too surprised.

After some time passed, I finally got out and walked right into the front door with confidence. I was greeted by the executive assistant to the CEO, who was the one who wanted to give me a warm welcome and tour. This was way different than my first day at the State House! Her name was Diana and she was so friendly, yet a little bit scattered.

"Am I going too fast for you?" She turned and looked at me, when we were halfway through the tour.

"No, not at all," I laughed. She had no idea what kind of craziness I just came from working in the Press Room of the State House.

She finally brought me over to where the Public Relations office was, along with the events and marketing team. It was a very large room with an array of cubicles in the middle. There were about five private offices lining the walls and we walked over to one of them. A woman was on the phone when we walked in and held up her hand.

"She's literally, always on the phone," Diana said. "But that's normal I guess. After all, she is the Vice President of Marketing/Public Relations. Let's go over to her assistant, whose name is Tammy and she will take over from here. Tammy will be your "go-to" person. She handles the students who pass through." We walked over to one of the cubicles and Tammy turned in her chair, with a huge smile. I already loved this job.

The day was filled with getting settled in the cubicle that they gave me, getting myself logged into the system, paperwork and my email set up. After the day was nearly over, the Vice President of the department made her way over to me. She was a very tall woman, even taller than my 5' 9" frame! Her hand shake was firm and her voice was loud.

"Hello there! I'm so sorry about this morning, we have a huge event tomorrow and I had so much to check on today for it. I'm Laura and you are?"

"Lindsay. I'm the new co-op from Northeastern," I replied, feeling a bit intimidated by her large presence.

"Ah very good! Well, I'm sure Tammy got you all set up. Glad to have you on board! Do you like traveling?" I nodded my head.

"Well, good! You will have the opportunity to do that here if we decide to keep you on board after your co-op," she winked at me and walked away. After she left, Tammy came into my cubicle and handed me some things to bring home to read.

"Isn't she intense? She's really loud too, I know," she said and we both laughed. "She's a really good boss and great leader. You'll learn a lot from her."

The first day went wonderful. Everyone was so nice and I was already making friends. Tammy ate lunch with me and a few other students who I met. Unlike the jerk from the State House, the two other students were guys, but they were nice young men. It would be a fun few months working with all of them. As I walked back to my car, a car alarm went off somewhere close-by in the garage and I nearly jumped out of my skin. Fumbling for my keys and silently cursing myself at how absurd my nerves were once again, I heard my name being called.

"Linds! You ok? I saw you just jump nearly ten feet in the air over that alarm!" One of the nice male interns came running over. Even though I knew he was a good person, I was so embarrassed over having such anxiety, that all I did was nod and finally manage to open my car door. Without another word, I jumped in and left. I looked in my rearview mirror and he was just standing there, scratching his head in confusion. *Ugh! I'm such a wierdo!* I was so frustrated with myself, especially after having such an awesome first day. *Will I ever be normal?*

The next day, that same intern who tried to help me in the garage avoided me. I didn't blame him, as I could only imagine how strange my response to him must have been like. Luckily, he transferred to another department, so I wouldn't have to duck every time he came my way. The weeks went by fast and it was soon March. My 21st birthday was finally approaching and I couldn't wait!

Kelly and my friends had a big party planned downtown and I was so excited! My birthday was on a Thursday and that night, my mother came up to have my official "first legal drink" with me. We went out for a nice dinner and toasted with my first legal cocktail together. I asked her if she was planning on staying the whole weekend and going to my big party that Saturday night with us?

"Oh, heck no Lindsay. Want me to drop dead? I can't keep up with that! When does Derek arrive?"

"Tomorrow night. He and Matt are planning on taking me out to dinner at a Mexican restaurant tomorrow in Cambridge. Margaritas and tacos! Then they'll meet everyone Saturday night for the big party. The city will be hopping anyway for St. Patrick's Day weekend. What a great time of the year to turn 21!" I said.

"Well, be safe. I better talk to Matt and make sure he knows to keep an eye on you," my mother answered, looking a bit worried.

I rolled my eyes at her and laughed. The next day, Matt texted me after mom called him:

More like, you might need to keep an eye on me instead. This weekend will be fun!

The night of my party went without any hitch and was a blast. Prisha and I stumbled out of the bar at 2 a.m. after hours of dancing and lots of booze. Everyone that I loved was there and we never laughed so hard as we did that night. Prisha and I managed to get a cab and meet Christian and Kelly back at their place. The next morning, Prisha, Kelly, Christian and I roared with laughter at the pictures that were taken. Christian was known for his picture taking skills. We had hundreds of pictures captured of our college days.

"Last night will go down in the books, Linds," Kelly said. "Along with CJ's 21rst! What an incredible night that was!"

I smiled at her and thanked them all for giving me such a special night. I felt so blessed to have friends like them to honor my 21st birthday. Later that night, as I laid in bed, thinking about the party more, I felt content. I thought about all the people that showered me with gifts and love. However, within seconds, something changed and my heart began to race out of nowhere. Darkness clouded over my happiness and I felt so guilty about this sudden change. I grew angry and stood up from my bed. I couldn't believe at how ungrateful I was! After having such a fantastic birthday celebration, there was absolutely no reason for this to be happening. I took a glass figurine that I had on my bookshelf and threw it against the wall, hearing it smash into pieces.

"WHY? Why can't I just be happy and STAY that way?" I screamed into a pillow. I stayed with my face buried in my pillow, crying with defeat until I fell asleep.

At the end of April, the following month, Kelly and I began to talk about living together with another friend of ours, Casey. Her apartment in Waltham with Christian was ending its lease and he was planning on moving in just with Allen to a smaller place. My lease with my roommates was coming to a close as well and Tara expressed she wanted to finally live with her boyfriend. Hannah and Rachel would remain living with each other for a while longer, but I felt it was best for me to move in with Kelly. My anxiety had begun to increase more and more since the night I snapped after my birthday party and I secretly just wanted to be near Kelly, where I felt the most secure. My roommates were great, but Kelly's presence always calmed me. It was the big sister relationship we had. In all the years that I had been suffering with anxiety, it was worse than ever and I didn't know what to do about it. I began to drink more, often alone, which was something I never did before.

Kelly wanted to live a little closer into the city again, so we began our search in Brighton, MA. Casey was studying abroad in France that semester, but she was all for getting an apartment with us and told us to just pick one out. So, Kelly and I set out to do just that. We searched for a few apartments with a realtor and the last one we looked at caught our eye. It was the bottom of a three-family home, with the apartments all stacked on top of each other. It was under construction, but the realtor assured us that the remodeling would be done in time for us to move in a few weeks later. We were willing to risk it because it was the cheapest one we saw and it included a parking lot behind it with no extra fee. Total win!

A few days later, while at work I received an email from Casey that she would be home by the end of the week and she couldn't wait to go see the apartment. I called the realtor and he said that it was no problem to go check it out and that he would give the carpenters a heads up that we were coming by on Saturday.

That Friday night, I hung out with my roommates and we went out to a bar. I was sure going to miss these girls, but I knew that I would still see them around. Tara stayed home as usual, but Rachel, Hannah and I sat at the bar, laughing until it closed. I was exhausted when we finally came home and fell asleep, I fell right into a dream that would forever warm my heart.

I heard a little girl giggling around me. I sat up to find where she was but I couldn't see her and noticed the rich aroma of Lily flowers that were all around me.

"Mommy!" I heard her again, laughing some more. She was still nowhere to be found. Mommy? Why is she calling me mommy?

Then I heard a different voice, singing in the distance. His Irish lilt was unmistakable. His accent enlightened my heart and I stood up to see who it was? I heard the little girl giggling again above the singing and I turned around. I saw her across the field, way in the distance running away from me, her blonde hair flapping in the breeze. She turned and smiled at me before fading away.

The singing grew louder behind me and I quickly turned around. I saw him, the man with the blue eyes walking towards me. He was holding a single red rose and sang lyrics I will never forget:

"Twas given to me by a girl that I know,

Since we've met, faith, I've known no repose,

She is dearer by far than the world's brightest star,
And I call her my wild Irish Rose
My wild Irish Rose, the sweetest flower that grows.
You may search everywhere, but none can compare with my wild Irish Rose."

I awakened from the dream, no sweat and no anxiety, just in complete amazement. That was the most beautiful dream! I had to write it all down. Looking at the clock, I saw that it was only 6 a.m., so I had time to write. As I turned on my light and reached for my journal, I yawned. I had only slept a little over three hours but after a dream like that, there was no way I would be able to fall back asleep. I wasn't surprised I was dreaming about the blue-eyed man again, but I was still taken back by it because of the song he sang. The biggest mystery of the dream though, was definitely the blonde little girl. So random, I thought.

Kelly, Casey and I went out to breakfast later that morning at a little diner down the road from our new, soon to be apartment. We were chatting away about Casey's semester in France and also about decorating our new apartment. I was also curious to see how the remodeling was coming along too. We finished breakfast and drove up to the house. It was nighttime when Kelly and I first saw the place, so this was good that we would see it in broad daylight. We heard one of the carpenters cutting wood as we got out of the car. He was just outside the front door and stopped when he saw us walking towards him.

"Well look at that! Three gorgeous ladies ye are!" His Irish accent boomed out of him. I inhaled quickly when I heard the accent, remembering my dream! He was a very tall man with dark hair and he extended his hand. "I'm Liam. Are you the broads who will be moving in this shack?" Shack? *Oh no, I thought, is it still a mess in there?*

"Yes, we are. I'm Kelly and these are my roommates Lindsay and Casey," Kelly answered him, shaking his hand first.

"Very good. Well go on then. Take a look," he nodded his head towards the door.

Once inside, we all gasped. The place had already shaped up very well in the past week since we saw it. Everything looked and smelled new and Casey already loved it.

"Wow! This is great!" Casey's face lit up as she looked around.

I heard more chatter in the rooms down the hall where other carpenters were. The apartment had a big, long hallway just past the kitchen that led you to the bathrooms and bedrooms. At the end of the hall was a door, which was to the laundry room that was shared with all three apartments. Kelly and Casey began to talk in the kitchen about who was bringing what and their voices began to fade out, as I felt a strong urge to go look in one of the bedrooms. I felt my body floating towards it.

The door to the second bedroom on the right, was halfway open and I heard movement in there. I slowly opened the door and saw a carpenter with his back facing me and on his knees, laying the new wooden flooring. For some reason, my voice felt stuck in my throat and I couldn't make a sound, but he knew I was there. He heard me come in and he slowly stood up. He turned around and I nearly fainted.

The blue eyes, the same blue eyes that I had seen everywhere, were staring at me. It was him. I still couldn't find the right words and stood there frozen. His demeanor was entirely different than all the times we ran into each other, but unlike me, he was totally relaxed. It was like he was expecting me. His face was soft, with a smirk on it and my mouth was dropped open. I had never been this close to his eyes before; it was like gazing into an ocean of magnificent blue. No matter how hard I tried to look away, I just couldn't. I felt as though our souls were hugging as our physically bodies stood still, facing each other. He made the first move and grabbed my hand, his Irish drawl so thick.

"Nice to finally meet you Lindsay. My name is Jason," he said, winking at me.

My eyes widened even more. *What?* How did he know my name? Even if the realtor told him our names, how did he know that was me? *Lindsay, this is when you just run out,* I told myself. I just couldn't believe he knew my name! However, I couldn't run, instead I continued to stand there, staring at him and studying his beautiful face. I knew I would never forget this moment with him. His eyes sunk into mine and the way he looked at me was almost as if he was reaching into the depths of my soul. As I helplessly stared back, still unable to move, I knew right then, that he was mine forever. That he had always been mine even before this very moment. An all knowing passed between us as our energies continued to reunite and intertwine, as if they were coming "home" to each other.

When he lifted my hand and kissed it, the all-knowing feeling confirmed itself that there was a love between us, so ancient and so true. A timeless, tale between old soulmates was about to dance into this lifetime together and I held my breath. I was about to be swept away into a love story like none-other.

Thirteen

I never said anything to him, even after he kissed my hand. I was just so taken back. Kelly had come into the bedroom and interrupted us, introducing herself to him and I was relieved she did. The intensity of what I was feeling when we were standing there, rocked me to the core. I had never felt anything like that before and I wasn't sure what it even meant. Whether I liked it or not, I was about to find out! When we left, after Casey thoroughly looked through the apartment, Jason winked at me and told me he would see me soon. I figured he meant out on the streets, randomly bumping into each other, so I didn't think anything of it. Little did any of us girls know, that these Irish carpenters lived on the second floor above us!

A few weeks later, on a warm Friday in May, I finished my co-op at the media company. The apartment was finally ready and the big move was the following day. On my last day, a party was thrown by the staff and it felt so good to have ended this co-op on a much better note than the last one. That night, Kelly and I went out to dinner and also planned to pick up some things for our new apartment at Costco after. At dinner, Kelly started to talk about the Irish carpenters. None of us mentioned them since that day we took Casey to go see the apartment and we still had no clue they lived upstairs.

"Weren't they dreamy with that accent?" She asked. I smiled and my mind instantly got lost in the image of Jason. A chill ran up my back, remembering how he kissed my hand. My stomach was in knots as I thought about it and I wasn't sure how to tell Kelly. I wasn't used to handling emotions like this so I did what I do best; I pushed it aside.

"Yeah, it was. I've never heard an Irish accent in person like that before. I really liked it too," I answered her. That was all we said about the Irish carpenters. We paid the bill and headed off to Costco.

Christian and Allen met me at my apartment with the moving truck late that night and packed me up. I had the least amount of stuff because it was just my bedroom things. We got back to their apartment and I stayed there with them. We got up early the next day and packed up Kelly's things. Casey was moving in the following weekend and her parents were coming up to help her. As I followed the moving truck, my stomach began to flip with nerves again. Why was I feeling butterflies? We all pulled into the driveway of my new apartment and I parked. Kelly pulled up next to me, blasting music and laughing to herself, while waving at me. This helped me to relax a little. Christian began to slowly back up the moving truck, trying to get it as close to the door as possible to make unloading it easier, but he was having a real hard time lining it up to the front door. Allen jumped out and began shouting directions at him on which way to turn the wheel. We were all cracking up at how hard this task was, when all of a sudden, I felt someone watching me.

I turned and looked up at the deck to the second apartment and there he was. Jason was leaning over the side of the railing on the deck and staring right at me. We locked eyes just like we did when we officially met that day a few weeks prior. It hit me all of a sudden, what he meant when he said, "see you soon." He pushed off the railing and made his way down to meet us in the driveway and stood right next to me. I felt an electric jolt run through me while we stood there. His arms were crossed in amusement, watching Christian try and back the truck up still. He started to walk toward it and up to the driver's side.

"Hey buddy, let me do it ok?" Jason said and Christian looked relieved.

Jason and Christian switched places and Jason backed in the truck flawlessly. We all laughed. Hours later, we were done and somewhat organized for the night. The boys managed to get our beds set up and sheets on them. Mom would be proud! We placed an order for takeout Chinese food at a place that Jason recommended and that was when the rest of the Irish group, who lived with Jason came bursting through the door. Kelly jumped up as the hostess in her couldn't sit still.

"I'm going to run to the package store for beer. Do you boys want some beers?" She asked and they all laughed.

"A bear shit in the woods, yes?" Jason replied and Kelly laughed.

"Ok then! I take it, that means yes!" Everyone gave her cash to pick up the food too and she left.

Once she was gone, more chatter broke out and I stayed quiet, looking down at the floor. I wasn't sure why I felt so shy. Finally, I looked up and Jason was staring at me, smiling. He didn't move to come sit next to me though, instead he looked at Christian.

"So, where are ye all from?" Jason asked him. Christian gave him a mini play by play of our lives together, from past to present. We all continued to exchange stories of our lives, but I remained quiet. I was still quiet and at a loss for words. Jason's presence was not only oddly comforting, it was nerve-wracking because of how drawn to him I was. Perhaps it was the accent and his eyes. I don't even know this guy! Kelly returned with the beers, some wine and the Chinese food. We all ate, talked some more and after everyone was gone, she and I sat out on our new little patio with our wine glasses and candles lit.

"I think Jason likes you," she said. I froze. I was hoping she wouldn't pick up on anything!

"Oh? I don't think so," I answered, trying to sound as calm and casual as I could, but she knew my words were untrue. She saw right through my act.

"Oh, I think so." She smiled at me. "I have a deep feeling about you two. I don't know why, but I just sense something. But even if I am wrong, he sure is hot. And that accent...damn. It wouldn't hurt to roll around with him for a while, listening to him talk, even if it doesn't last!"

"Oh my god, Kelly!" I laughed.

"You and he will date and be together for a LONG time. I just know it," she replied.

I didn't answer, instead I sat deep in thought for a while and we both gazed up at the night sky. Kelly stood up finally and said she was heading to bed and I cleaned up. As I picked up everything off the table and walked to the door, something caught my eye on the ground. I bent down to get a closer look in the dim lights from inside. I gasped! It was a rose, one single red rose sitting in the grass right outside our door. I couldn't believe it. Another rose? Where did that come from? I brought the stuff in my arms into the kitchen, loaded the dishwasher and went back outside to get the rose. I brought it to my room and looked at it, so beautiful and perfect, just like every other rose that came my way. I did what I usually do with them and hung it upside down on the doorknob to my room to dry out. I figured it might have been dropped by one of my neighbors who lived on the third floor albeit surprising to see laying on the grass. I looked over at the basket of dried roses on the floor near my window. A beautiful, dried collection of the many roses I had come across in the years I had been in Boston. So beautiful and mysterious.

The next week, Kelly and I spent nights unpacking when we were home and trying to organize. I was also interviewing for a nanny job for the summer, along with the store for more money. The store only had about fifteen hours a week available and most of that was on the weekends. I wanted to take on more work for the summer instead of more summer classes. It was a long year of co-op but a good one, so my brain was toast and needed a break. Being a nanny would be a fun, along with the store and both easy.

Tammy at the media company surprised me with an offer for a part time regular staff position to begin there in the fall, as an editorial assistant. I knew that my days at the store were numbered because I couldn't do that, take classes and work as an editorial assistant. I told Sam, that I would be leaving them at the end of the summer. She was excited for my new job which would give me a lot of experience, but sad to see me go.

I didn't see Jason the first week we lived in the new apartment. I saw his car come and go but we didn't see much of each other face to face. That was just as well for me because he made me so nervous. Perhaps Kelly's prediction would turn out to be wrong, although something still stirred deep within, whenever I thought about him. We did, however, get to know the girls who lived on the top floor and absolutely loved them. They were fun and rowdy and liked to party like we did, so we quickly befriended them. We spent many nights together that first week, drinking wine and chatting. They filled us in on the gossip of the house and even the Irish boys that were sandwiched in-between our apartments. They had known them for a year by that point and said they were fun guys, but a little crazy.

The following weekend, Casey moved in and more chaos of trying to get organized and settled began. It didn't take long to get her stuff organized and a few days later, we were flattening our last moving box. Pictures were hung and all of our décor was laid out. The apartment looked fabulous. I landed a job with a great family to nanny for the summer and things seemed like they would be better for me. My anxiety was still raging, but I was feeling a lot more comfortable with Kelly near me more.

June came and brought sweltering heat, which for New England was on the early side. We had no air conditioning in this apartment but because we were on the bottom floor, the place wasn't too hot. When Jason and I did see each other, we only exchanged few words still. This raised my curiosity about him. I couldn't deny the fact that my strong attraction to him was growing, but I didn't talk about it, not even with Kelly. There was nothing I could do about it, so I just waited to see what would unfold.

One weekend in mid-June, Katie and I decided to sit in the driveway and sun bathe and paint our nails. It was a really hot day and we didn't feel like driving to a beach, so we stayed home instead. Casey was on campus, getting some studying done and we all planned to head out that night to go dancing downtown. Just then, as we were drying our nails and letting the sun soak in our skin, Jason's car roared into the driveway. I noticed all the Irish men drove superfast when they came home. He got out of his car and Kelly chimed in first as he walked toward us, his sunglasses on, looking extra sexy. Shifting uncomfortably in my chair, my words were stuck again. Thank goodness Kelly was with me chatting away.

"Well hey there neighbor. What's going on?" She asked.

He stopped in front us, took off his glasses and looked right at me first before he smiled. *Oh Lord, breathe Lindsay. Just breathe!* My mind was yelling but I tried to look calm.

"I just had some things to do around town. What are the two of ye doing here in the driveway?" He looked at me again, with a smirk on his face.

"Oh, you know. Mani and pedis and soaking in the rays. Hey, listen, we are headed downtown tonight. Want to join?" She asked him. Kelly no! I felt my heart start to race, but I didn't feel anxious. I felt...*excited.*

Jason was quiet for a moment until he finally answered.

"Sure, I'd love to," he smiled at her and took one more look at me before he headed up the stairs to his apartment. I erupted once he was inside.

"Kelly! Why?" She laughed.

"Calm down buttercup. I'm just trying to be a friendly neighbor," she said, with a wink. She knew I didn't buy it. "Ok fine, if you aren't going to attack him, then I will for you!" She cracked up. "Ok no, for real, this is so you two can hook up. You're welcome." She put her sunglasses on and leaned back to snooze. I wanted to slap her but also thank her at the same time.

Casey got home a few hours later and we all got ready for the night ahead. Kelly made a quick dinner, some spaghetti and meatballs, which she was really good at.

"I hope ya'll love balls! I made some delicious meatballs! Let's eat up this pasta, so it can soak in the booze ladies! Get ready for an epic night!" She called out to us, as she filled up our plates. I laughed as I texted Prisha to let her know which bar we were going to. She was going to meet us there. We called a cab a couple hours later and Kelly made me be the one to go upstairs and get Jason. He answered the door. It was finally time to face my fear and talk to him. Enough of the staring games.

"Hello there, love," he said and I nearly collapsed on his feet. What is with this accent? It was so incredibly alluring. I also caught a whiff of his cologne and it smelled divine.

"Hey Jason. So, um, just you coming? What about your roommates?" I looked past him, searching for them.

"Why would I do that?" He moved past me. "Then I wouldn't get you all to myself," he smiled at me. Oh shit.

A short while later, a cab pulled into our driveway and we piled in. We were meeting some of Kelly's friends from college at the bar as well, so it was going to be a fun night. Jason sat in the front with the cab driver, asking him all kinds of questions and the cab driver just nodded in response, not understanding a word of his thick Irish brogue. I laughed because I didn't either. I found myself smiling and nodding a lot too! Kelly and Casey were giggling and joking with each other next to me, and I kept my eyes glued to the back of Jason's head. He must have sensed it and turned and winked at me. Oh, shit again. *I'm in trouble!* I tried to smile at him, but my face was frozen in nerves.

We got to the bar and once inside, we all began to drink and Kelly and Casey went out to dance floor right away. I finally made my way to dance after I had a drink in me, and within seconds, I felt hands on my hips. I spun around and there was Jason, dancing with me. I started to tremble, but his smile and the way he moved with me, calmed me down. I leaned into him and we were inseparable for the rest of the night. I don't even remember hearing the music and all I could do was stare into his eyes. The same eyes I had been seeing off and on for years, finally captured my heart completely as we swayed together. Butterflies rose in my stomach and it felt so good to experience a feeling like this. I didn't exactly know what was about to unfold, but I knew one thing: What was happening between Jason and me, was enthralling and absolutely beautiful.

Once we got back to the house later that night, the fun continued. Kelly and I went up to the third floor and hung out with the girls. We were all together on their deck and Jason's roommates all came to join too. It was turning into one big family in the house. Jason came over to me and pulled my hand to get me up from my chair. He led me downstairs to his deck. He began to move me into a slow dance with him, as I relaxed into his arms. The intensity of the mutual feelings that were growing in both of us was a lot for a girl who had spent the last five years in silent suffering. My mind was battling it, urging me to run and telling me no, but my heart said yes. He swept me off my feet that first day I met him and now I was beginning to fly with him.

"Aren't you a romantic," I managed to say. Jason's mouth turned up in a small, sexy smirk and he shook his head.

"No. I'm not a romantic. I'm a man who is completely mesmerized by a woman who is his soulmate. A woman who I have known for what seems many lifetimes and a woman I have seen for two years now, waiting for the right time to make his move. Romance is the only response there is to have with you," he said, his eyes softening, as his gaze looked down at my lips.

"Make his move, huh?" I teased and he laughed, twirling me around. "Oh, Jason you are impossibly charming."

"And impossibly falling for you, darling," he said and with one quick gesture, we were face to face again. With his eyes still locked in mine, we shared our first kiss and my world as I once knew it, would never be the same. It was a kiss of promise. I didn't know what our journey would look like, but I knew it would be forever. This, was love.

"It has always been you darling," he whispered in my ear. "My search is over. I found my Lindsay." *His search?*

I didn't think to question him. Love was too heavy on my mind and sinking into my heart, which distracted me away from what he said. I put my head on his shoulder and we sat on the chair together on his deck, looking up at the stars. This summer would be something I had never experienced before. The magic of love was about to show me its miraculous powers. I was slowly unfolding, blossoming to love's miracles like the radiant roses that always found me, since I was sixteen-years-old. He very quietly whispered ear again:

"Twas given to me by a girl that I know,
Since we've met, faith, I've known no repose,
She is dearer by far than the world's brightest star,
And I call her my wild Irish Rose."

I was speechless as tears brimmed in my eyes.

Jason Gibson continued to surprise and astonish me as our relationship kept going. I became lost in love with him that summer. We spent hours conversing late at night, in that same spot on his deck, growing more in love by the minute. He made me laugh and at the same time, challenged me with his wisdom. I had never met a man so open and connected with his faith like him. He would spend hours talking about God and his life story with me. I sat listening, engrossed in his words and inhaling his strong faith in like oxygen. God was someone I had fallen away from since the rape. He sensed something was underneath my smiles and laughter, no matter how hard I tried to hide it. He wasn't afraid to challenge me with these spiritual talks, but my response was always met in silence. This only turned the wheels in his brain to find more ways to reach me. He was committed to me in ways I had never known before.

July 3, 2005, was when he took me on our first "official date." We went to a Red Sox game and I remembered the season before at the State House when they won the series. We sat at a bar next to Fenway and toasted each other for finally making our first date in public. We couldn't help but laugh as we were just so content being at home and talking.

"I'm glad to finally be out with you in public and show you off as my girlfriend," Jason said as we sat down in our seats, ready to watch the game.

"Oh? Your girlfriend huh?" I said, teasing him with my smile. He leaned in real close.

"Admit it darling, you wanted to really show me off," he winked and I laughed.

After the game, we went out to eat and sat on a patio at a restaurant on the harbor, talking until they closed for the night. We held hands as we walked down Boston's cobbled stoned streets, quietly watching everyone around us. I couldn't believe the relationship we were forming. It was so incredible and I lost myself in it. Our love felt like a big band aid on my damaged heart. I was hoping it would be the band aid I needed to finally end all of the pain I had been suffering with. It was certainly doing a good job slowing my anxiety down. Or so I thought. Finally, we hailed a cab and went home.

The rest of the summer under the stars with him, brought more talks and greater love. I even moved upstairs and lived with him by the end of the summer. Things were moving at warp speed, but to us, it was a long time coming. We didn't care about timing or the pace of our relationship. Time stood still when I was with him. We had decided to sublet my room out so Katie and Casey could save even more money, by splitting it now four ways.

The fall semester was beginning and I started my part time job at the media company, along with taking five classes. I was really packing it in and enjoying life! However, Jason still saw through a lot of it. The closer we became, the more he saw the young girl hiding in a shell inside of me. He knew not to push me to talk about it. There were many nights, I would be awakened by a nightmare and Jason would ask me what I dreamed about?

"I can't remember." Was all he ever got in response. He knew it wasn't true.

Finally, one night in late October, after we finished dinner, something shifted. We got comfy in our favorite spot on his deck, enjoying the cool fall night air. He grew serious when he looked at me.

"What happened to you darling?" I looked at him, puzzled and thought he meant earlier that day when I didn't call him back for hours.

"I'm sorry, the day was so hectic. After my morning classes, I squeezed in some hours in the library after I went to the gym. Then I had to get to my job and..." He cut me off.

"No, what happened to you as a teenager?" He said without a beat. *What? Oh no!* Fear iced all over me, causing me to shiver against my quickening heart.

"Jason, I...I can't," I began to stutter, looking away.

"You can't or you won't?" He turned me head to face him again. "You were hurt, weren't you?" *How did he possibly know that?*

I also couldn't believe how bold he was being and it started to anger me, but I knew the anger was not at him. I was angry at myself for letting that night still haunt me like it did, eating at me slowly as the years went by without any healing. Why would he even want to bring this up? Besides, I felt like I was doing so much better, except for the random nightmares here and there. All I could do was nod my head and he knew by that reaction that I couldn't tell him the whole story. I didn't even remember it anyway. I had totally blocked it out. As he continued to look at me, waiting for an answer, for the first time in years, I actually tried to remember and I just couldn't. It was completely buried inside of me. What he said next nearly pushed me over the edge.

"And how have you lived your life since?" I looked at him completely dumbfounded. "Okay, let me rephrase. What are you accountable for from that night? Have you faced the truth yet?" *Accountable?* I felt my face flush with anger and I quickly found my voice.

"Jason Andrew Gibson, how dare you! That's the worst question you could have possibly asked me! Goodnight!" I screamed and stormed downstairs to find Kelly.

She was asleep in her room and I quietly got in beside her shed many tears, as I tried not to awaken her. My tears weren't out of anger from his question, it was out of realizing he was right. However, I not in a place to receive the truth of his words. I didn't know yet that Jason's words would ultimately save me. His love was slowly beckoning me to come out of the darkness in my soul. I fell asleep, quietly cursing myself for how incredibly weak I still was and how I reacted to him.

Fourteen

It took me a little over a week to approach Jason after I stormed off from him that night. He gave me the space I needed and never pushed me to talk about it. I was very distracted with school and work, so that helped with the intense anxiety that emerged all over again since that conversation with him. I was desperately trying to understand what he was trying to say and why? Finally, one night after dinner, I opened up the discussion again.

"Jason, I'm sorry. I just can't handle talking about my past. It's better that way," was all I could say. He was quiet for a while, which was something he did when he was cooking up just the right thing to say.

"Don't be sorry to me Lindsay, be sorry to yourself. That's your choice to ignore it, not mine, but in response to what you just said. That's fine. Topic closed." I was surprised at how I did not feel angry at what he said. Instead, it had me think for the very first time about the word "choice". As a rape victim, I felt like my choice was taken from me that night as well as my innocence. Where was the choice for me then? I was lost in my thoughts and I didn't notice Jason was staring at me, searching my face with his own thoughts.

"I'm not talking about that actual night. I'm talking about now. Right now, what choice are you making to move forward?" He asked. I didn't answer. I wasn't quite sure because a big part of me, in fact most of me, was still so angry and victimized. I felt like choices didn't make any difference for me because anxiety and nightmares ruled me, no matter what I would choose. I sighed out a huge breath of frustration and got up without answering him. I went to the bedroom to write in my journal. When I opened it, instead of diving into a long entry, I wrote one thing:

Whose fault is it that I am still so sad?

I didn't answer it. Instead, I grew angrier. I wanted to scream. My rapist was at fault not me! I also wanted to scream at Jason too. Why did he put these thoughts in my head? I started to cry into a pillow, trying to muffle the sounds of my heartache. I missed who I was before that night, a young girl trying to find herself. My rapist took that away from me and therefore left me without any choices, but only to be in pain! I threw my journal across the room.

Tears were falling down my face as the night was heavy on my mind, but I still couldn't recall very much. What I did remember began to cycle through my head: his voice, the whistling, and parts of the room I was in. As I sat there, allowing myself to release some tears, more pieces of that night for the first time came into view. I started to panic. I heard the late summer crickets and it even felt like blood was dripping down my legs. My heart was pounding through my chest as I saw the convenience store that I limped towards. NO! I sat up and I started to choke. I couldn't breathe. Why did I always choke like this whenever I remembered anything from that night? This is exactly why I don't *want* to remember! I couldn't handle the memories or the pain. I realized that the more I cried, the more I remembered, so I forced myself to turn everything off. Sitting on the edge of the bed now, I wiped away my tears, holding my breath until all the memories stopped.

Jason had heard me choking and came into the room and when he saw my face, he ran to me and we hugged for a long time. He took my hand and led me to the bed and turned on the television to help distract me. As we watched a movie together, I leaned into him and felt so safe. I still wasn't too sure what he meant by all of his questions, but I knew he meant to help. I didn't care to understand either. He loved me. Wasn't that enough?

Thanksgiving seemed to come fast and I decided to take Jason home to meet my family for the first time. Mom especially, was very interested in talking with him as she didn't get to the first time she saw him. She had come up shortly after I moved into the apartment with Kelly and Casey, but she only got a glimpse of him. We were sitting at my table outside the apartment, after a day of shopping and Jason had come out to his deck. He was leaning over the railing, smiling at us. When mom saw me look up and smile, she turned to see who it was. When she saw Jason, a striking, yet much older Irish man, she figured something was going on between us. It must have been her motherly intuition, but she was cautious. She was worried I would get my heart broken.

"Lindsay, slow down. I see how you are looking at him. He has heartbreak written all over his face. He is too good-looking, plus he has an accent," she warned me. I laughed at her reasoning.

"What does his accent have to do with anything?"

"Everything. It spells out HEARTBREAK!" She said, but she couldn't help but laugh herself.

Eight months later, they were face to face again but this time over Thanksgiving dinner. My mom had been eying him since we walked in the door, still not sure about the idea of the two of us together. My brothers took on to him very well and they were chatting away about soccer and drinking some beers.

"I like that guy!" Derek said when he came in the kitchen to get some more beer, where mom and I were cooking. "He's really funny Lindsay!"

Mom turned from the stove and looked at Derek, eyes narrowing.

"That's nice you like him," was all she managed to say and I rolled my eyes.

"Mom, go talk to him," I said.

She ignored me and kept mixing the batter for a dessert she was making. We all sat down a little while later and stuffed ourselves fully. Finally, mom and Jason began to talk. Within an hour, Jason had her in tears laughing. They finally warmed up to each other and I breathed a sigh of relief. The night ended as a success!

"I can see why you like him Lindsay. I like him too," my mom whispered to me in the kitchen at the end of the night. I gave her a hug in response. "You feel hot." She placed her hand on my forehead.

"Yeah, my chest feels tight and my head is pounding. I think I'm coming down with something," I said.

The next day we were back on the road to Boston and I was exhausted. I woke up in the middle of the night sweating and coughing. I was definitely sick with something and felt awful, but I had so much to get done over the next few weeks with school. No time to rest! My work was so understanding and cut my hours in half to help me get through my finals, but even with that, I was still swamped.

When we got back to Boston, my favorite holiday was in full swing. Christmas! I was really looking forward to it as I was planning on taking a break from Christmas Eve through New Year's Day. I couldn't wait! Finals that semester, with five classes were going to be tough, so I got started on one of my three final papers, right away, once we were back from Thanksgiving. Whatever I was sick with quickly turned into bronchitis a few days later and all I could do was pop in some antibiotics and keep going.

Over the next few weeks, I lived in my computer when I was not in class or work and hardly even had time to talk with Jason. I would usually collapse in bed late at night next to him and most nights he was already asleep. I missed him so much and finally one night, I decided to take a break and go Christmas shopping with him. I was finally feeling better and I had completed four of my finals. I had one more the next day which was an exam. I had already studied all day, so I needed to clear my mind.

We went out to a very romantic dinner and had a lot of fun looking at all the lights downtown. We also discussed our New Year's Eve plans and enjoyed catching up with each other. Jason was so incredibly understanding of how my busyness. The next day I finished my last final and headed into work. There was a Christmas party that day and I was looking forward to that. I had such a bad headache and wasn't sure how long I would last, but I stopped at a drug store to pick up cards and a gift card for a nice restaurant to put into the Secret Santa pull.

Once I was there, I heard the Christmas music playing from the back room where the party was. The bigger executives were all going out to eat that night to celebrate, but they were throwing the rest of us a party at the office. It was a very big company, so they couldn't accommodate all of us at a restaurant. Tammy greeted me as I came in, looking very excited.

"Lindsay! I'm so happy you're here. I think someone is getting an offer for a promotion! And that someone is you!" She was practically jumping up and down with excitement for me.

"Me? I only started working here three months ago!" I told her.

"Well, yeah but you did the co-op too and they love you! Plus, you are really good at writing those media scripts. I think you are going to be moved up into the PR department!" She had a huge smile on her face.

We walked into the party and the next few hours were spent stuffing ourselves with catered food and playing corny games and finally the Secret Santa. I received a nice handmade pair of earrings from a local vendor in the city and the party was overall very nice. We all received raises too and then Tammy was right, in my letter for a raise was also a promotion offer. I couldn't believe it! Of course, I said yes! They planned on meeting with me after the New Year to discuss the details more.

A few days later, Jason and I were on the road and heading back to Connecticut for Christmas. We were discussing the idea of getting a place together, just the two of us. My big Christmas gift from him was a brand new, German Shepherd puppy that we named Darcy. We weren't technically allowed to have a dog in the apartment, so it made even more sense to move. Even though we had been sharing a room for the past ten months together, I still felt a little nervous talking about a place of our own. I felt a jolt in my belly, like something was telling me it was going to happen regardless of my nerves. I didn't say anything to Jason about it and was very quiet the rest of the drive.

Christmas was really fun and lots of gifts were exchanged and mom and Jason continued to build a relationship together. She couldn't believe I owned such a big dog, but I assured her that Darcy was a sweetheart. We left Darcy home with Jason's roommates who were not leaving the city for Christmas. A few days later, we headed back to Boston to celebrate New Year's Eve.

The day before New Year's Eve, I was downstairs helping Kelly pick out an outfit for the following night. We were all going to hit up the bars and I was excited. I had not gone out in a while and it was time to get out. The next night we partied our hearts out and had a blast. Everyone from the house went out together and it had been since the summer that we all did that. I was really looking forward to the New Year, especially with the new job offer. My finals from school had been so much work mixed in with my job duties, that I hardly noticed my anxiety anymore. I had successfully stuffed it away again and that was how I wanted it to be.

One Friday afternoon, in mid-January, I came home absolutely exhausted. I was feeling unusually tired the past few days and on and off queasy. It must be some virus and I was glad it was Friday. I couldn't wait to just go snuggle on the couch with Jason and then go to bed. I fell asleep the second my head hit the pillow later that night, not at all expecting what was about to come next as I fell into a deep sleep.

The scene was blurry at first and finally I made out where I was sitting. I was in the same field full of Lily flowers again and this time, Jason was sitting right next to me. He was smiling at me as he put his arm around me. I smiled back at him and he said, "Our sweet Lillian is here." Who?

I woke up with a start and sat up fast. Who was Lillian? The queasiness I had been fighting for a couple days, woke up with me, except it was much worse. I felt so sick to my stomach, so I got up to go to the kitchen to make some peppermint tea. After I turned the water on to boil, I ran to bathroom and got sick. Jason heard me by that point and woke up too. He came into the bathroom to check on me.

"Sick baby?"

"Yes, ugh. I must have a flu," I said. He went into the kitchen to finish making my tea. Darcy was excited that Jason was up and was jumping around all over him, clearly not caring that I was not feeling well.

"I'm going to let her out. I'll be right back," he said and placed the tea next to me.

We were supposed to look at apartments that day, but I wasn't sure I would make it. I felt a little better after I got sick and was able to fall back asleep. Maybe whatever virus this is, was finally making its way to the surface. I woke up a couple hours later and felt surprisingly better. Since my stomach wasn't hurting as much, we decided to head out and at least look at one apartment. A little while later, we were just walking out of an apartment and the realtor was chatting away about it, when nausea struck me again out of nowhere.

"Jay, we need to go home. I feel sick again," I said and was tugging at him. Too late. I got sick all over the bushes, outside of the apartment we just looked at. I sheepishly look at them. "They probably won't choose us to live here now," I said and they both laughed.

Jason took me back home and decided to leave again to go look at the other apartments with the realtor. I went downstairs and sat with Kelly.

"I'm just feeling so weird the past few days. On and off sick to my stomach and I had such a weird dream last night about Jason and me. He told me in my dream, 'our Lillian was here' so that was odd. I don't know anyone by that name," I said to Kelly, as I laid on her bed. She was quiet and deep in thought.

"When was the last time you got your period?" She asked.

"What? What does that have to do with any…" my voice trailed off. "Kelly, what's the date?"

"It's January 21st," she answered. I froze. When was my last period? December was a blur with finals and the holidays. I just couldn't remember. I knew I got it sometime very soon after Thanksgiving, but it was now late January and no period had come yet this month. Without hesitating, Kelly jumped into action.

"Come on, let's go. We're going to get a pregnancy test," she grabbed her purse and we were out the door.

An hour later, I was slumped on the bathroom floor in shock, staring at the two pink lines on the stick. Kelly put her arms around me as I started to cry.

"Lindsay, it'll be okay. I promise, just breathe," she said, trying her best to reassure me.

"How did this happen?" I asked in a daze, with tears brimming my eyes. I was not ready to be a mom!

"Do we need to have a little talk about the birds and the bees?" She asked, with a small smile on her face and I threw the bathroom towel at her face.

"Stop it, I'm serious! I'm on birth control. Seriously, I think I'm going to pass out," I said and leaned over, trying to get more air in. Kelly hugged me again.

"It'll be okay Linds, just try and calm down," she said. I got up off from the floor and looked at her.

"I need to see Jason," I said and she nodded.

I walked outside still stunned. Pregnant? What was I going to do? I opened the door to his apartment, walked into our bedroom and sat on the bed. He wasn't back yet from looking at apartments, so I laid down, feeling woozy again, only this time I think it was more from my nerves. A car pulled in a short while later and my heart skip a beat as I heard him come inside. I held my breath. He paused at the bedroom door, leaning up against the side of the door frame with a serious look on his face. Then a smile spread across his face.

"So, my love. You're lucky I love babies so much," he said and my mouth fell open. "I'm just sorry it didn't dawn on me until after you got sick all over those people's bushes." He winked at me. He knew. That man had an intuition like I had never seen before.

"Jason..." I couldn't find the right words to respond. I stood up and he walked toward me, standing directly in front of me now. I handed him the positive test and he looked at it with tears forming in his eyes now too.

"We're pregnant," he said calmly and bent down on his knees, facing my stomach, kissing it over and over. I laughed and cried all at the same time. I wasn't sure what to do next, but I knew one thing, Jason would never leave my side.

Fifteen

Mom was anything but thrilled with the news at first. I was only twenty-one years old and was at the height of my college career. Her reaction was like the fury of a tornado, strong at first and then the wild winds of her shock eased back down. Pretty fast too! Two days later, the tornado passed and she was hell-bent on supporting Jason and me. The rest of my family was equally supportive, but as for me? I was scared and not sure what to think, despite Jason's loving support.

During the first couple weeks before we saw an obstetrician, I quietly took in this new information, but my mind was on full speed. My head felt jumbled trying to organize what I was going to do. Jason and I are "planners" by nature, so we were out of our element. My young age and college responsibilities made this harder for me. It did help to have him working full time and making good money, so I knew that we would get through. However, even with his solid salary, it wasn't helping me mentally and emotionally wrap my head around being a mother.

Mom was there for me to cry with, when I was at a loss for what to do. She cut to the chase during my meltdowns and was not afraid to share her opinion, pushing me to work through each one.

"Lindsay, becoming a mother is a time of emotional, physical and spiritual challenges. Work through it," she would say because tough love was the way she raised all three of us. "I'm going to be support you and be here as much as I can, but you both need to figure it out, not me." Those were the best words she could have ever said, yet at the time I felt so abandoned with her words.

"Mom, I'm only twenty-one. How am I supposed to do that?" I asked her, feeling my anxiety start to rise through my anger. I wasn't angry at her, I was angry at myself for being in such a difficult position, though I didn't tell her that. I was scared and wanted her to "fix it". Luckily, she knew better and knew that the only way for me to learn to swim through motherhood, was to just jump in without her holding my hand.

"Let your strength push you and your instincts guide you. You and Jason will figure this out. You're both good people," was her answer. That's it? That is all she has to say? I realized it was time to put my big girl panties on.

The night before the first ultrasound, Jason and I were laying on the couch, mindlessly watching television. I couldn't focus on school work or anything else besides being pregnant. Jason didn't want me working and going to school while pregnant, especially when I wasn't feeling well during the first trimester with strong morning sickness and fatigue. I wasn't so sick that it was debilitating, I just felt really lousy, like most moms do in the beginning of pregnancy. That was not entirely the reason he wanted me to cut back on working though, it was mainly because my stress and anxiety had heightened. He was afraid I would completely fall apart. I was close.

I was scared I would ruin this baby's life, if I didn't get a grip on my emotions. Maybe Jason was right, I just needed a break to think through things and rest. I told my boss what had happened, gave my notice and watched my promotion slip away from me. That saddened me, but it also took a lot of pressure off. I was grateful to Jason for giving me that choice. He taught so much about relationship and commitment, but I was worried that I couldn't give anything back to him. His patience was remarkable and I realized that my personal problems took a back seat to my pregnancy. We needed to prepare for this baby and that was all we were focusing on. However, there was one night, that it came out.

"Jason?" I looked up at him, while laying on him. "I'm scared."

"I know you are," he said. "But I told you, I've got this. I will handle all the bills, just relax." I couldn't have been more thankful to have him tell me that, but my fears ran deeper.

"No. I'm scared I won't be a good mommy. I have no clue where to even start once the baby is home with us," I explained.

"Do you think anyone does?" He was right.

"True, but I'm not sure I know how to love a baby," I responded. He leaned in and kissed my forehead, but I still wasn't sure he understood just how perplexing this fear was for me.

I had been fixated on this concern for days now, which was pulling me into a really low and negative state of mind. I hardly scratched the surface of understanding love as a couple, but now a baby? We had made really great strides together in our relationship and I was certainly growing from it, but I was nowhere near ready to challenge myself with a baby.

I tried hard to envision myself holding my baby in my arms, but I couldn't see it yet. My inner darkness made me feel numb to connecting. It wasn't the baby, in fact I love children, especially babies. In school, for my psychology requirements, I was always drawn to infant and early childhood development, but this was different. *Much* different. The news of this pregnancy was pushing me to be present and aware of myself like I had never done before. That was why I wasn't ready. How could I bring my emotions out for this baby, when I still couldn't see what was going on inside of me?

What I failed to accept while lying on the couch with Jason, was that loving this baby would be a challenge because I didn't know how to love myself first. Of course, I would love and care for this child, but there was something missing. I couldn't extend love out for my child the way that was needed because there was nothing to draw from in me. I was so empty and so blind to all of this, so it was easier to just blame my inexperience and young age with my fears of motherhood. This seemed to the most logical and what kept me from facing the truth. Lost in my thoughts, I faced Jason who was staring at me. He knew exactly what the battle was about in my head.

"Being a young mom isn't what's scaring you. Age isn't the problem here and you know it." Scary how he can read my mind sometimes.

"What are you talking about? I just don't think I can give this baby what it needs. I'm hardly an adult myself," I said, trying to reason with him. I grew annoyed at what he said, but it was really me I was annoyed with. I could never handle criticism well or when he pushed me to dig deeper within. This was why the progress between us was a slow one, despite how fast we fell in love.

"I think you need to get some help before our baby is born. You need to learn what love really means and I'm not talking about how you feel about me," he sternly said and I didn't like it.

"Get some help? Really Jason? Like I'm a bad person? I go to school and have maintained a 3.9 average since the first day of college. I have completed co-ops and worked my butt off! I'm a responsible person and your telling me I need help?" My voice had escalated to a high-pitched scream. As usual, he stayed cool and calm. I wanted to slap him.

"So, what's the problem then Lindsay?" He asked, but he knew the answer. "Since you're so put together, why can't you love this baby? Obviously, age isn't a problem then since you're accomplishing all of that. Right?" Cornered! This was my cue to shut it down completely and Jason knew it. Before I even stood up, he pointed behind him. "Go ahead, run off then."

"Jason Gibson! You're such an ass!" I shouted, in defense, which only made me angrier. I went into our room and laid on the bed, looking around at the boxes and feeling uneasy. We were still in the middle of planning to move because we needed our own place, especially now. I took a deep breath, trying to cool down, while staring at the boxes to distract me.

Living in Boston was expensive and I wasn't sure how we would afford our own apartment. Jason made good money, but he still had some planning to do to be able to provide for the three of us on his own. He kept reassuring me he would figure it out, but he didn't have any answers yet. I was nervous how this would all play out and that made me angry all over again. Trust, was one of my biggest challenges. Gripping a pillow, I threw it against the wall. How could I have let myself get pregnant? Jason gave me space and we didn't talk the rest of the night. Angry thoughts spun in my head, as I fell asleep.

"Mommy catch me!" The little girl called down to me, her blonde hair sparkling against the sun as she smiled at me so big from the top of the slide. She was absolutely gorgeous. Was she mine? I bent down at the bottom of the slide.

"Okay Lillian, come on down! I'll catch you!" I called up to her. Just as I was bending down, getting ready to catch her, I felt someone grab me. The next thing I know, I was falling into a deep, dark hole and I heard his evil laughter.

"MOMMY! COME BACK!" I heard the little girl scream with fright.

Waking up and shaking from head to toe, I was breathing hard as the morning sickness hit me. I ran to the bathroom and vomited. Sitting on the floor, waiting for my stomach to settle, I thought about the little girl, Lillian, from my dream. There was that name again. Jason knocked on the door and came in with some toast. I started to cry. Maybe it was the pregnancy hormones or his persistent love, even after a fight like the one the night before, but the tears kept falling.

"I love you, Lindsay," he said when he saw my tears. "Let's get ready and go see our baby today, shall we?" It was really all we could do at this point. At least for today.

We hugged each other while standing in the bathroom. We didn't know what the next move would be or all the answers, but Jason was good at showing me how to slow down and take things as they come. He was an independent man and because of this, he didn't run from challenges as easily as I did. He wasn't afraid of the lack of money for the baby, but I was. We were such opposites. My anxiety kept me running from everything difficult and challenging. The "planner" in me kept me so busy, that sometimes I made decisions without thinking through them. When plans fell apart, I ran to my mom to "fix it," but for the first time that was not an option for me. She wisely, let go and challenged me to become a mother, which was so scary. Until now, I would just cover up my bad choices with alcohol. This pregnancy was taking away a lot of those habits and crutches and I felt vulnerable and weak.

Having a baby was one of the biggest challenges of my life, so I was on overdrive. Therefore, my anger the night before, was the result of being overwhelmed and anxious. I needed help, but I wasn't ready to ask for it. So, I got in the shower to get ready for the ultrasound appointment.

We were in better spirits by the time we finished breakfast and got in the car to drive to the hospital. I was under the student health plan at Northeastern still, so I didn't have a private obstetrician yet. Therefore, this initial maternity visit, would be done in the hospital. As we pulled into the parking lot, I got nervous. Would this doctor be male or female? The idea of a male doctor examining me, freaked me out. Why was I feeling like I was in danger all of a sudden? After all, doctors are safe people.

"Jason wait," I snapped out of my daze and turned to him. "I can't do this."

"Baby, we have to. It's just an ultrasound. I think you're going to feel so much better when you see her on the screen." *Her?* The name Lillian came to me again.

"How do you know our baby is a she?" I asked him. He smiled at me.

"Because I have been waiting on our little girl for a long time," he said and winked. "Come on love, let's go. I'm right here with you." I was still nervous, but with no time to ask him about it, I got out of the car and followed him through the sliding doors of the hospital.

I never got to finish explaining to him why I was nervous, but I realized he was right. I had to do this. We went up to the floor that the office was on and I held my breath. Inside, we sat down and filled out all of the paperwork and Jason was trying to make me laugh with one of his dumb jokes. I couldn't even bring myself to smile, my nerves were so jittery. He sensed it and put his arms around me

"It'll be okay, just breathe," he assured me. I heard my name called and I wanted to slide out the back door.

The nurse was really sweet and smiled, which helped a little. She led us to our examining room and told me to undress completely. *Oh, my god! No!* I nearly passed out.

"Wait, all the way? Why?" I said and felt vomit creeping up from my stomach and into my throat and headed for her feet.

"Yes, the doctor wants to do a pap smear and breast exam as well as an internal ultrasound to see how far along you are," she said without looking up from her chart.

What the heck was an internal ultrasound, I wondered. *Didn't they just rub gel on your belly to look?* She didn't see that all the color had drained from my face. I usually went home to Connecticut to have a pap smear done with a female doctor I have known for years. Even then, I asked mom to come in the room with me. Jason caught on fast where my fear was stemming from and jumped in.

"Is the Doctor a male or female?" He asked.

"Male, but I can ask for the female doctor if you'd like? You just might have to wait a little longer," she said.

"That's fine, we will wait for a female," he said. She nodded her head and left after she took my blood pressure.

We waited for what seemed like forever and finally the doctor came in. She was a young, attractive doctor and looked nice, so I calmed down once I saw her smile at me.

"What's an internal ultrasound?" I asked her right away.

"The baby will be too small to pick up on an abdominal ultrasound, so I will insert a wand inside of you. This type of ultrasound will get closer to the sac to see and measure," she explained and held it up for me to see. Since she was so gentle in her approach with me, I felt I could get through it. I was so thankful Jason spoke up for me, requesting a female doctor because I would not have been able to let a male doctor do this exam.

"I'm so confused as to how this happened!" I blurted out to her as if she was my therapist, while she turned on the ultrasound machine. She paused and looked at me, waiting for me to continue. "I was on birth control and took it at the same time every day. Or maybe I messed up? I just don't know anymore. I was so stressed out last semester with five classes of finals, that I can't remember." I felt the frustration and tears building. I was clearly still so surprised that this happened and for some reason, spilling my heart out to this strange new doctor felt comforting. It was like she could make it all disappear somehow.

"Did you throw up any pills?" She asked and I shook my head. "Were you on any other medications, like antibiotics in the past couple months?"

"Not that I…" I started to say but then my voice trailed off. "Wait… Yes! In fact, I was on an antibiotic for bronchitis that I developed after Thanksgiving."

"Well, that could be your answer then. There's a lot of studies that say antibiotics can lower the effects of birth control but I'm not

100% certain. However, with all of the stress you had going on with finals, you may not have taken it properly like you thought. Either way, I have patients who conceive on the pill a lot more than you may realize. Fact is, you had a positive test, so let's check things out, shall we?" She smiled at me, patted my hand and turned to the machine to get it ready. Then she looked back at Jason and me. "Are you two ready to see your baby?"

Jason reached for my hand and I closed my eyes as she inserted the wand. I heard her click the large keyboard and felt her moving the wand around. Jason leaned over to my ear.

"Open your eyes darling and look at this miracle," he whispered, so I finally did. The doctor turned up the volume and at that moment my life changed. I heard the fast-paced heartbeat of our baby and it seemed to breathe life back into my lungs. I released the breath I was holding and looked at the screen.

"There's the heartbeat, so strong!" She froze the screen to capture measurements and pictures with her other hand. When she turned it back on, she pointed to where the heartbeat was and I saw it flicker on the screen, filling the room with new life again. *Oh, Wow!* I thought, *there really is a baby in there. My baby!* Tears stung my eyes, but they weren't tears of sadness. I wasn't quite sure what the tears meant. All I could do was stare at the heartbeat on the screen. *Lillian.* The name jumped out at me again. The heartbeat was like a golden light illuminating the screen. Like a lily flower whose golden essence shines brightly in the sun, so was this little flicker. I knew then, that I just became a mother.

"My sweet little baby." I whispered in complete awe. I heard Jason choke next to me with his own tears, as he watched the screen with me.

Instead of turning to him, I continued to sit there mesmerized with the sounds and what I felt inside. The tears were now falling down my face. Were these tears of joy? I could feel my heart leap and my stomach follow in response.

"There's the yok sac and fetal pole," she pointed out. "You're about 6 weeks along. Everything looks really good so far!" She continued to measure a little more and take pictures. "I'll be right back to do the pap smear and give you two a few minutes," she smiled and stood up to leave.

Amazed, I still didn't look at Jason. Then I sensed her golden spirit move through me, echoing the sparkle that I just saw on the screen and my heart stirred with immense motherly love. It was an anchoring moment that finally put my feet on solid ground. I was going to be a mom and all of my fears the past couple weeks dissolved. There was new life growing inside of me and this new life was all mine. I was absolutely astonished and speechless. Lillian's voice, broke into my consciousness from the dream I had the night before, calling me "Mommy" and also the dream with Jason in the field of Lily flowers from a few weeks back. It all made sense now. She has been trying to tell me that she was coming! My tears turned into cries of gratitude. I was so thankful for what this new life was already doing for me. Her spirit was so vibrant, beautiful and such a blessing. It was a girl, Jason was right. I knew it too! Finally, for the first time since the ultrasound started, I turned to look at him.

"Our Lillian," I said to him and he nodded, bursting into tears again, as he bent down to hug me.

Sixteen

In the first few days following the ultrasound, I soaked everything in. The doctor printed some ultrasound pictures for us, so I sat and stared at them for hours. For the first time, I was able to envision holding her. I was beginning to be get really excited! However, something was still lingering on my mind. It was the second dream I had of Lillian, where I fell into a deep dark hole at the end of it. It puzzled me because dreaming about my daughter was supposed to be beautiful, so why would it end in such an ugly way? Putting it out of my mind, I thought about the fact that she was coming and that was all I needed to focus on!

As the weeks went by, I went into complete "mommy mode" and my love for her was growing every day. I often touched my stomach and couldn't wait for my belly to pop out. Jason was true to his word because he found a better job, with much more pay. We were still trying to decide if I would be able to stay home with her after she was born, so we were working hard at trying to figure it out. At least for right now, I didn't have to worry about it and was able to be home resting, or rather nesting. The baby books said that nesting didn't usually happen until the final weeks, but I was in full blown "nest mode." Mom followed close behind, immediately helping me to prepare. I realized that the first thing I had to take care of was school.

My classes for that semester were paused because Jason and I needed our own place to live. He needed time to save up for our own apartment, so he stayed in Boston with a friend and I went back to Connecticut for a couple months. I didn't mind because time home with my mom was so refreshing and I was able to get organized, with her help.

Finally, in April, Jason put a deposit on an apartment outside of the city in a town called Belmont, MA. I was looking forward to finally having our own place. Belmont was more of a suburban town with lots of families around and still accessible to the city. There was even a park right down the street to walk to with the baby after she was born. I couldn't wait for him to pick me up and head back to Boston.

I was about four months along and all of my first trimester symptoms were gone. I was feeling pretty good and now with our own apartment, a little more positive about everything. I did not have a bump yet, which disappointed me, but everyone told me first babies "pop out" a lot later. The cute maternity clothes mom bought me while I was in Connecticut, would have to wait. I started stocking up on all things girl and hid them. Jason and I never told anyone that we knew the baby was a girl or the dreams I had of her. It was our special secret! I still was curious as to what he meant during the first ultrasound when he said, "I have been waiting a long time for her." However, I was too busy to ponder on it.

The female Doctor that we saw in the hospital was nice, but we didn't want to have to go into the hospital every time we needed a checkup. I was given the name of a midwifery group associated with Brigham and Women's Hospital by the nurse at Northeastern, which seemed good for me, so I set up my first appointment for when I got back.

Finally, it was moving day! Jason came to pick me up and mom planned on following us, with more of my stuff. We also had to get Darcy! During the two months of transition, she had to stay on a farm that we found near mom's house. Her place did not have enough room for a German Shepherd and she also had an indoor cat that would not par well with Darcy.

We piled ourselves and the dog into the truck. With the back loaded and mom following, we caravanned to Boston to start the next chapter of our lives! Putting my hand on my stomach, I pictured my little baby in there, growing strong and I couldn't wait to feel her kicks. Darcy sniffed my belly and kept licking my face. She was so happy we were all together again! She was such as special dog because she was the first big gift that Jason bought me. As we drove down the highway, I pet Darcy's head, thinking about the day we got her.

December 2005

Jason surprised me for Christmas with a picture of a liter of German Shepherd puppies, telling me we were going to go pick one out. He remembered that I mentioned a couple months prior that I wanted a puppy, but I never thought he would actually get one for me! I especially didn't think he would get a German Shepherd out of all the breeds. He was absolutely set on that kind of dog. Kelly made sure to remind us about a dozen times before we left to go buy her, that we weren't allowed dogs in the apartment.

"You guys are nuts," she said as we got into the car. "The landlord will be so pissed!"

"I know!" Jason said and smiled at her as she shook her head.

He was beyond excited about this new fur baby and I couldn't help but laugh. Kelly was right, this was crazy! We were leaving to go home to Connecticut for Christmas in a few days, but he wanted to get the dog prior in case they were all gone by the time we got back. Buying this dog for me was his way of symbolizing our new love for each other. I looked at him while he drove, smiling from ear to ear.

"You know Jay, a necklace would suffice too, for a Christmas gift."

"Nope! Jewelry can never trump a German Shepherd!"

"I beg to differ," I rolled my eyes. "Are we really getting a German Shepherd? What's wrong with a nice teacup sized, Yorkshire Terrier, with a little bow in its hair?"

"What the feck' is a Teacup Yorkshire? Sounds like chocolate pudding." I pulled up a picture on my phone to show him.

"Woman, that looks like an oversized rat. If we're getting a dog, then we are getting a real one. Can you picture me walking that thing down the streets of Boston?" I burst out laughing.

"Okay, fair enough," I agreed.

The farm was out in in Western Massachusetts, so it was a long drive. Once we pulled up, a large German Shepherd was barking at us in the front lawn.

"That must be the mother," Jason said and his face lit up at the sight of her. I nearly dove under my seat.

"What the WHAT is that?" I exclaimed. "Jason Gibson, NO! That's NOT a dog, that's a small wolf. I will not. NOPE!"

"Oh yes you will little lady," he said and got out of the car to my side and nearly pulled me out.

"She looks like she's going to eat us," I groaned, timidly putting my feet on the ground and hiding behind him.

The mother dog came running over, barking some more. Even though I was scared for my life, Jason did have a point, these dogs were very beautiful. She was striking with her black and tan coloring and strong ears sticking straight up; a very classic looking Shepherd. Once Jason got to the fence, he let her sniff his hand and she calmed down.

"See?" He looked back at me. "She won't hurt you. Aren't they so lovely?"

"Charming," I said sarcastically. "How will we bathe that thing?"

"Bathe it?" He shook his head laughing.

A lady came out of the house and greeted us. She brought us around the back to the barn and an all-black puppy, came bouncing over to us.

"This is the last male we have left. The father was all black like him, that's why he has that coloring," the woman explained. "And over here, we have the last female. However, you may not want her. She was the runt of the litter and her ears never went up." She pushed open the barn doors and there she was, our Darcy! She stood up and went straight to Jason, wagging her tail and looking so adorable. I loved her instantly.

"I don't mind the ears," I said to Jason as he continued to pet and play with her. He was smitten too.

"Neither do I," he said, as she kept licking his face, kissing him over and over as if to claim him. "Since she's the runt and her ears are down, is she full price?"

"You really want her? How about 50% off?" The woman offered.

"Sold!" Jason said and followed her inside to sign paperwork and pay her.

I stayed outside with Darcy and bent down to talk with her. She wasn't as jumpy with me, but she licked my face a few times and cautiously wagged her tail while looking at me. It was like she knew I was hesitant.

"Ok sweetheart, you're all ours. I don't have the slightest clue how to take care of you, but we will love you with everything we've got," I told her and she seemed to like that statement and licked me again, even barking a few times.

Jason came back out and we were ready to take her home! On the drive home, I sat in the back with her and she chewed on the seatbelts, making me laugh.

"Darcy," Jason said and the dog perked her ears up at him.

"She seems to like it," I said laughing as she licked my face over and over. "Why Darcy?" I asked and Jason laughed.

"Darcy is a name that the old farmers use back home in Ireland a lot for their dogs. The name always made me laugh when I would hear them call it out. So, it's a perfect name because this dog will certainly bring lots of laughter to us," he said, eying me in the rearview mirror. "I love you Lindsay and this dog, is my first symbol of that love and commitment to you." I nearly melted right there, unaware how far that commitment would be stretched in the months ahead. As I came back from my thoughts on that first day with Darcy, I noticed she was looking at me.

"Do you remember that day too, girl?" I asked her and she licked my face in response.

We arrived at the new apartment and spent the rest of the day unloading and of course mom made sure the bed was made and food was in our kitchen before she headed back to Connecticut. Darcy ran all around the apartment, sniffing every single corner and even peed in a few rooms to mark her territory. This did not impress mom and I laughed every time she did it because I would hear her swearing from across the apartment. Darcy would come running out of a room with her tail tucked!

That night, Jason and I were laying in our new bed that he bought us. It was so comfortable and big! He bought an extra-long, king sized bed and the mattress felt heavenly as I laid on it.

"Jason, this bed is wonderful! Why did you buy such a big one though? I mean, I know we are both tall, but this thing can fit like four people in it," I asked him.

"I just thought it would be more comfortable for you as you get bigger and bigger. Besides, with all this room, I don't have to feel your pregnant, sweaty body as much," he teased and I threw a pillow at him. It was only April, but I was already sweating like a pig and went through a lot of deodorant.

"Don't remind me," I groaned and rolled over to go to sleep, peacefully, with no nightmares to disturb me. It seemed my nightmares were really dying down, but I didn't question it. I was afraid to jinx it.

As the summer of 2006 came, so did my belly. I finally popped around six months and my goodness, did I ever pop! It was the Fourth of July and I stood in the bathroom, staring at my growing abdomen through a sun dress I was wearing. We were going to a barbeque at his Aunt and Uncle's house that day. They lived south of Boston and were the only family Jason had in the United States. The rest were in England and Ireland. They had four children who were around our age and their son Jonny, was particularly close with Jason. We loved having them near us and they were very supportive of us, ever since I met them.

"Jason, I'm not sure how much more room there will be for this baby in there. Look how big I am and I still have three months to go!" I shouted from the bathroom.

He was laughing from the kitchen as I waddled my way in, where he had a plate of food waiting for me. Behind him were the ultrasound pictures from a couple months before when we found out that our baby was indeed, a girl. We both tried to act surprised by the "news" when the doctor told us.

Lillian had been making her way into my dreams a lot more over the past few weeks and the nightmares still stayed away. Instead, my dreams were beautiful about her and I woke up feeling calm every day. Each dream was entered in my pregnancy journal I had for her, to make sure I never forget them. My little girl was going to be absolutely hilarious because in my dreams, she was about five or six years old and was so funny. I couldn't wait to meet her!

"Want a snack before we go?" He held up a plate filled with fruit and half a bagel with cream cheese.

"That's a snack?" I groaned, thinking it would make me fatter, but took it anyway.

"You look so beautiful," he said and came up behind me, putting his arms around my belly. "Oh, she kicked me!" He jumped back a little and I laughed at her strong kick in response to her daddy's hugs.

"She's quit a jokester this little one, I can promise you that," I smiled up at him.

We were both so happy and the initial shock of becoming parents was fading away. I felt so blessed to be with him. He worked side jobs to save money and had even received another promotion. It was because of his hard work, I was going to be able to stay home with Lillian and finish school. He was truly a man of honor.

The summer ended with a beautiful baby shower and by September, the nursery was complete. All there was to do now, was wait! Mom came up to Boston a lot in those final weeks, helping me get last minute things and talking to me every chance she could about becoming a mother. I was really grateful to have her love and support because even though I was ready, I was becoming a little nervous the closer we got.

Finally, early in the morning on September 29th, 2006, I got up to use the bathroom and felt a pop! My water broke and shortly after that, early labor finally began. Lillian was on her way! I was so relieved because I was ten days past my due date and miserable. Mom was already in Boston and we set up a bed in the nursery because we knew she and my mother-in-law would be using it a lot in those early months.

I crawled into bed with mom after my water broke. My midwife, Annie, told me to labor at home and come when contractions were closer together. This didn't worry me because my instincts told me the same and I also trusted their advice. It had been such a wonderful six months under their care. They introduced me to natural mothering and I had spent the rest of the pregnancy researching all things organic and natural. I was hooked. They were also so calm and reassuring the entire pregnancy, which raised my confidence tremendously.

"Remember though," Annie said to me over the phone after I called her. "Today is the Red Sox and Yankee play-off game here in Boston, so we have to get you here either before or after the game! Don't come rushing down here in the middle of that mess," she teased.

Mom told me to rest with her and I left Jason to keep sleeping because I knew I would need him alert and rested. I labored at home all of that first day and finally by 9 p.m. that night, the contractions were five minutes apart. It was time to head to the hospital.

Jason had sweat on his forehead from nerves as he rushed down route 9 to get me there ahead of the game getting out. However, he still managed to make a pit stop at Dunkin Donuts to grab his coffee and cheer with a few Red Sox fans that were in the parking lot! Even the lady at the drive through window couldn't believe he did that after she saw that I was clearly in labor. Really Jason? "America may run on Dunks", but apparently, so does my Irish man.

Lillian made her way into this world, after a very long and difficult birth on October 1, 2006 at 1:23 a.m. When she was finally placed in my arms and looked up at me, it was an instant, soul-sister connection. My eyes burned with tears as I looked into her blue eyes, the same blue eyes that Jason has and I cried with happiness. Looking up at him, as he held both of us in his arms, I could barely get the right words out.

"Thank you, Jason. For giving me such a gift. I can't believe how in love I am with her. I don't ever want to leave her side. Not even for a minute," I said, as I held her to my breast to nurse. Tears of love were still pouring down my face.

"And you won't ever have to," he said, as he wiped my tears. "Just be a mom sweetheart. I'll handle the rest." And he did.

Part Three
Love Wins

"Love wins, love always wins."
Mitch Albom

Seventeen

December 2013

I sat staring out the window in my favorite chair of my bedroom, pausing between thoughts as I finished up a journal entry before Lillian got home from school. I kept peeking out to see if her school bus was pulling up. It had been a few weeks since Joseph's memorial service and the memories of Boston had been playing out in my mind little by little. With each memory, my heart opened more and more to everything I recalled. I wrote everything down in my journal that came to me because even though I had kept a journal in Boston, it was nice to finally reminisce about all the good times. This was because my journals from college were mostly about the anxiety attacks and flashbacks. By writing all these memories down again, I was able to reintegrate them with happy times.

PTSD kept not only the bad memories hidden, but the good ones too. There was never any rhyme or reason to the pattern of my PTSD symptoms in the earlier years of Boston, before Lillian was born. It had a mind of its own, lashing out and forcing me to replay bad memories when I didn't want to. I looked out the window again. Still no bus. I always missed her when she was at school.

Despite the critics I had of being a young mom, I took to motherhood naturally after she was born. When I brought Lillian home from the hospital, all my worries during her pregnancy proved to be incorrect because my maternal instincts immediately guided me. It certainly helped that she was also a very "easy" baby, sleeping through the night right away and eating like a champ. Once she learned how to smile, that was all she ever did. She loved people and interacting with them in public and to this day she is still very social. As I continued to wait for her school bus, I closed my journal and smiled at some of my fondest memories as a new mom with her.

Motherhood also put an end to some very destructive behaviors because it anchored me. It stopped my party days and drinking. With a sober mind, I began to notice some of the damage the years of PTSD had done to me. I discovered an autoimmune disorder with my thyroid, migraines that had been developing and became constant, and eczema appeared out of nowhere. Thus, began years of healing my body that had fallen apart because no matter how much I ignored myself, my body knew where the hurt still remained. It knew my truth, even when I didn't.

I also became aware of just how well I had mastered concealing my pain. However, this continued, even when the drinking stopped after she was born. I was still afraid of feelings, so even though I wasn't drinking like I once was, I often missed it. Alcohol certainly has a clever way of hiding the truth from us. What would I hide under now? Motherhood. That's what. I used my job as a mother to stop drinking, but also to mask my pain. For a long time, it worked very well. Lillian's lively personality also made it a lot easier and the dreams I had of her the summer before she was born, came to life as I got to know her.

Her charisma and unforgettable smile could light up an entire room. Her humor began to come out at the age of one, when she was starting to put her baby babble into words. She is one of the funniest kids I know. No matter what we had been through together, she has always made me laugh. Her wit could turn anyone's frown upside down. I appreciate my incredible girl so much. She is intelligent and has a caring heart like I have never seen before. No matter what mood

I'm in, the second I look at Lillian's face, all my troubles fade.

For years, I thought there was nothing wrong with this. Especially because there were only a handful of times in the seven years with her, when a panic attack gripped me out of nowhere. To me, this seemed like I was healing, but the chaos was still there, ready to attack anytime. She became the topic of most of my journal writing, which kept my focus off the havoc inside me even more. Being Lillian's mom fit me like a glove. I was young and that made it challenging in its own way, but the love I have for her handled the rest. But what about me? Who was handling "the rest" of me?

My emotions were like a bubbling pot of water, waiting to boil over and spill out. Deep down I knew that, but Lillian's light was what I chose to follow instead of my own. I thought I was protecting her from my past, but she knew I was suffering. She cast her light on me as strong as she could for many years, but it wasn't enough.

One time, when she was especially bright, was during Jason and my separation. She was three-years-old at the time and was the glue between me and him. She was always there to remind us that no matter what, we were still a family and, more importantly, that we still loved each other. One day, about six months after Jason and I split, she crawled up on my lap and looked at me.

"Mommy, you know that Daddy loves you right?" She asked me and I smiled.

"Yes, baby, I do," I told her.

"Ok, just don't forget that," was all she said. The maturity of her words for a three-year-old was amazing. She was right. Jason continued to work his two jobs and prepared for his company that he has now, which is hugely successful today. He was still there, taking care of us and loving us beyond measure - even from a distance.

Life with Lillian had been nothing short of growing into motherhood, with a daughter who was ready to show me the world.

But did I see it? She taught me how to be a mom. She taught me that laughter is truly medicine to our souls. She was my surprise, firstborn baby who gave me a reason to try again at life. But was I trying? I loved every minute of my mothering with her, even if my own self took a backseat. When she took her first breath, all hope of looking into the mirror of my past, was put aside collecting dust. For the first time since I lost Joseph, that mirror was in my hands once again. I had my first glimpse of myself in it, while in the hospital birthing him. I held it now with shaking hands, terrified of what would I will see next.

Still waiting for her bus to pull up, I took a deep breath and shook off the anxiety that was building. I longed for the days before we lost him, safe in my comfort zone, hiding from all the inner pain. A sinking feeling came when I realized, how lost I really was. All of this time I wanted to believe I was healing. What happened to me? Tears began to fall and I scrunched my eyes, rubbing my face to hold back the answer to that question.

"Rape," I whispered. For the first time in thirteen years, the words left my lips.

Falling onto the floor and holding my head, I sobbed for the girl I lost. My mind began to go back to that night and I tried to stop it.

"No!" I shouted. I wasn't ready.

I sat deep in my sorrow for the sixteen-year-old girl and my son, neither one, I ever got to know. What do I do now?

The buzzer in our apartment rang and startled me. The sounds of young voices outside made me realize that Lillian was home and I forgot to go out and meet the bus! Lillian was standing outside the door with my neighbor, Tanya, from another building and her son Kai.

"Oh my gosh, thank you so much!" I said to her and she looked at me, her eyes squinting.

"You okay, doll?" Tanya asked. It was hard to hide anything from her. As a single mom, ex-army person and one tough personal trainer, she can see through almost anything. In other words, she's good at bullshit.

"I'm good! Just tired and fell asleep," I answered, avoiding her eyes.

"Uh huh. Okay, I have a client coming. See you later!" She waved and headed off.

"MOM! I thought you forgot me!" Lillian said as she walked inside. It was freezing outside and the smell of snow sat in the cold December air. I paused for a second before I followed her in. The icy breeze felt good against my clammy skin.

Once inside, Lillian dashed off into her room to play. I went into the kitchen and stared in the freezer, wondering what to take out for dinner. I heard my phone buzz and saw that Jason was texting me.

Let's go out to dinner tonight. I sense that you need some distraction. I'll be home in an hour.

Relief washed over me, as I sighed. It's like he can feel everything I feel no matter where he is. Even though his thoughtful text helped me to relax a little, the underlying feeling of uncertainty was still shaking me up and I wasn't exactly sure why? This undefined feeling felt like: I was a soldier coming to the frontlines in the final battle. Not wanting to reflect on this feeling anymore, I headed into Lillian's room, where she was playing with her Monster High dolls. Sitting down next to her, she lit up.

"Hi Mommy!" She perked up even more when I grabbed one of the dolls. "Which one is your favorite? I like Clawdeen Wolf." She held her up. I studied the wolf-like doll, dressed in a sleek and tight dress with huge ugly boots. "She has a brother who always protects her, named Clawd Wolf and is dating this one, Darculaura." I noticed as she held up the other two dolls, her eyes stared down at the male one named Clawd. That was my cue.

"That's her brother?" I gently asked her, pointing to him.

"Yes," Lillian stayed still, looking at him before she looked back up at me, smiling again.

"Lillian, I'm so sorry you lost your brother, sweetheart," I said, swallowing the huge lump in my throat. My heart felt like it was burning as I said it. Lillian's smile faded and her eyes began to water and within seconds, she was sobbing on my lap, still holding onto her dolls.

We stayed there for a long time, just holding each other. I wasn't sure after a while, who was consoling who anymore. My mother instincts were fighting hard to stay in control and help Lillian. Another part of me wanted to hide. After all, that had been my "go to" response for so long. Just stop the tears and hide in fear.

"Hi girls!" Jason's loud voice broke into our moment.

"Daddy!" Lillian jumped off my lap and was in his arms in what seemed like one single leap.

"Hi! Yes, it's me, Daddy!" He held her tight and looked over at me. "What are ye two doing in here?"

"We were just playing with her Monster High dolls and then something made us miss Joey," I explained.

"Well, then that just means he was in here playing too," Jason replied, which saved the day, as it always does with his quick responses. Lillian's face broke out in a huge smile and she looked absolutely fascinated at what he said.

"Wow! Really? Joey, are you in here? You can play with Clawd!" She was now standing and facing the room and holding up the male doll.

"Ready to get some dinner?" Jason asked. "I'm starving, so let's eat early." Lillian looked even more excited. She was a big 'foodie' like me and loved to go out to eat.

"Yes! I'm hungry too Daddy! Joey, I'll leave Clawd in here for you to play with. I love you!" She said, as she bounced out of the room.

"Come on baby, stand up." He pulled me up and put his arms around me.

"Thank you, Jay," I said, breathing in his love and exhaling my sadness.

"We got this, my love. Together. Me and you," he said and while the pain of losing our Joseph was still so raw, his words brought me comfort. We did have this. We were doing it together, one step at a time. Whenever I fell down, I will still able to stand back up.

Eighteen

Christmas festivities of 2013 was dull, dark, and sent me right back into the deep waters of grief. That made me so angry. Christmas is my favorite holiday and time of the year. But not this year. Basically, I wanted to push "delete" and get past it. When I first got pregnant with Joseph, Christmas was also one of the very first things I thought about. Getting an ornament for him to match Lillian's and dressing my bump up in cute holiday clothes for Christmas parties. All of that would not get to happen.

Instead of happily playing Christmas music over and over, which drove Jason and Lillian nuts, our house was silent. Decorations stared at me from boxes and there was no laughter or anticipation. Worst of all, I was completely exhausted. Nightmares, flashbacks, and anxiety found me again and I was at the verge of a mental breakdown. No way would I find the energy to hang Christmas décor, so all of the Christmas magic stayed trapped under the lids of the boxes they were stored in.

On the last day of school before Lillian's holiday school break, I decided to do some online shopping for Christmas gifts before she came home, when I stumbled across a picture of a baby boy. He was about six months old, smiling in an ad for the Toys R Us website. He had a Santa hat on and Christmas pajamas and an adorable smile across his face. Before I could click off the picture, I snapped. I slammed my computer shut with rage and hot flashes blurred my vision. Standing up, I went into the kitchen and grabbed a mug sitting next to the sink, smashing it all over the floor. Then, as I reached for more, something felt like it grabbed my arm in midair. I turned, but no one was there. What just happened? Who grabbed me?

Even though I couldn't see anyone, I felt it and knew I was not alone. Sinking down to the floor next to the shattered pieces of the mug, I began releasing tears, washing out the anger. My heart was still broken in hundreds of pieces, just like the mug and I didn't know how to get it back together. The dining room table was stacked with moving boxes and looking over at them, I sighed. We were moving after Christmas to Southbury, Connecticut and it was all just too much to handle. These outbursts of anger made it feel even more impossible.

Pent up anger is like a prison sentence, only I was punishing myself. True happiness eluded me because I still thought I didn't deserve it. Lillian and Jay still made me happy at times, but it never lasted. Deep down, I didn't want to see what life could be like if I was happy again either. One night, the week before, I shouted at Jason in pure frustration.

"Jason, why? Why can't I just get over this!" I screamed.

"You know the answer to that, Lindsay. He's our son. You'll always love him, that's why," he said, matter-of-factly, which only pissed me off more. I buried my face into a pillow in frustration because that was not the true extent of my question. It wasn't just his death that was making me angry, it was something deeper that made me feel naked and vulnerable. Just like in the car, driving home from his memorial service, this anger was very apparent again.

"No, Jason! That's not what I meant!" What did I mean? Words were forming, but it was difficult. "It goes so much deeper than Joe. There's this nasty hate just floating around me. I don't like the way it feels." I paused, trying to catch my breath from all the shouting, when suddenly, it just spilled out. "I thought when we got back together that I was healing and ready to give you what you needed!" *Check. That felt good to say!*

Jason smiled at me. *Dammit! There's that smile again.*

"But were you ready to give you what you needed?" *Checkmate.* Clearly, I wasn't. I didn't see what I needed. I just wanted Joseph back. No, that wasn't all of it - I wanted myself back. What was I afraid of? The answer came quickly to my mind: *Love.* I realized then, that I was afraid of love because then I had to be responsible for receiving it.

Christmas came and went and the New Year began. We were moved into our new home in a very familiar town, Southbury. It's funny how life circled right back around to my hometown after all the trauma. This was where my roots were and I felt like I could catch my breath once I was back. The schools are some of the best, so I knew it would also be good for Lillian. Things were looking really positive for Jason's career too. After five years of building his company and after the move, he was finally where he wanted to be, no longer needing to work two jobs. Therefore, I felt like Southbury would be a good landing spot for the time being with all of the good the move should bring. However, our demons follow us no matter where we go.

After the New Year, I went back to work as being alone made me feel worse. My business, *Healthy Mom Happy Baby* had picked up speed prior to the pregnancy, but understandably slowed down when I got hyperemesis with Joseph. I didn't want to start back with consulting one-on-one, so I dove into teaching group educational classes for moms. Consulting privately seemed intimidating because I didn't feel strong enough from all the grief. Teaching also gave me an opportunity to create classes that could be used for years to come. I also learned, that teaching was something I really liked! I jumped right into more research, study and developing more and more programs. I taught classes in a nearby baby store as my first attempt to break back into the working world and began to hire other practitioners to contract with to handle the private sessions for the moms.

While working was a great distraction during the day, the nights were an entirely different beast. Each night, tears still flowed with sorrow that never seemed to end. Crying on Jason's shoulders until I fell asleep and fighting diligently to push everything aside. It never worked. My anxiety kept going strong and welcomed the day each morning. All I knew to do was just hope that I could make it through my day.

One night in February, it was snowing very hard as a Nor'easter blew through. The winds were fierce and Lillian and I were cuddling on the couch under a blanket. The new home we moved into was in a very old farmhouse in the Historical District of the town, so it was really drafty. We were watching a movie and Jason was practicing his guitar in the other room. Lillian looked up at me and smiled. I could tell her mind was running through all kinds of thoughts.

"Mommy?" I looked down at her and she smiled. "Good thing you aren't pregnant anymore."

"What do you mean?" I asked.

"Well, it's such a bad storm. Imagine if Joey was born now? You would have to sled to the hospital!" She giggled at herself, but I couldn't even bring myself to smile. Poor child, was trying so hard still to cope with her own sadness, so I hugged her tight in response. Every now and then, she would push on my still-swollen stomach, almost like she was checking to see if he was really gone. As the movie played, I drifted off to sleep on the couch.

Looking out into the ocean, I felt the ocean breeze hug me as it blew around me. My feet were bare and I curled my toes to feel the warm sand under them. A tiny hand slipped into mine and I looked down to see a little girl at my side. Her blonde hair billowing in the breeze and when she looked up at me, her smile made my heart dance. I felt another hand grasp my empty one and turned my head to look. It was my Lillian, standing beside me. She too, looked at me with a wide smile and bright eyes. Turning back to the little girl, I bent down in front of her, cupping her beautiful face with my hands. Lillian came and bent down behind her, holding her.

"Mommy?" The little girl said. Mommy? She pointed to the water. "Come with me! Hold my hand and don't let go!" She grabbed my hand and pulled me to the water, laughing as she ran.

Where had I seen her before? Her face was so familiar.

"Layla!" Lillian shouted and ran towards her. The little girl laughed even more when Lillian reached to pick her up. I watched as the two girls twirled joyfully around in the water.

"Mommy!" She shouted over Lillian's shoulder. "Wait for me!"

I woke up with my heart racing. The movie was over and Lillian was asleep next to me. I knew that little girl from my dream, but from where? All of a sudden, it dawned on me. The stage nightmare. It was her! She was that random little girl on the stage! She had come to me twice now in a dream! I could still hear her laughter, as it echoed all around me. Taking a deep breath, I stood up to get some water in the kitchen. I leaned against the counter, deep in thought. Why did she call me mommy?

A week later at the store where I taught, I bent down in front of a Valentine's Day display, looking for a box of cards for Lillian's class. I felt a tap on my shoulder. Looking over, I saw a little girl, about three or four years old, with blonde hair and blue eyes staring at me.

"Hi." She smiled at me. She looked just like the little girl in the dream from a week ago and I caught my breath. I was taken back with the similarity between the two girls. Finally, I smiled back at her.

"Hi, sweetheart," I said.

"Layla!" The girl's mother came over to us. "Layla, come on, baby girl, time to go!"

"Layla," I whispered, as she left, hand-in-hand with her mother.

I was stunned and something in my stomach rolled, as I watched them cross the street. A familiar peace came over, the same peace that came while birthing Joseph. My feet were pinned to the ground, forcing me to stand still and allow this warm feeling to penetrate my mind. At that moment, I knew everything would be okay again. I didn't know how or when, but I just knew. *Be still,* was all I heard in my head. The little girl was now skipping with her mother as they continued down the street.

"Lindsay!" The store manager called. "You want me to start setting up the chairs for the class?"

I snapped out of the daze I was in and turned around. Trying to reorient myself, I noticed this amazing feeling stayed with me. When I taught my class, it kept me grounded, as I savored its delicious warmth.

Driving home later that afternoon, I was lost deep in thought. The class went smoothly, mostly about pumping breastmilk and returning to work. I was relieved when they didn't have too many questions so I could go home. Questions circled around and around in my mind: How was it that I dreamed of a little girl named Layla and then see another Layla in the store a week later? Who was Layla? Why was she coming to me in my dreams? What did she want? Why was she calling me mommy? I was not pregnant, so I was baffled. A recent conversation between Jason and I crossed my mind, as I pondered over this mysterious little Layla.

"Jason, I just don't know how I can ever endure another pregnancy," I said to him, coming out of our bedroom after Lillian finally fell asleep. Lillian had good days and bad days and she was still sleeping in our bed with us. She was so afraid that she was going to lose someone else and was not sleeping well, even with us.

"I think you have more strength in you than you even know," he said, testing me. We wanted another baby, but the thought of actually doing it was way too frightening to me.

My obstetrician had already told us right after we lost Joseph, that whenever my menstrual cycle returned for a couple months, it was safe to try. She did, however, also inform me that in the case of a stillbirth, it was probably best to wait as long as we could to make sure we spent enough time healing our emotions. At the time of that conversation, I simply let it go in one ear and out the other. I didn't even want to begin thinking about trying again for another baby. Now, a couple months later, the question came up: should we try again? Jason and I sat in silence for a little while, thinking through the two perspectives we both had on our situation.

"I'm broken. I'm just so broken," I said back to him and leaned into him, letting myself cry, feeling my sadness wash down my face.

As I drove, thinking about that night and that discussion, I put one hand on my stomach. My breath began to quicken and my face grew hot as anxiety struck me out of nowhere, making me dizzy. Pulling into a nearby parking lot, I turned the air conditioner on full blast to try and cool my already sweaty body. The beautiful moment of bliss that I experienced earlier, was gone. My heart was pounding, as I began to wail against my hands, crying for relief from this suffocating grief. But what was the point? I felt like the tears never really helped anything.

"It doesn't matter!" I yelled through my sobs. "Nothing matters. My life's just going to be nothing but this!" Despair. Sadness. Anxiety. Worst of all, relentless anger. My anger since Joseph died just kept escalating and between all of the reoccurring nightmares of my past and my mourning, I was teetering on the edge of staying in control most days or falling into the abyss of the unknown.

Now, as I sat in my car trying to breathe through the anxiety, anger boiled like hot lava. It churned within, hungry for destruction, and I knew it was too much for me to control. I let out a vicious scream, slamming my hands down on the steering wheel and wishing for my life to just end. My phone rang, snapping me out of the wrath that was taking over. It was mom calling and while I didn't want to talk to anyone, I knew that I needed to get myself home.

"Mommy," I answered in between my sobs.

"Lindsay, what's wrong?" She asked, surprised at how bad I sounded.

"When will it stop? I can't take any more of this," I said, eyes watering over once again. I didn't need to explain to her much more than that. She knew. As my mother, she could feel everything, even through the phone.

"Honey, it won't ever stop completely. We are all hurting for the missed opportunity of meeting our Joseph. I will stay with you on the phone until you get home," she replied. Feeling like I was in slow motion, somehow, I made it home. Walking into the house, I heard Jason and Lillian in the living room, chatting and laughing.

"Hi Mommy!" I heard Lillian call out. I stood in the entryway and stared at them. My heart was nowhere near mended, nor was I sure it ever would be. Yet, I knew that I needed to keep going for the daughter I had and for my husband whose love for me, has never faltered.

Nineteen

Summer of 2014 came fast. After that day in the store and my dream of Layla, I continued living on autopilot. Waking up each day, just wanting to go back to bed still, never knowing what kind of dreams would greet me. I often woke up so dizzy and nauseated from nightmares, that I kept my trash can close by. I hardly ate, never called anyone back and everything made me jump. Sleepless nights, grief and PTSD were at its all-time high, which only increased my anxiety even more. One nightmare, replayed itself at least once a week: It started and ended exactly the same.

I would be walking down the hallway of a busy hospital, bleeding but none of the nurses or doctors noticed me. I would open the stairwell and instead of it being the hospital's large set of stairs, it would be a small, carpeted staircase. I would begin to climb these frightening carpeted stairs, always reach the top to a door that I knew so well and wake before opening it.

If it wasn't nightmares or daytime anxiety, it was endless baby shower invitations or new baby announcements from friends. Day and night. I had nowhere to hide.

Nothing was working anymore. Not Mother's Mary's message of peace. Not roses. Not my career. Not dreaming of a little girl named Layla. Not Lillian's humor. Not even my husband – could help me climb out of this darkness anymore. There were no more breaks from the PTSD like it once used to do. While my mind played the pretend game of "this isn't happening," my heart and body were not loosening their grip so easily. Physical symptoms of hypothyroidism and eczema worsened. The more I tried to stuff my emotions, the worse my condition became. My body reminded me every time I looked in the mirror, that my heart still needed to fully purge this ugly poison.

June came and Lillian completed first grade. We were leaving for England in a few days and I was looking forward to the break. Jason's brother Sean was getting married there. I was unpacking Lillian's backpack after she got home from her last day and thought about how much she had grown and how well she transitioned into her new school. She was excelling in reading and writing and I was proud of her. The school psychologist was notified right away about the loss of her brother and stepped up to help her during this delicate time. Lillian's emotions were still up and down, but at least she was back to sleeping in her own bed. For that, I was grateful.

She took to drawing to express herself, whereas I always journaled. She drew stories of how she was feeling inside with mini cartoons, often portraying her feelings into the characters. She also enjoyed reading children's short devotionals and was not afraid to ask me about whatever thoughts popped into her mind about life and death. We found ourselves healing on separate paths, but together as a family.

Since Lillian had to come to grips with death at such a young age, it matured her well past many of her peers. She was much more in tune to her emotions and became very compassionate. Each day, along with Jason, she still tried very hard to make me laugh, through my tears. Her humor never stopped and I always joked with my friends that one day, we would see her in a comedy movie. She was interested in learning more about death, asking questions such as: Where we go after we die? Does God hear our prayers? She started to pray more. She wasn't able to share this with her friends, but she kept the lines of communication open with Jason and me.

The day before we left for England, I was excited as I prepared to pack the suitcases for our first trip of the summer. Marrying a man from Europe had been quite an adventure. Jason had been a traveler his whole life, something he planned on doing more and more with me as the years went by. As I was coordinating outfits to wear, I thought about what I would need. We were heading over to see his father's side of the family after the wedding, since they were not going to be attending. It dawned on me that I would be needing some nicer undergarments for the dress I was wearing and so I opened the top drawer where I kept my fancy stuff. An electric shock, traveled through my body, sending me backward. My stomach burned with nausea. Joseph's pictures were right on top. I don't know who put them there or why in that particular drawer, but they were not something I wanted to see. Ever. I backed away from the drawer and sat on the edge of the bed.

I spent a long seven months struggling daily, sometimes hourly, to keep my mind away from his death and locked in a box. In one second, as I stared at his pictures, that box was opened. Like an ant working day and night, to build her nest of safety, my nest was exposed. Grief just kicked my nest away. Yet, like a hardworking ant, I was determined to build my anthill again. I refused to stop even though my body was so tired, that my muscles were sore from all the effort.

"Well, that goes to show how often you wear anything sexy for me," Jason's voice broke through my thoughts and I jumped. He always just showed up out of nowhere. I looked up at him and he winked at me, taking the pictures out of drawer. He walked out of the room and returned a few minutes later. I didn't ask him where he put them and didn't want to know either.

"Jason, I'm really worried about myself." Fresh tears sprang in my eyes. When were these tears ever going to stop?

"I'm not," he said and he kissed my forehead. "There's no such thing as a "right way" to heal. I think you are handling it the best you know how to right now."

I wasn't so sure anymore what I was exactly handling. There was so much happening all at once.

The three of us left for England the next day, crossing the wide-open Atlantic Ocean together. I was glad to get away from everything at home. Traveling certainly couldn't erase everything that has happened, but it was an escape from everyday reminders. That was another reason Jason and I loved it so much. Darcy was left in the care of my mom and a hired dog sitter, but with all of the tension and stress since Joseph died, she had been hyper lately. Her protective nature, common for a German Shepherd, had been enhanced greatly and she was always by my side. I really hoped she would be okay while we were away, but I knew we had to go, so I didn't dwell on it too much.

It was early morning when we landed in London, which was always my favorite part when we travelled overseas. I enjoyed watching the sunrise as we descended onto foreign soil. I loved looking at the land below, as we crept closer and closer and in this case, over the rooftops of the infamous and very large, city of London. It might be my writer's mind, but once in a new country, I became a new character; absorbing the culture and new life all around me. This made it easy to leave my grief behind. We touched ground and I breathed deeply. It felt like the first real breath I was able to take since I said goodbye to Joseph.

The first adventure upon arriving was going to be the wedding. His brother was marrying an English woman, which was what brought the wedding here in the first place. Her family was hosting a lavish affair and I couldn't wait to see what an English wedding was like. Like most of Europe, the countryside was stunning. Other than being freezing cold and lack of sunny skies, which was always a bit startling when we were visiting in the summer months, it would be a wonderful visit.

The wedding weekend proved to be absolutely amazing. My new sister-in-law, Joanna and her family threw a marvelous party and the wedding décor was everything you would imagine with an English wedding. Her parents held the reception on their property with a professional tent to fit it all, including the dance floor! My anxiety had taken a back seat so far during the trip and my mind was too distracted by endless champagne, laughter, and fun to think about anything else. Lillian was also having a blast, dancing all the way until the early morning hours the night of the wedding. I couldn't believe how late she stayed up!

The morning after the wedding, we headed north to just outside Newcastle, England to meet the Gibson family. I was so excited because this was my first time meeting them all! I had heard a lot about this part of the family roots, but wasn't sure when I would ever get a chance to meet them. I had met everyone on his mom's side in Ireland and spent many visits getting the know them, so this was my chance to meet Jason's other half on this side of pond.

Once we arrived at his aunt and uncle's house, the first thing I noticed was the massive difference in English slang. I stood there, speechless, not knowing what to say when we all hugged and they spoke to me. Jason knew that was his signal.

"Don't worry babe, I got you this week. This Geordie accent is tough," he whispered to me.

"What's a Geordie accent?" I asked him and he laughed.

"Northern English dialect. Believe me, even I have a hard time following it. Just do what you did with me the first few months when you had no clue what I was saying. Smile and nod. A lot," he said. I laughed and while I felt like a foreigner within my own language, I really liked his family so far.

We spent ten more days in England, getting to know the Gibson's and exploring the Tyneside region. On one of the rare, sunny days since we arrived, we headed to the beach. Unlike back home, where I would be sweating before we even laid our towels down on the sand, I sat shivering in a sweatshirt. I couldn't believe the locals were walking around in just their bathing suits. They must have thick skin to block out the cold. Either that or their friendly and generous hearts kept them warm. The Gibson family was so nice and I was really enjoying being with them. Lillian braved the North Sea and dived right in with all the locals. She came running up to me, laughing at how bundled up I was because I was all but frozen in the wind.

"Lillian, have you lost your mind? You'll lose limbs from frostbite in that water," I told her.

"Might as well get the full experience! Beach-bound and icicles, English style! I feel like Olaf in Frozen when he dreamed of the beach! Wahoooo!" She shouted and ran off again, back to the sea.

Our wedding anniversary was on the last night we were there and his family offered to take Lillian for the night. Off we went! We took a train to the city of Newcastle and had dinner at one of the restaurants by the famous Jamie Oliver and explored the city. Jason's favorite soccer team was Newcastle, so of course, we had to go by the stadium. His eyes lit up with delight when we arrived. Living in the States for so long, he certainly missed his professional soccer games. After we took what seemed like a hundred pictures there, we went for a stroll. It was nice to be holding hands and not have anything to worry about in that moment.

"You've been so much better since we got here," he said to me.

"Yeah, I know. It's easy for me to put everything on pause when we travel. I wasn't sure how I would handle this trip with how bad I have been, but it has ended up being the best thing I could have done. I feel rested and I actually feel the air going into my lungs. I can breathe here," I said. Jason was quiet for a moment.

"No, darling. While it's true you are sleeping better here...you were always breathing," he stopped and looked at me, holding me close in his arms.

"Oh, Jason, obviously I'm not dead. I know I'm breathing, you don't understand what I mean," I said. He waved his hand and cut me off before I could continue.

"I understand perfectly, love," he said, staring deeply into my eyes, as if he was making sure I was truly listening. "It's more like you aren't following me. Relief, healing, happiness, it's all still in you. It never went anywhere and it will always be there waiting whenever you slip away again. Nothing can ever take away what is in here," he said, pointing to my heart. "No matter what happens to us. Like the sky, the joy in your heart stays put. It never goes away. What happened to you at sixteen," I pulled back, trying to stop him.

"Jason, please don't," I pleaded with him.

"Lindsay, I'm not letting you run from me right now. What happened to you at sixteen, what happened to our son and the pain that followed are like the dark storm clouds that temporarily covers that joyous sky. But just like clouds in the sky, they pass. Problem is, you made the choice to follow them," he said. He was holding my arms so I wouldn't walk away. Tears were falling down my face. Great, now my pretty makeup job for our anniversary was washing off with my tears. I tried to say something, but I couldn't. Instead, I closed my eyes, trying desperately to block out his words. I couldn't face this truth, but he was relentless.

"Do you remember when you first told me about the rape? I know you do. I asked you something then. Do you remember?" He asked. *Yes, of course I remembered*, I thought. Instead of responding, I stayed completely silent. "I asked you what you were accountable for since that awful night? Who is the one that is really following those dark storm clouds of pain? Who is the one that is creating such misery? Reliving that night over and over? Who is it Lindsay?" I was now crying. Sobs were choking my throat. *Some anniversary,* I thought and now boiling with anger.

"It's *not* that simple Jason. I can't just pretend like that night never happened!" My voice barely coming through my sobs. "Jason let me go!" He didn't let go and his eyes stayed even with mine. Neither one of us was going to break the stare.

"Lindsay," his voice was a lot calmer. He stroked my face, wiping away the tears and ruined makeup. His eyes, those blue eyes that I knew so well, seemed to lull me into a daze that calmed my frayed nerves, like a soft melody sung to a newborn baby.

"The problem is, pretending is all you have ever done since that night," he said quietly. I felt dizzy and sick to my stomach. I bent down, trying not to pass out. The truth of his words struck me like a lightning bolt. However, I still wasn't exactly sure what they meant. I may have forgotten most of details, but I knew what happened to me at sixteen; so how could I be pretending it didn't happened? Jason must have known I needed to sit because he pulled me over to a bench where we sat in silence for a while, watching people pass by. I leaned onto his shoulder after the tears stopped and I felt calm again.

"Remember the first day we met?" he asked me. Relief washed over me that he changed the subject.

"How could I forget?" I replied. "It's still so crazy to me that you said my name before I even said anything." Jason laughed.

"Not to me. Someone or rather something maybe, told me to come find you at twelve-years-old. So, once I grew up, I did just that." He smiled down at me.

"You never told me that before!" I exclaimed. I sat up to face him and a smile spread across his face.

"Well, you never asked," he said. He was right! In all the years and everything we had been through together, I never once asked him exactly how he knew my name on that first day. I sat for a minute, letting this new information sink in. I didn't ask anything more about it, leaving the mystery to this part of our love story, to be simply a beautiful moment. I thought about the handful of times we ran into each other in Boston before we formally met and how when we did finally meet, it was like I knew him all my life. I especially remembered all the times when he would know how I was feeling, even when we were in two different places. It was remarkable how he knew everything about me and vice-versa.

"Jason Gibson, you surprise me every day," I said and leaned back onto him. "Thank you for all you do for me. You really put up with me, don't you?"

"I would do it all over in a second, except the only thing I would do differently, is love you even more than I do right now," he said and I felt butterflies in my stomach. "I see who you really are, despite that your hiding. I knew at twelve-years-old to come find you and that you were someone really special. There are thousands of Lindsay's in the world, but I was guided to find the right one - you. I feel so lucky that I'm the one who gets to love you. So, I don't put up with anything. I can tell you all of these things, but until you believe it yourself, it will only be words," he paused for a minute and finally continued. "So, to your earlier comment, I say yes. I know you are breathing better since we started this trip – just like you already knew how to do. You have been shining underneath, with strength like I have never seen in anyone before. I love you, Lindsay Marie. I love you for all you do, all you are and all you will be again. Happy Anniversary," he said and kissed me.

"Now let's get you back to my aunt's house. I have a feeling that the next nine months are going to be really rough." Wait. *Say what?* Nine months?

Twenty

"Ladies and gentlemen, welcome onboard Flight 194 with nonstop service from London to JFK. We are currently third in line for take-off and are expected to be in the air in approximately seven minutes time. We ask that you please fasten your seatbelts at this time and secure all baggage underneath your seat or in the overhead compartments. We also ask that your seats and table trays are in the upright position for take-off. Please turn off all personal electronic devices, including laptops and cell phones. Smoking is prohibited for the duration of the flight. Thank you for choosing Delta Airlines. Enjoy your flight," the flight attendant said through the speakers. Her voice seemed extra loud to me.

"Mommy? Can I watch a movie now?" Lillian asked.

"Not yet honey, the movies will come on when we're in the air," I replied and I felt my stomach roll. I had been nauseated since the day before and all I wanted to do was get home and curl up in my own bed. It had been a long two weeks away and while I loved the experiences we had in England, I was very ready to be home. I figured the foreign food was finally catching up to me. I looked over at Jason who was almost nearly asleep already. I rolled my eyes. That man could fall asleep in the middle of Times Square.

Seven long hours later, we touched down in New York and I couldn't have been more relieved. The flight was not terrible but my stomach was still screaming at me. I spent the better part of it with those white, pathetic sick bags under my face, listening to Jason snore. He woke up and looked over at me.

"How are you feeling love?" He sat up and looked at me.

"Oh, you know. Just grand. I nearly blew chunks all over the back of the seat in front of me about nine times, everything on this plane reeks and I'm hot and sweaty. You're driving home!" I snapped at him. Why did it smell so awful? I felt the color drain from my face. It wasn't the foreign food or the flight that was making me so ill. Jason knew what I was thinking because when I looked over at him, he was smiling at me with tears building. He put his finger to his lips to keep me from bursting at the seams. I needed to get to a pregnancy test immediately! However, first, I just needed to get off this damn plane!

A few hours later we were walking into our house and Darcy couldn't have been more excited! She was so relieved we were back. Her tail wagged hard enough to knock down everything in its path as she inspected our luggage.

"Okay, girl, okay," I said to her as she jumped all around me.

"I'm going to take her outside to run off her excitement and energy," Jason said and I nodded. I retreated to the bathroom to shower and then my plan was to park my butt on the couch, possibly forever. After my shower, I felt the rolls of nausea churning again and I almost felt like a flu was coming on because my entire body felt achy. I finally decided to turn on my phone and let all the texts and emails load in from being away. I expected the first ten to be from mom but surprisingly, it wasn't. It was my sister-in-law Melissa whose text came in first:

Hey! I hope England is fun. Funny story. I had a really interesting dream. I dreamed you had another daughter. In the dream, I was at the park and I saw you pulling her out of the backseat. Anyway, just thought that was funny.

I laughed because I felt like everyone knew I was pregnant. Lillian came into the living room, all clean from her shower and sat right next to me. The smell of her shampoo was what finally did it. I got up and bolted to the bathroom where I sat next to the toilet, gagging and groaning. After a while, I heard Jason come in. He helped me splash my face and sat me on the toilet. I reached over and opened the drawer, where one single test sat. We looked at each other and I nearly threw up all over again. A few minutes later, we were staring at a positive pregnancy test. I wasn't sure what to feel, which was odd to me as I stared at the two pink lines.

"That's why you said the next nine months will be rough," was all I managed to say. *Well, duh, Lindsay!* Without answering at first, Jason scooped me up and hugged me so tight. He was clearly excited.

"Of course, I knew. I know everything," he winked at me teasingly. "I'm so happy we're pregnant! Wahoooo!" He cheered, as we walked out of the bathroom.

"Jason!" I grabbed his shoulder, "Shhhh. Let's not tell Lillian," I whispered.

Instead of going back into the living room, we went into the bedroom and sat down on the bed. Jason bent down and kissed my belly, just like he did with Lillian and Joseph. While Jason jumped for joy, I felt sad. For the first time, his loving gesture did not help me. I couldn't believe how sad I felt. What kind of monster am I?

"Hi, little baby of mine. Daddy's here," he said, kissing my belly again. "I love you." He stood up and kissed my forehead. "I'm going to go check on Lillian." I felt like I was in the twilight zone watching him walk out of the room.

I felt numb inside, lifeless even. Maybe I was just tired? I was still holding the test and I looked at it. The two little pink lines stared at me as tears spilled out. All I could think about was my Joseph. Guilt from this thought made the nausea even worse. Then came in the anger and I stood up and threw the test into the garbage. As I paced around the room – anxiety was making me sweat. My thoughts were starting to run wild: *I couldn't be pregnant because what if I get HG again? I couldn't handle that again. What about Lillian? How would she handle another pregnancy with me if I get so sick? Why was I so upset? All I wanted was another baby. We were so ready to have more children, so why was I acting like this?* Joseph. My sweet angel. His little face was all I could see.

My temper increased thinking about him and I started grabbing pillows, throwing them everywhere. Holding my head, I tried to breathe myself to calm down. It didn't work. My lungs felt like they were collapsing when I realized - I didn't want this baby. I wanted Joseph! I stopped dead in my tracks. I can't believe that horrible thought just came into my mind. Guilt again. I was a bad mommy. Feeling defeated within these negative thoughts, I put my hand on my belly and sat down, crying so hard. This innocent new life growing inside of me didn't deserve this. I had never felt so ashamed in my entire life. This wasn't me. Who is this person I had become? This, right here - was reality of a grieving mother.

"Sweetheart, it's okay," Jason voice interrupted my anxious thoughts. He came back in the room, sat next to me and put his arms around me. His strong hold on me felt so good. I softened into his arms, allowing myself to just keep crying.

"I miss Joseph. I miss him so much Jason," I said in between my sobs.

"I miss him, too. It's okay. Just let it all out," he whispered to me, trying to keep everything under control so Lillian didn't hear us.

"I..." the words were there in my heart but the guilt was keeping them locked in my throat. Jason squeezed me tighter. I felt my heart beat faster against the anxiety, fighting for the words to just come out. Finally, they did. "I don't think I have any love left for this baby," I blurted out and nearly got sick on his shoulder, from crying so hard. He stood me up, hugged me and started to rock me from side to side, kissing my cheeks and neck. This comforting movement helped me to eventually calm down. He stayed silent for what seemed like hours, until he finally spoke.

"See, that's the crazy thing about love, baby. It can be found in places you never knew it could be. It can sneak up on you without you ever expecting it to. It's everywhere, in everything and all around us. But you know what's even more incredible?" He paused, stroking my hair. I felt him take a deep breath before he continued, "A mother's love. It conquers things like I've never seen before. It brings miracles. It's always there, never running out no matter how many times she's challenged. You see, darling, there is *already* love for this new baby because that's what your heart was created to do. It's not a matter of having love for this new baby, it boils down to a choice of wanting to give the love that's already there, to her. It's all about choice. You release the fear and allow your heart to do what it already knows how to do or you don't. And this little one?" He laughed, as he smiled in thought for a second. "She's been speaking to you through your courageous, motherly heart for months now. You're already a part of each other. Talk to Layla, my love. She's listening." I gasped. Layla. My dreams! Layla's little face flashed in my mind and I could hear her voice echoing in my head.

Wait for me mommy...

I sat down, completely in awe of his words and the profound truth to his statement. All I could do was just cry. Jason bent down in front of me and let me cry for a quite a while. The dream with Layla on the beach. Lillian, holding her hand and swinging her around and around on the sand. Her face. Her giggles. Even as I still felt so sad, I also felt her energy around me. I put my hand on my womb and felt a chill run down my spine. My Layla was in there.

"Jason, my god. You're right. It must be that little girl in my dreams. I feel it," I finally said to him and he just smiled knowingly at me. I leaned in and kissed him.

"Talk to her, baby," he said. "She can hear you."

Looking down at my stomach, with tears still sliding down my cheeks, all I could do was whisper, "Sorry, sweet girl."

"Mommy? Daddy?" Lillian's voice behind us seemed so loud that it felt like she was screaming. I jumped back, startled. "Mommy? Why did you run so fast to the bathroom before? Are you sick? And why are you two just standing in here hugging and kissing? Gross." This broke my tears and I couldn't help but smile at Lillian.

"Mommy is just really over-tired from all the traveling. It made her stomach hurt a bit," Jason explained and Lillian eyes narrowed. *Oh boy.* I knew our daughter. She had always been one to read right through people and know when lies are being told. She was a lot like Jason.

"Uh huh. Sure, Dad. Because Mommy always gets sick when we travel," she met his response with her quick sarcastic wit. Luckily, she didn't push us much further than that and walked out of the room. Jason went to make dinner and I decided to lay down on the bed and write in my journal.

An hour later, when I heard him call us to eat, I realized a majority of my journal entry were questions. Despite the beautiful moment Jason and I shared, just before Lillian walked in, fear was still lurking heavily behind me. Fear I would lose this baby too. Fear I would get HG again. How do I tell the fear to back off now? Seeing Layla in my dreams, just like I had with Lillian, was nothing short of miraculous. While it should have brought me reassurance and comfort, I didn't fully trust it. No, that wasn't entirely true. As Jason so wisely put it to me, I didn't want to trust it. I didn't want to love her and get my heart broken all over again if I lost her, too. Before I closed my journal to go eat dinner, I decided that for now, it would be easier not to love her. That was my choice.

As I walked into the kitchen to grab my plate of food, I felt small waves of queasiness reel in again. *Here with go again. I hope it doesn't turn into hyperemesis.* As I sat down at the table, trying to muster up just enough strength to fake it for Lillian's sake, I noticed them both staring at me. Green-faced, I smiled and Lillian burst out laughing, followed by Jason.

"Mom, seriously? You look like you're going to hurl. I know you're pregnant. I'm a pro at all of this by now," she said without missing a beat and she looked directly into my eyes, not afraid of my response. It was like a stare down at the table between the two of us. Finally, I looked at Jason helplessly and all he did was shrug, nodding his head.

"Lillian, I literally just found out," I said and before I could finish, she jumped out of her seat, cupping her mouth with her hands.

"So, I'm right? You're pregnant? YESSSS!" Like her father, she jumped up and down in excitement. Maybe she could handle another pregnancy with me after all. She was clearly excited. I tried hard to match her happiness. I didn't want her to know that inside, I was crying for her brother. Lillian was still happily cheering, when I caught eyes with Jason. He knew no matter what he said at that moment, it wouldn't change how sad I felt, so he stayed quiet.

A week later, Jason dropped me off at mom's house. I wanted to tell her by myself. Jason understood and told me he had a major business meeting he had to attend anyway at work. We planned on a fun way to tell the rest of the family, but I needed to talk to mom in private first. After telling her the news, I told her the truth about how I felt. Mom was silent as I told her how scared and sad I was about this pregnancy. Not because I didn't want the baby, not because we couldn't handle or afford it, but because I was terrified to love this baby. Mom hugged me with tears in her eyes of happiness. Like Jason, she was so excited I was pregnant.

"It will be okay," she assured me. "The baby is going to be just fine!"

I thought about my little Layla in my womb, who I know was feeling everything I felt and hearing what I said to mom. That made my heart break for her. She was just so innocent in all of this and I felt like I didn't deserve her. This baby needed a mommy that could give her so much more. I knew Jason was right and that it all came down to a choice of giving my love to her or not. However, it was a choice that I still couldn't make.

My first appointment with the OB was still a few days away and luckily this time, the nausea and vomiting was not as strong as it was with Joseph, at least not yet. Once Hyperemesis with Joseph developed, it proceeded with such intensity! So far, this one was a slow build up, but the fact that it was gaining strength was concerning mom. I admitted to her that over the last two or three days, I wasn't able to keep any fluids down.

"Not as bad as Joseph, yes, but bad enough!" Mom said.

My doctor was not responding to my constant requests that I needed a script for anti-nausea medication early. She explained to me on the phone that she wanted to "wait and see" and refused to do a thing about the increasing nausea, until she saw me at my first appointment. *Wait for what? Wait for me to slide into her office half dead from dehydration?*

After crying and talking to mom for what seemed like hours about my feelings, I also told her how the doctor was ignoring my requests for meds and IV care. That got her to jump into action.

"I hear you. I know Jason hears you. We both understand how sad you are with this pregnancy. However, the first thing we need to do is get your sickness under control. You don't look well Lindsay. You're so pale. How often are you getting sick?" She asked. I couldn't even remember. She had me lay down on her couch and she came in with her laptop. "So, your appointment is not for a few more days? And your doctor is ignoring your calls about how you are feeling? This isn't right." I didn't know what to say in response, so she turned on her laptop, as I began to doze in and out of sleep. "Lindsay, check this out. It's called the HER Foundation. It is an organization all for hyperemesis gravidarum. I'm going to call them. They have volunteers and all kinds of helpful things on their website. I wish we knew about them with Joseph!" Leave it to my mother to find that in a matter of seconds.

Minutes later, she called them. She was redirected to call a man by the name of Lyle, who was the head of the volunteers and left a message. As mom hung up the phone, the room spun and nausea was creeping up on me again. I sat up and before I could take another breath, I ran to the bathroom. There I sat, for a long time, trying to fight back the tears that were building. I didn't even know what the tears were for anymore. Were they for Joseph? Were they because I was sick again? Were they because of the PTSD that was once again, trying to destroy me? Or were they because of the rape itself? The only word that came to me right then was failure. I felt like I somehow, failed this baby already and I was only about six weeks into the pregnancy. Mom's voice was talking to someone on the phone in the living room, which got louder as she came toward the bathroom.

"Yes, she's right here," she said to the person on the phone. "Lindsay, this is Lyle on the phone from that organization. He wants to talk to you." I shook my head. I was too sick to talk. Mom got back on the phone and walked away. My face was on the tile of the bathroom floor, cooling my hot, sweaty skin. My nerves were on fire because HG scared me so much. The word abortion came to my mind. I felt absolutely disgusted as soon as I thought it. How could I have even allowed my thoughts to go there? I hated myself even more now. Mom came into the bathroom.

"Lindsay, he was so helpful. He talked me through a few things. We need a new doctor but right now? We need to get you some hydration." She helped me get up.

She called Jason and within minutes we were on our way to the ER. *Here we go again for real.* My thoughts were on overdrive as we walked into the hospital. With my permission, Jason continued with his meeting knowing mom could handle it. Besides, I had done this song and dance before and just needed to get some hydration. However, walking into the hospital, especially the one I birthed Joseph in, might not have been such a good idea to do without him after all There was no turning back, though. My mom was practically pulling me inside.

Two nurses in the ER at the check-in counter jumped up when they saw me. They remembered me very well and I remembered them all clearly.

"Lindsay!" One of them said and put her hands to her mouth. She knew. "Are you? Oh, my goodness!" Her face lit up like it was Christmas morning. I started to panic as the sight, smells, and sounds of the hospital sunk in, bringing memories back. Grief sliced into my heart. I reached into my purse and clutched my phone, ready to call Jason just in case. Mom helped me take some deep breaths. She was like a charge nurse, talking to the medical staff, so I knew I was well taken care of with her especially.

The same nurse that spoke to me came around the desk, hugged me hard and took my blood pressure. After she saw how low it was, she put me in triage immediately, where another nurse who recognized me came in. Before she did anything, she ran over and hugged me too, telling me that everything will be okay. Their faces were unforgettable due to how many trips to the ER we made within the first couple weeks of Joseph's pregnancy. Many of them came to Labor and Delivery to check on me when we couldn't get the HG controlled at home and I was admitted for many on and off weeks.

"I couldn't even believe it after a nurse in Labor and Delivery told me about your son. I'm so very sorry. You were already gone by the time I went upstairs to see you. I'm not happy you are feeling so sick again, but I'm glad you're here so I can finally hug you. When did you find out?" She nodded towards my stomach.

"About a couple weeks ago, so it's still very early," I answered.

"You poor thing. You look pretty weak, but not as bad as you were with your son. I'll put you in a room right away and have the doctor come in soon. I'll also get some Zofran going in your IV as soon as the doctor sees you," she said. Nurses are amazing. They truly run these hospitals and I would not have gotten through Joseph's birth without them.

The ER was not busy, so the doctor was able to come in quickly. She was a very short and stocky woman that I had never seen before. She rolled up her sleeves and I noticed the dozens of tattoos all up and down her arms. Mom was staring at her arms too. She also had a look on her face, like she was going to eat me for dinner. She had absolutely no bedside manner, picking up my chart to glance through it.

"So, you've been here before, it looks like," she finally said, her voice was deep and heavy and her face never changed expressions. Mom tried to say something, but the doctor quickly put her hand up to stop her. "I'm talking to my patient here." Okay, now I was getting mad. Who was this lady?

"Ms. Gibson, are you married?" Married? Couldn't she read my chart? How was this woman possibly a doctor? I nodded in response, stunned at her stupid question. "I see here that you have done this before?" I stared at her in disbelief. Done "this" before? Did she mean, had HG and deliver my dead son? She put my chart down. "Look, I am going to be rather frank with you. We're giving you hydration and we'll give you some Zofran, but that's all we'll do. I don't want to see you back here. You need to leave here and go to the store. Find a drink, any drink that you like and can get down. Drink 3 liters of it a day. I don't care if it's not water." She sighed out a frustrated breath and I wanted to hit her. "Lindsay, do you even want this baby?" She was staring at me now, without a single change in her face. I met her eyes with the rage of a threatened wild animal. Actually, I came close to attacking her. Was this woman for real? I felt the repressed hot fury flush my cheeks. Only hours before, the idea of abortion came into my thoughts, but now all I wanted to do was protect my baby

"How *dare* you ask me that. What's wrong with you? Are you insane? I refuse to even answer you or partake in this dime store psychological assessment from a doctor who clearly only has half a brain cell floating inside her head. If I could drink anything at all, I wouldn't need to be here, now would I?" I said, clenching my teeth, sitting on my hands. I had a strong urge to punch her. Thank goodness, Jason wasn't here or he would have let her have some of his Irish fury.

"I don't know Mrs. Gibson, would you? I ask because right now, you're not doing a very good job protecting your baby. You need to get it together and take care of yourself. Go see your OB doctor and confirm the pregnancy, find a drink you can drink and get over this sickness you think you need to be in here for," she said and walked out of the room without another word. I was shaking from head to toe in complete rage. I was not a violent person by nature, but it took every ounce of strength in me to refrain from strangling her and I was glad mom witnessed it.

She jumped up and came next to me and tried to hug me, but I was stiff with anger. The nurse came in fast and knew instantly something was wrong. She must be used to this doctor, I figured, but it wasn't in her place to say anything. My body was still shaking, as I leveled a lethal stare at the innocent nurse. I was ready to draw blood with the next person who dared to come near me.

"I want out of here. Get me my discharge papers immediately please, so I can go," I spat through clenched teeth. She nodded and left.

"Lindsay, just stay calm. If you lose it, they will send you to the psych department. We just need to get the discharge papers so insurance will cover this visit and leave," Mom said, holding my hand. The nurse was fast and came in a few minutes later with the papers for me to sign. After I did, she leaned in to hug me and whispered that she understood why I was so upset. I knew there was nothing she could do about it, so we just left.

Once, inside the car, I erupted in tears and cried for a very long time. The doctor's rude questions made me realize how much I already did love this baby, but it also infuriated me because I didn't think I could survive another day pregnant. I couldn't believe I had just encountered this person, who called herself a doctor. Mom had her arm around me, feeling just as angry. My cell vibrated as my OB doctor called. I answered it, hoping that she could help.

"Lindsay, the attending physician from the ER just called me," she said and I finally exploded with anger.

"I'll never step foot inside that hospital again, do you understand me?" I screamed, unleashing all of my anger at her. I told her what happened and she was quiet as she listened.

"Lindsay, ER doctors are not exactly up to date with maternity care. It's also very possible that you have built up having HG again in your mind because of the last pregnancy. This is a very common belief amongst many doctors, in fact," I hung up before she could finish.

That was the last straw and the very last time I ever spoke to her. I was stunned at her insensitive comment. She thought I made it up. Mom thought it would be good to call Lyle and while I was hesitant, not sure what he would say, I decided to call anyway. He answered and in seconds, his understanding and gentle tone put me at ease. My desire to give up was at an all-time high after that visit to the hospital, but he calmed me down. He confirmed that both doctors' reactions to it all was actually very common in the HG world. I was just surprised because with Joseph, she seemed more on top of things, although mom had to tell her how to order home care nurses - so maybe not.

I cried as I listened to Lyle, remembering the day this OB told me Joseph had no heartbeat. It made me so sad to know, that she could not be my doctor anymore. I simply could never look at her face again, after what she just said. Although, I was thankful for all she had done for me, I knew she was not the best doctor for my condition. Lyle laid out all of the facts about how HG sufferers are treated this way. He even validated my feelings of abortion, telling me I was one of many sufferers who struggle with that decision. What hurt the most though, was the fact that some doctors think HG is all in our mind. That was ludicrous to me.

I felt much better after we hung up and Lyle was so relieved Mom found him, but I still had work to do. I needed a new doctor immediately. My phone had several texts from Jason and I needed to respond, but I was completely lost in thought and still trembling. Even worse, the nausea was coming back again, as well as the anxiety. I got out of the car for some air. Mom came out of the car with me and we walked a few laps around the parking lot, trying to settle my nerves. It felt like I was spinning out of control.

"Mom," I said to her after a few minutes, "I'm not sure I can do this pregnancy." I burst into tears and sobbed on her shoulder as she hugged me.

"Yes, you can, and you will do this pregnancy. This baby will be all right and so will you. All I see is white light in your womb. We will get through this." She held me tight.

"I need help," was all I said in response.

Twenty-One

A couple weeks later, I found a new therapist and had a brand-new OB doctor who took over my pregnancy. He got the HG under control and very quickly and was extremely proficient, sensitive, understanding and aggressive in my treatment. He also put me in high risk because of my history with Joseph and wanting me to feel secure with the added visits. I felt much more supported and my anxiety about the HG had lessoned, however, my fears and sadness were still spiraling further into the darkness of despair. I was losing touch more and more with everything that I had come to learn and understand since Joseph's birth. The nightmares were almost nightly now and I was so overtired with stress that I couldn't even remember them when I woke up. Tears never seemed to stop as I kept thinking I was bleeding. I mostly stayed at mom's house during the day, waiting for the hours to pass.

Lyle and the volunteers from the *Her Foundation* continued to be incredibly supportive. Soon, letters flooded into my mailbox of other HG moms with sweet words of encouragement and support. He checked on me almost every day and even sent someone local to come visit me. Her name was Melissa and she suffered severe HG with her daughter years ago. She had even been the one who recommended the OB that I was now using. She came and held my hand as I cried, fixing me broth and kept me company. It was a major switch from the lonely days on the couch with Joseph. There were a couple other women in Connecticut that contacted me, who were also survivors of HG and they all formed a circle of love and protection around me. Hyperemesis gravidarum is such an isolating disease and no one around me really understood the horrors of it, besides Jason and mom who were witnessing it live. Occasionally, Derek sat with me, trying to make me laugh. At least this time with it, I knew what to expect and how to fight it.

Even with all of the added support, it still felt like I could lose control in this pregnancy, at any second. My life felt like a giant maze, running from something or someone. A maze that I had been in since sixteen, running in only one direction to get out. Joseph's birth was a pretty big crossroad in this endless maze. It was an enormous emotional break, showing me that there were different options. He showed me that I have a choice and could get out of this maze a different way. Almost like he was saying, "Follow me Mom!"

Better yet, his death showed me to trust and that once I did get out, I would be safe. It seemed following the love for him, would lead to peace and joy. Those exhilarating minutes of happiness I felt in the hospital room during his birth, was a break through within my traumatized soul. It was like a lightbulb turned on inside of the broken cracks, showing me the door to a new life. A door to the other side of my healing journey, however I was way too scared to see what would happen. I often stood outside of this "door", still deciding if I had the courage to walk through. Now, with this new pregnancy well underway and feeling fragile, I was running in the complete opposite direction, away from Joseph again.

The day of my first visit to the new therapist, I was somewhat comfortable and drugged up on Zofran. Her name was Kate and from the second I saw her, I knew that she could reach me on the level I needed. Jason was waiting outside in the waiting room. I needed to go in alone first. I wasn't sure why, but I trusted my gut and walked into her office without him. Her warm smile was nice, but her calm presence was what struck me. She didn't try and overly talk or ask any awkward first visit questions, she just smiled. Tears began to fall down my face, but I didn't offer her any explanation. She handed me a tissue.

"Tears are good Lindsay," was the first thing she said to me. I nodded as I wiped them away. I took a deep breath and let the words spill out of my mouth before I could stop them.

"I don't..." I said at the end of about ten minutes of rambling. I was stuttering trying to get what I really needed to say, off my chest. "I don't want this baby." It finally came out and I was in complete disbelief. Did I really just say that?

"You don't want this baby or you're afraid to have this baby?" She asked.

"I'm so scared," I began to sob. She sat, calmly and patiently as I cried, while the tears fell down my cheeks and off my face at a rapid speed. Then to my amazement, Kate got up off her chair and came over to me, bending down, and placed her hand on my stomach. The energy I felt from her hands felt so good. My tears began to slow and we sat in silence for a few minutes, with her hands still on my stomach.

"Repeat after me," she finally whispered. "I am safe right now. My body is safe right now. My baby is safe right now. There is love for this baby right now." We sat and repeated this mantra a handful of times as the tears dried on my face. I felt calm and ready to talk again.

After the session was over, I walked out to Jason and all I could do was hug him. Standing there in the waiting room, we hugged for a long time, not caring what anyone thought. Tears of relief came with this hug. Was the sorrow in my heart gone? No. It was still there, gripping me hard, but I felt like I was at least slowing from a full run to a light jog now. Kate was a blessing and became a weekly gift, who helped me ride out the deep pain I felt. Pain that still was screaming at me to fully let it out. I couldn't help but wonder how much more I needed to empty? I was constantly crying now, falling back down this mountain of PTSD and grief. As we walked out to the car, I clenched my teeth, trying to not get sick and fighting off the hatred. Where was this hatred coming from and who was it directed at?

Me.

It was directed towards me. I absolutely hated myself for having such horrible feelings toward my baby.

The next month was filled with distraction. Every pain, twinge or gut feeling that I told myself I was having, led me to constantly believe I was still miscarrying. Even I was aware that those "gut feelings" were a myth from fear and not truth. It was also a busy month trying to keep my HG under control. There were many more doctor appointments than anticipated and Jason was doing everything in his power to be home with me as much as he could. He also jumped right into taking care of me, just like he did before with our son, but everything just seemed so surreal. What was the most eerie was that everything was lining up with the same dates and timing as it did with Joseph the year before. Kate reassured me that having previous PTSD, HG and the same due date as Joseph's pregnancy, probably put my triggers on overdrive.

Jason and mom also made sure to get me as many other kinds of appointments as possible to could to keep me comfortable. Everything from acupuncture to massages, whenever I was having a better day with the nausea. Unlike with Joseph, there were some days I could actually get up off the couch, so I was at least thankful for that. Even though I was well taken care of and blessed to be able to be home resting, it wasn't helping the pain inside. Jason, mom, Kate and all of the doctors and practitioners I saw were not enough to stop the inner demons. At this point, I was just plain confused. What was I not doing? All I do is shed buckets of tears and wake up each day to try again. I made sure to get to my weekly appointment to see Kate. Short of more pills, what on earth was left to do, to help me feel better inside? It wasn't like I was turned off from my feelings anymore like I used to be. I felt everything. Or did I?

In reality, I wasn't. I was just feeling more tense through each agonizing memory and flashback. Each day challenged me in a tug-of-war between complete desolation and the HG. Nothing was pulling me out of this awful place I was in and eventually, I concluded that the beautiful moment in Joseph's birth was too good to be true. Before this pregnancy, I was falling apart, but I hadn't hit rock bottom yet - I was now inching closer.

By twelve weeks, the HG was still hanging on. We just had the twelve-week check-up and the doctor decided to perform weekly ultrasounds, informing me that when I reach the third trimester, weekly stress tests will be ordered too. Looking at my baby on the screen as she wiggled about, should have made me elated, but I wasn't.

"Looks like your rainbow baby in there is doing awesome!" The doctor said and turned off the screen. A rainbow baby is supposed to represent hope after a loss. I had been hearing that term from everyone since I got pregnant again. While I understood why people called it "rainbow", it didn't click with me. Jason and I walked out of that appointment and he was smiling from ear to ear, but I was feeling nothing. My phone was constantly beeping with messages and notifications from past clients and friends asking me daily how everything was going? I just ignored them all. I was so ashamed that I felt the way I did. There was absolutely nothing "rainbow" about this pregnancy and baby. In fact, it was black and white and motionless. I didn't want to connect to this beautiful new life, growing in my womb. I wanted an abortion. This was officially now the second time I thought about abortion. Before I could stop myself, I said it out loud.

Jason was opening my car door when I blurted it out. He grabbed my shoulder and spun me around to face him.

"Lindsay, what did you just say?" He was looking at me dead in the eye.

All I could do was fall apart. I sat down in the front seat of the car and sobbed in my hands, telling him over and over how sorry I was. Expecting him to yell, I instead, felt him wrap his arms around me, loving me without judgement.

"Okay, okay, let it all out. Let's just sit here and let this moment pass. It will pass. You're so scared and confused and sick, how could you not want to do that? I didn't mean to respond that way," he said and even though he was supporting me and my feelings, I felt worse. Not because of him but because of me. I felt like such a horrible person and a part of me wanted him to scream at me for saying it. We finally began to drive home and I dozed off. Car rides were a source of sound sleep for me since Joseph's memorial service, yet what greeted me in my dreams was distressing.

I ran to the door, but he got there first. Slamming it shut, he turned around and faced me. It was just he and I. I was alone in an apartment with a complete stranger, who looked anything but safe. My heart was pounding so fast that it was nearly up and in my throat. I started to back away from him and tripped over the coffee table. Like a hungry lion, he leaped across the room towards me, slamming me to the floor with my arms over my head as he held them. The room heavily spun and I saw white spots. I was so dizzy from hitting my head and my left shoulder was throbbing he smashed it on the wooden floor. Laughing, he stood up to take a long drink of his beer. I tried to get up and he kicked me back down to the floor. I froze, not daring to move again. Whistling, he picked up a bottle of half-drunk vodka and handed it to me. I didn't take it.

"What a rude little guest you are! Come on, have a drink...NOW!" He pulled me up and shoved the glass to my lips, forcing me to drink and I nearly choked on the sting from the strong alcohol.

"Lindsay, wake up!" Jason was shaking me out of the nightmare. I woke up coughing as though I was really drinking the vodka. I could actually taste it in my mouth. We were home and I opened the car door and vomited. I couldn't stop gagging, both from the HG and the nightmare. Jason came out and around the car and helped me inside.

With shaking hands and a foggy brain, I grabbed my phone and called mom in complete hysterics. She answered and tried her best, to calm me down. It didn't work. I was screaming through my tears, trying to explain the nightmare, the doctor's appointment, my feelings and thoughts about abortion. Jason took the phone from me and talked to her. Getting down on the floor, all I could do was continue to sob. Mom told Jason she was going to make some phone calls and within what seemed like a few seconds, she called him back and told him that she contacted an organization by the name of *Hope After Loss* that was here in Connecticut. Someone from there was going to call me any minute. I wasn't sure how I felt about it but I knew that I needed immediate intervention. Otherwise, I was going to end this pregnancy. The phone rang and with every ounce of strength, I answered.

It was the phone call that saved Layla's life.

After hours on the phone with one of their staff members, I was much calmer and my body had stopped shaking. I never told her about the nightmare, but I did tell her everything else. She reassured me that a lot of women with pregnancy after loss feel the way I do and I wasn't a bad mother. Her affirmative words calmed me down.

Mom had been watching Lillian while we were at the doctors and since she still had her, Jason and I laid down on the couch together after I hung up the phone.

He held me tight and I relaxed against him. Just as I was falling asleep, he began to list off every single reason why he loved me. I took a deep breath as I continued to calm myself. We both took a long and, by the grace of God, peaceful nap.

Twenty-Two

Layla Donna was born March 25, 2015 at 10:42 a.m., after what felt like a pregnancy that would never end. She was born large and healthy at 10 ½ pounds, pink and blonde, just like Lillian. Unlike the pregnancy, her labor was very peaceful. Jason and I took hypnobirthing classes and we used those techniques until the end. We had to have a C-section because of her positioning and being stuck in the birth canal. It was a beautiful experience to labor that way, which made the C-section much easier. However, things went south the second she came out.

For the first ten minutes, I went into shock. When I heard her first cries, all I felt was confusion. Was it Joseph? I looked at the nurse and asked her if *he* was all right? The nurse handed Layla to Jason, who held her while the anesthesiologist worked with me to help me come out of the shock while I was being stitched up. I didn't feel any pain nor was I scared; I was just in a weird daze.

Finally, I was able to regain my bearings and Jason placed her across my chest so she could find her way to my breast. As I watched her nurse, I knew something wasn't right. The disconnect that I felt throughout her pregnancy was even more obvious to me now that she was here. It almost felt like an out of body experience. I saw her, but felt nothing. I was completely detached mind and body. We were wheeled into my postpartum room for recovery and all I could do was stare straight ahead. I could not look at my beautiful and perfect, sleeping newborn who was naked against my skin and trying so hard to bond with me.

Once we were inside of the room, I looked out the window and saw that it was snowing. I heard Layla begin to shift and bob her head, looking to feed again. I didn't move or say a word to her. Jason watched me with tears forming in his eyes. He didn't know what to say or how to reach me but he was also not surprised. After we called the volunteer from *Hope After Loss* that day, he knew there was nothing more he could do to wake me up. All he could do was wait. Hiding in my silence throughout the pregnancy gnawed at Jason as he tried to fill the gaping hole that I had fallen into. It was the kind of silence just before a funnel cloud, soundlessly spinning faster and faster; dropped to the ground with a loud crash and consuming everything in its past.

He also trusted that a big change was about to come, so all he could do was give it God, despite how hard that was to do. He remained as calm as he could be witnessing it, trying not to shake me up. In fact, he treated me like a queen, but I felt like I was a peasant. Despite his heroic and very nurturing ways, there is only so much that a person can take. One night, about a month before we went into labor, a heated argument broke out in our bedroom.

"No, Lindsay!" Jason shouted at me. "The girls need you to be HAPPY!" I didn't care what he said, even though, I needed to stop with all of my emotional breakdowns and stay in control. I walked away from him and into our bedroom and he followed.

"Don't you remember the day we found out Layla was indeed a girl? Same for Lillian! We already *knew* they were both girls! All your dreams? Don't they mean anything to you, after a lifetime of all those incredibly miraculous dreams you have had? What about us, Lindsay? Do you think the kind of love we share is just luck? Or how about when your therapist had your mom clear out the nursery a few months back, so you can just sit in it and connect? Remember the first time you found the courage to do that? That *same night*, Layla showed you in a dream what nursery colors she wanted! Don't you see the phenomenon in all of this? What do you think all the wonder is about?" He shouted, grabbing my shoulders. I had forgotten about the nursery dream and the love I felt for the few minutes after I woke up from it. Jason continued, "Love, Lindsay, it's all about LOVE. Stop running from yourself because that is where the love is! All you have to do is be still, baby, in order to handle the fears, the negative and all the ugly things this world can bring. Stop being afraid of your past, your tears and your fears. They're not you! Be calm, be still, and be with God. Most importantly, like Joseph showed you how to do when he died, let your past surface and JUST BE!"

"Stop it, Jason, just STOP IT!" I screamed and asked him to leave the room.

The memory faded from my mind and Layla was now nursing again. I was so tired, emotionally drained and lost that I didn't even feel her latch to my breast. My body started trembling with anxiety and the feeling of wanting to run out of the room overcame me. I detached Layla and handed her up to Jason.

"Take her, Jason," I said to him. He took her and soothed her with his finger. She was clearly upset and still wanted to nurse. I rolled over to my side with tears falling down my face, angrier at myself then I had ever been.

"Show me, God. *If* you're even there, show me what to do," I whispered.

The next eight weeks felt like a blur. Once we got back home, I walked around in a daze. All throughout my pregnancy, we received countless gifts and cards and now that she was born, there were even more. Mom helped me open a lot of them and putting everything away, but there were still many unopened cards. I sat down at the kitchen table one day, staring at the basket that was completely full of them. Jason was in the nursery holding and rocking Layla. While he never seemed to put her down, all I wanted to do was stay away from her. Every time I nursed her, Jason would have to sit right next to me, to keep me calm. While I forced myself to do skin to skin in those early weeks, it took everything inside of me to hold it together while she was on me. Postpartum Depression had found its way into my life. What more could I take?

Postpartum Depression or PPD, made me feel like I was a ghost. My body felt like it was floating from room to room around the house, disconnected from reality and watching my family from a distance. Perhaps it was just me wishing I was dead from the guilt I carried over having PPD with a rainbow baby after a stillborn.

Still looking at the basket, I finally reached for a card on top and opened it. A gift card fell out and when I looked at the words, the first thing I saw was: *She is finally here! Your Rainbow baby is here!* I threw the card across the room and stood up, knocking my chair over. I began to pace around the room angrily. Where was the "hope" that everyone kept telling me I would find? Was Layla a mistake? Lillian heard the commotion and came out from her bedroom. She picked up the chair and the card I threw and came over to me.

"Mommy?" She put her arms around me. "Mommy, what's wrong?" I pushed her arms off me and retreated to my bedroom, slamming the door. I was even slipping away from my Lillian. Eight years of bonding and I felt like I was losing that too. I didn't even know what to do at this point because I felt like I had tried everything. Nothing was working. Little did I know, Layla was about to show me the answer.

A few days later, Jason left early for a meeting at work. He told me he would have his phone glued to him and would be back by lunch time. I was still not doing well and between him and mom, I was never alone. Mom was also at a meeting at work, Lillian was at school and so it was just me and Layla. Alone for the first time and I was very nervous. As a second-time mom, this felt silly to be so scared. What was the problem? I realized I can take care of a baby, but I couldn't take care of myself. I was fighting minute by minute to keep my mental state and my emotions in control, ignoring it as much as possible. I had a brand-new baby who needed my full attention and I didn't need a break down.

The morning started off with minimal drama. Layla had a long feed and was sound asleep. Like Lillian, she was a fantastic sleeper, so that was a blessing in and of itself. Every mother knows how crucial sleep becomes after your first baby is born and so any long stretches of sleep are pure heaven. I knew Layla would be out for a few hours and I looked at the clock. It was just after 9 a.m. and I sighed in relief. Jason would be back sometime after 12 p.m., so perhaps I would make it through the morning just fine.

I walked into the living room with a book and my journal and decided to write for a while and then read, two of my most favorite activities. Both would help to keep my anxiety down and my thoughts from going haywire. I looked down at a basket of the girl's folded clean clothes. Layla's tiny little outfits were on top alongside a pile of clean bibs. Layla was a "spitter," in fact her pediatrician diagnosed her with reflux and so we decided to handle it with a mixture of herbs and diet changes. We went through about a dozen bibs a day, so a smile broke across my face when I saw them. This made me feel stronger.

"Okay Lindsay, you got this. Just stay calm," I told myself out loud. I heard my phone notify me of a text. It was Jason.

Hey baby, you still alive over there?

I smiled again and answered him that the house had not burned down yet. Right as I put the phone down, the room spun.

"Whoa," I said. I grabbed the coffee table in front of me for support and waited to see if another dizzy spell would hit. When it didn't, I laid down with my feet up and decided to put on some meditation music. Closing my eyes to let the relaxing sounds soothe me, I figured the dizzy spell was just hormones mixed in with nerves and feeling so mentally tired. Just then, a strong smell of roses hit me, stronger than ever before. It was so powerful that I sat back up, half expecting to see a fresh bouquet next to me. I turned off the meditation music and looked around the room. Layla's sound machine on the monitor hummed, as a car drove by outside. I took another big breath and didn't smell anymore roses, so I laid back down on the couch.

A calm sensation came over me, which was almost unnerving after so many months of breakdowns. It had been since that day in baby store when I saw that little girl, where I felt this much peace. Instead of putting the meditation music back on, I listened to the sound of Layla's sound machine on the monitor, soaking in this peaceful relief. Suddenly, I felt an all-knowing sense, that everything would be okay and to trust that the strength of motherhood would come again. Postpartum Depression robbed me of that strength with Layla so far.

When Lillian was born, I felt that kind of strength right away. Like any firstborn, they will always be the one who surprises you, with all the challenges of "firsts". There were, and still are, so many "firsts" with Lillian: The first time I heard her cry, the first sleepless night at home from the hospital, the first smile, the first time she crawled or walked, the first time she ate solid food, the first laugh, hug, kiss and the first time I hugged her goodbye when she got on the school bus. I'm still learning that motherhood is an on-going lesson with Lillian. Eight years in with her and I realized, I'm still learning be a mother with her and of all of these "first" experiences. I needed to give myself compassion and stop judging. Layla was my second baby and it didn't mean things would be the same. This awareness complimented the peace inside of me. No two babies are the same after all.

Once a mother is in tune with this powerful motherhood force, she begins to transform. She becomes someone new, as the woman becomes a mother. This is different with each pregnancy and birth. At that moment, I knew that once again, I was being transformed with Layla. In the darkest moments of my life, including this murky season of postpartum depression, I was still changing. What was I still missing then? Why was I still suffering so much?

I heard Layla begin to cry on the monitor, waking up earlier than I expected and snapped out of my thoughts. I got up quickly to get her and even after this incredibly grounding moment, my heart began to pound. Why am I anxious and why is her crying triggering me? Why do I keep flipping from peace to panic – All. The Time? Then, *I lost it.*

"Get your shit together, Lindsay!" I screamed, grabbing a picture frame from the wall in the hallway and throwing it as far as I could. Layla, of course, heard this and was now fully awake, crying louder for me. I stood up and began to walk up and down the hallway outside of her room, trying desperately to reason with myself that everything was okay and Jason would be home very soon. Walking into my bedroom to look at the clock; it was almost 11 a.m. I pulled my phone out from my pocket and texted Jason to come home immediately and dropped it to the floor, without waiting on his response. I knew he would come.

Standing outside of Layla's nursery door, I froze. She was crying so hard now and my tears matched hers as they slid down my face.

Breathing was difficult and the room started to spin again, this time faster. I put my back against the nursery door and slid down to the floor. My life flashed through my mind at a rapid speed, something that had never happened before during any of my previous panic attacks. I put my face in my hands and sobbed uncontrollably.

"Mommy!"

Where did that voice come from? I looked up and no one was there.

"Joey?" I whispered.

I knew it was him. He was here. I couldn't see him, but I felt him with his presence so incredibly strong. My heart was racing at full speed and I knew that something was about to explode in me. Layla kept screaming on the other side of the door. Hearing her cries, broke my heart all over again and in this terrifying and panic-stricken moment, all I could do was clutch my legs with my head buried in them. My demons were relentless. While I had thought about it before, the notion of suicide as an option became real in my mind just then. I was terrified of my thoughts and shame flooded me. How could I let myself think such a thing? Visions of suicide continued to spiral around and around in my head. The funnel cloud, after Layla's birth, had landed. In truth, it was a massive storm that had been spiraling since the rape and it finally crashed to the ground.

Outside, Darcy had erupted in constant barking. She was so protective and in tune with everything that was going on in our family, that she somehow knew I was slipping away into the darkest thoughts of my life. Her persistent attempts to communicate with me snapped me back to the present and stopped any attempts to actually harm myself. I felt a jolt in the pit of my stomach and it was so strong that it prompted me to stand up. I could almost feel a set of hands underneath me, pushing me up. My tears stopped abruptly and I wiped my face, opening Layla's nursery door. Taking a big breath and slowly releasing it, I walked into her room.

Fighting my tears away, I didn't want her to see my pain or cry in front of her. My mission was to feed her and get her back to sleep, to protect her from all that was happening with me. Trying to be her mommy, protect her, and be the wiser one, but it was Layla who was wiser. She had another mission in mind. She was about to finish what Jason, Lillian, and Joseph all had begun. Leaning over her crib, she saw me and she started to calm down. I picked up my precious baby girl up and held her against my cheek, as we walked over to the rocking chair. Astonished at my ability to hold it together at that moment, we rocked and relaxed so she could latch onto my breast. I held my breath. *Stay calm, Lindsay, just stay absolutely calm and still.*

After Layla nursed for a few minutes, I decided to peek down at her. What I saw surprised me. Instead of sleeping, which I expected, she was wide awake and looking directly at me. Startled, I gasped, not just because I was surprised she wasn't asleep, but this was the very first time we locked eyes. We saw into each other's soul. As our eyes met, she reached her tiny hand up and placed it on my face. I wanted to pull back but I didn't and felt her warm hand against my skin. I was completely stunned. Without any thought or attempt to stop myself, I began to cry. Wet tears fell onto her soft skin as she continued to nurse with her hand on my face. This was unlike any other tears I had ever shed. They were tears of release, tears of letting go and surrendering to deeper love. As I cried, I told her how much I loved her and how sorry I was. It seemed that her touch not only offered *release*, it opened my heart to *receive* - an abiding love full of joy and peace. Everything in my life up until this point was in its final unravel. It was almost surreal.

The emotions I was struggling to hold back, not just since her birth, but what seemed a lifetime since I was sixteen years old, came pouring out. I didn't fight it, question it or judge it anymore. I just let the emotions flow through my tears. I cried without a single thought in my mind. I didn't know how long it lasted or when Jason got there, but when I finally looked up from Layla, I realized he was there and felt his arms holding us all together. Layla never moved her hand. With this incredibly powerful gesture, my tiny infant showed me that hope was still alive. Hope comes with surrendering to what just is, in the moment, and that is where my joy still was, waiting for me to let go. Just like Jason had told me to do so many times. I realized right then, that I had the power to *choose* to be in this stillness. However, just like being in the eye of a hurricane, there was one more blow to withstand before I could finally stay in peace. I knew what I needed to do and what was going to happen. I was ready.

Layla fell back asleep and as the tears continued to flow, Jason took her and rocked her for a few minutes before placing her back down in her crib. We went to our bedroom. I couldn't stop crying and for the first time, I didn't want to. I knew now, that Joseph took my hand when I lost him to give me the courage to finally face this demon.

An intense amount of fear come over me, but for the first time, I didn't fight it. I finally understood that I was safe with love all around me. Falling to the floor, I let out the loudest scream ever, as Jason got down next to me, repeatedly whispering:

"You are safe. Love always wins."

I could hear the whistling vibrating through my ears mixed in with loud ringing. The night that my innocence was brutally and violently taken began to flash in front of me, fully replaying itself without one single pause. The sounds of whistling grew louder before it stopped. I heard the voice of my rapist somewhere behind me, calling my name as if he was coming out from the deepest hiding spot of my soul. I looked up as I continued to clutch onto Jason.

Twenty-Three

August 13, 2000

The carpeted stairs were in front of me as I made my way up them and finally to the top. My friend was already inside the apartment and I stood outside of the door, feeling an urge to go back to the car. Instead, I opened it and followed the voices to the kitchen where my friend was with him. His back was toward me and when she looked past him at me, he turned around and I was staring up at him.

"Come on, Lindsay, let's go." My friend handed him something and walked past him. He put his hand on her shoulder, stopping her.

"You go on to the club, let me take Lindsay home for you," he smiled at her. She shrugged and said okay and continued out the door. Before I could even reach the door behind her, he was in front of me, gently closing the door so he didn't startle her to be suspicious. I started to back away from him and tripped over the coffee table. Like a hungry lion, he leaped across the room towards me, slamming me to the floor with my arms over my head as he held them. The room heavily spun and I saw white spots. I was so dizzy from hitting my head and my left shoulder was throbbing he smashed it on the wooden floor. Struggling against his grip, he ripped my clothes off.

A chill went down my spine because I could vividly feel the cold wooden floor beneath my naked back and my left shoulder throbbing in pain as he smashed it to the floor. I heard myself begging him to stop. I was an innocent sixteen-year-old, virgin. My young voice pleading with him became louder, as did his laughter.

"Don't do this to me, please. I've never done this before!" I begged with every ounce of courage I could find. He paused, intrigued by this new knowledge, but it didn't stop him. His hand gripped my throat, the room grew dimmer as I struggled to breathe.

I felt myself floating; the moment my rapist took my body, as I was strangely separated from myself. He had his way with me, the pain of my virginity ripping away and bleeding out the aftermath. He began to choke me harder, enjoying the struggle as I fought to escape. He finally let go and I gasped and coughed to breathe again. I got sick with one final cough and he sat still, watching it all in amusement. He studied my face as I continued to fight to bring air back into my lungs.

Laughing, he got up and began to whistle as he opened a beer and took a long sip. I tried to get up to run, but he kicked me back down, holding me down with a foot on my chest. I froze, not daring to move again. He picked up a bottle of half-drunk vodka and handed it to me. I didn't take it.

"What a rude little guest you are! Come on, have a drink…NOW!" He made me chug it and I could feel the sting of the alcohol going down my throat. I started whimpering. "Aww, you look so scared. Don't worry, because once you're dead, this will all be over. You're just another worthless girl who would grow up and serve this world with absolutely nothing. I'm doing everyone a favor by ending you." His words sliced through me, breaking my heart into pieces.

Dead? I began to cry silently as tears spilled down the sides of my face and my body wracked in uncontrollable shaking. My mother's face was the first to come to my mind and how devastated she would be. I knew he was going to kill me next. *Someone please help me!* I screamed in my head, but no sound escaped me. I was too shocked to move yet. Setting the empty beer bottle aside, he grabbed a half-empty bottle of vodka from me and got back down on the floor. He began to trace his finger around my face, smelling my hair. I couldn't stop coughing as I choked it down.

"Your hair smells good, like an innocent little girl. A virgin, oops! Not anymore!" He laughed loudly. He continued to trace his finger until he got to my heart. "Wow, it's beating so hard. Shhh, just relax, this will be over very soon."

Whistling again, he put his hands back on my neck and slapped me. I saw stars. The image of my mother came back to my mind again. I knew she was most likely frantic now, wondering where I was. Adrenaline began to pump through my veins. NO! He would *not* have his way and do this to her! A flash, from the corner of my eye, raced across my vision. What was that? I felt oddly calm after seeing that.

Out of nowhere, a banging from the apartment above us startled him and he loosened his grip, his face was still inches from mine. My calm feeling vanished and adrenaline replaced it again. Except this time, I was angry. I locked eyes with him, fire burning up my spine. I was ready to fight. The banging continued.

"Funny, that apartment has been empty for months." He let go, stood up and looked up at the ceiling. I struggled, silently gasping for air because I didn't want him to put his focus back on me. My will to live was overcoming me, a will that I never knew I had in me.

"TURN DOWN THAT MUSIC!" A voice yelled, muffled by the floor in between us.

Music? I was so shaken that I hadn't noticed the sounds of the angry rap bursting through the speakers of his stereo until now. He started whistling again, as he made his way to the stereo to turn down the music. Gasping for more air, I tried to get another deep breath in so I could get up. With every last ounce of strength, I could find, I finally got up and ran. I grabbed whatever clothes I could. His laughter loud behind me.

I didn't make it far, only to his bedroom before I slammed and locked the door. After putting my clothes back on, I fell against the door. Blood was all over me. I slid to the floor, with the door against my back and my legs pressed hard on the wall, guarding it as he tried to break it down. I was in a full-blown panic, but my heart was beating more and more with my will to live.

Suddenly, he stopped pushing on the door. He began to tap. *Tap. Tap. Tap.* Laughing to himself, he began to whistle again.

"Look up!" I heard a voice say.

I looked up and saw the landline phone on his dresser. I didn't have time to debate if it was safe to stand up. The whistling grew louder on the other side of the door. I covered my ears to block it out as much as I could. Suddenly, the whistling stopped again. I took my hands off my ears, feeling my heart pounding so hard that it felt like it was nearly inside my ears, about to burst them.

"Lindsay...." he whispered.

He laughed again. Without any more debate, I jumped up and off the door, feeling something powerful push me to the dresser. I turned around thinking it was him and that he got in, but no one was behind me. With shaking hands, I dialed the phone. I heard the comfort of my mother's voice on the other end.

"Mommy, please, help me! Come get me!" Without any questions, my mother was off the phone and in her car. I never told her where I was.

He heard me make the phone call. He knew he lost. But he still laughed with enjoyment because to him, this was all fun and games.

"Ok little girl, you win this time."

"Run!" The voice was louder this time, almost shouting in my ear. I covered my ear in response. Who the hell was talking to me? "RUN NOW!" It said again and another flash dashed across my eyes, nearly blinding me for a second.

With my body violently trembling, I opened the door and leaped out, flying past him while he smiled, holding the bat that was probably meant to end my life.

Outside the air was heavy with August's humidity, but it felt fresh and light to me. I was free. I heard crickets, the kind you hear in the late summer. It brought me back to my childhood days and I felt nostalgic for a moment, wishing I was a child, instead of a victim of violence. I looked over my shoulder, half expecting to see him following me but he wasn't. All I saw was the distant light of a 7-11 down the street, so I started to make my way there. With blood dripping down my legs, I began to limp towards the store.

I saw recycle buckets on the side of the road, waiting to be picked up. It had rained earlier that day so there was some water underneath the contents inside of them. I picked it up and washed the blood off as best I could. Then seconds later, mom's car pulled up beside me. How did she get there so fast? Without knowing how she found me, I saw the look of worry on her face that said it all. There was no time to ponder who guided her to me as I ran to her parked car.

Mom sensed my terror and began yelling, "Lindsay! Lindsay, what happened? Where were you? Oh my god, Lindsay, talk to me!" She begged me to answer her, but I said nothing. Relief began to wash through me, but I didn't feel fully safe yet. I realized I was in her car, but we were still close to him and instantly found my voice.

"Drive Mom! Go! NOW!" I screamed and then sat back against the seat. We drove in silence all the way home, with my body shaking nonstop. Mom's instincts knew to keep quiet in that drive home, so I could regain my sense of control, but she was completely frozen in shock seeing me like this. It was dark so she had not seen the blood underneath my clothes or the bruises that were forming all over my legs and face.

We arrived home and my brother Derek came flying out of the house, with a look of panic and relief that I was home. I ran past mom and into the house, with Derek following. He was first to see the bruise on my face, but he knew stay quiet after he saw the look on our mom's frantic face. Something in him caused him to be calm, which is what I needed from him. I was so afraid to call the police, in fear my rapist would find me again. Derek told mom he would help and quickly got me inside to my room. Once there, he stared at me and as he looked at the bruises and blood, anger filled him.

"Tell me where you were right now!" He demanded and tried to stifle his shouting. I was silent and he grew angrier.

He sighed in frustration, realizing how scared I was. I told him I just wanted to take a bath and so he went to fill the bathtub for me. He sat outside the door of the bathroom, listening as I cried and cried, and the fresh water quickly turned dark with the dirt and blood washing off my body. The evidence of it all vanishing into the pool of water. My mother was in her room, in her own state of fright, pacing and trying to figure out if she needed to call the police and what to do next. She still had not noticed the blood and bruises because if she had, the police would have been at our door already.

After my bath, I laid down and fell asleep within minutes. Waking shortly after, in a full fledge panic, half asleep and screaming. Derek had decided to sleep next to me so he jumped up when I woke. He woke mom and they got me into the backseat of the car. Derek drove, while mom sat in the back with me, racing us to the emergency room!

The worry my mom had, was finally turning into sheer terror as we rushed to the ER, in hopes that someone would help us. Now that I was fully awake again and being admitted, I begged to go back home. The solemn looks on all of the medical staff was not comforting and besides that, my rapist's face kept flashing into my mind. What if he found out I told them anything? He would surely find me and end us all. I decided it was best to just stay quiet.

After they saw the condition I was in, they put me on constant monitoring and my body never stopped shaking. I was in the safety of the ER, but they treated me as though I was the one who did something wrong.

"Tell me right now why there are bruises all over your face, back and legs," the first doctor demanded.

There was no slow warm up with this doctor. He was straight to the point and it silenced me even further. They asked my mother to leave the room and began to question her, as if she was the one who put those bruises there. They also refused to let my brother come in with me, even after I begged them to.

"I want my mom and brother in here!" Was all I kept saying over and over.

They continued to ignore me. I felt invisible. When my initial bloodwork they took came back, things became even worse. In the hands of doctors, whom I thought would protect me, became an extension of my nightmare.

"Speak up!" The same voice that was with me in my rapist's apartment, suddenly came back, the minute I was alone. I looked over to the door, where I thought the voice was coming from.

"Hello?" I called out. No one was there.

Minutes later, the doctor came back in, looking suspicious. Behind him was a female social worker and the police. The vodka that my rapist forced me to chug, was found in the bloodwork. They both stood on either side of me.

"I want my mom and my brother," I said to the social worker, in hopes that maybe she would let them in. She ignored my request too.

"Lindsay, you need to start talking about what happened to you tonight. You have bruises all over your body and alcohol in your blood. Your mother is requesting a rape kit test, but I haven't heard from you if that's necessary," she said to me, without a hint of compassion in her tone. I stayed completely silent and looked away. I focused instead on the clock on the wall in front of me.

"Lindsay," the doctor began. "If you don't start talking, we are going to call in the psychiatrist from upstairs. We want to help you, but you'll have to tell us what happened. Did you just drink at a party and fall down? Are you afraid you'll get into trouble with your mom? She gave us the name of the apartment building she picked you up in front of, but we want to know exactly which apartment you were in," he said. I wanted to scream at him for his ignorance. Fall down at a party? Oh, how I wished that was what really happened. I began to cry and my body shook even harder. They both left, not saying another word to me

When the psychiatrist came in, I turned my back to him as if he wasn't even there. Every question he asked was met with silence. All of his questions were the same as the others. He too, wanted to know which "party" I drank too much at. Ignoring him made him angry and he nearly slammed the door when he walked out. My visit in the hospital turned me into a victim all over again in a healthcare system that didn't know how to help me. I was labeled a teenager with a drinking problem and sentenced to an outpatient rehab by the very people who I thought would save me.

Too defeated to defend myself, I agreed to the sentence, just so I could leave. My life as I knew it was over. How did I go from an innocent high school girl who loved to go to the movies, have sleepovers with her girlfriends, watch basketball games, and play soccer, to this? Hospital staff didn't save me; they didn't protect me. They labeled me guilty and sentenced me to a year of alcohol and drug rehab. With my body bruised, broken and in pain, I narrowed my eyes at the hospital personnel and a deep, relentless anger began to stir within. Clenching my jaw as an inner wall, built with rage, embedded itself around my heart. Mom had always told me that if I was hurt, the doctors and nurses would help me, but I wasn't safe there either. As I continued to stare at them, my spirit completely shut down. I fell into a black hole, which is where I stayed trapped in silent denial for thirteen years.

Mom scrambled to get discharge papers, signing me off to outpatient rehab five days a week and crying with frustration. She knew intuitively that something awful had happened and no one could reach me, not even her. As I laid in the hospital bed, waiting for discharge, my door opened and a new male nurse came in. I turned my face away and hoped he would do whatever he needed to do and just leave.

Instead of doing vital checks, he sat down on the edge of my bed. I turned and glared at him. His eyes were a brilliant violet-blue, piercing through mine and I gasped. It was as if his eyes could see into my soul. His face was flawless and I could not help but stare at him. He smiled and reached for my hand, but I quickly withdrew it. Turning over in my bed away from him, I heard him then say the oddest thing.

"Lindsay, say something to them. Don't be afraid." *Say something?* "Tell them. Right now." He urged me and this made me madder. He was just another nurse sent in to try and get me to tell them what happened. He wasn't done. "We helped you get out. *Say* something," he said again.

My mouth fell open, but no words could come out. Helped me get out? Who was this man? I turned to look at him again, wanting to ask him what he meant. However, when I turned, he was gone. Another female nurse came in.

"Ok hun, let me do one more check before they let you go home," she said.

"Where's the male nurse? Can he come back?" I asked.

The nurse wrapped the blood pressure cuff around my arm, looking confused as she replied, "No male nurse on this floor."

"That's not possible, I just saw him. He was even wearing the same blue scrubs as you," I said. She continued to take my blood pressure, looking at me like I was completely stoned, but I was quite sober. "No, there isn't a male nurse that works in this entire department." She finished and left after that. *Great*, I thought, *she probably thinks I'm a crazy, drunk teen too.*

As we left the hospital, the mysterious male nurse's words faded and disbelief took over again. I just couldn't believe all of this happened to me. I was so cold and numb. My heart was shattered and an icy, blank emptiness had settled in it; where it once had such innocence, love, and trust. I could hear my footsteps walk against the sidewalk to the parking garage and mom was crying and wiping her eyes. Everything around me began feel far away.

I felt Jason's hand gripping mine and I opened my eyes. My throat stung with dryness and was hoarse from the screaming. Coming back into the room from the full memory of that horrible night, he was very calm. Despite how scared he was, he never let go of me.

"Just stay still, sweetheart, and breathe," he said to me gently and pulled me closer. My body continued to tremble through the aftershocks of the flashback.

"Do you know what just happened?" He asked, barely in a whisper.

"The eye of the storm," we both said together and I looked at him amazed.

"And don't you see?" He smiled at me before he continued. "That even though the memories are there, it's over. That night is over. It has been over. You are safe. You are here. You are still you."

"Jason," I tried to respond, but paused, not knowing what to say.

"Shhh. Just breathe. Don't try and control the memories. Let life revolve around you and not you around life," he said as he held me tight. "Choose to be in the center of your life, always. Just like right now."

Suddenly, the realization of his words became clear. I stayed perfectly still, just as he told me to and we both grew completely quiet. I felt the cool drips of sweat sliding down my back and forehead. My body relaxed into his arms. It felt as though my anxiety was melting away, as my body stopped shaking. In fact, I was so calm, it was almost unsettling. It was like nothing just happened.

This tranquil moment of silence between us was the groundbreaking realization I needed. I finally understood. I was the one choosing my life, not him. Not the man who hurt me. No one was to blame for my pain, except me. I surrendered and the hostile winds of my past finally blew over me. That is what my stillborn son taught me in the birth room. Choose life. Choose love and that this is what I have been struggling with all this time. I looked up at Jason with new eyes.

"Be Still and Know that I am God" Psalm 46:10

The cardinal chirped louder as Lillian continued to splash through the water. I heard her laughter and smiled. Layla's cooing voice on the monitor stirred me and I opened my eyes. Turning on the screen, I looked at her. She was sitting up and clapping her hands. My heart burst with love and I got up to get her. I walked up to the door of her nursery and paused, listening to her soft voice and little giggles. I took a deep breath to soak in the present moment. Hearing her and Lillian's laughter brought so much happiness to my heart. When I opened the door to her nursery, I was taken back by what I saw. Layla was standing in her crib, leaning over the side and pointing to something in the corner of the room.

"What is it baby?" I asked her and picked her up. She immediately put her head down on my shoulder and I breathed in her fresh baby smell from her hair.

I sat down in the rocking chair with her, silently, hugging each other so tight. I felt tears of gratitude with Layla's arms around me. It has taken me so long to get here with her, something I wasn't sure I could ever do. I took a few deep breaths to really draw in the moment. She finally pulled back and put her hands on my face and a deep sense of love and appreciation melted my heart. She pointed again. A chill, so strong ran down my spine. I wasn't sure what prompted me, but I knew to just say it.

"Hi, Joseph," I whispered and Layla's face lit up.

"Joe," she said, her mouth moving in a big "O" to try and get the name right. Tears sprang to my eyes and I smiled, nodding my head.

"Yes, sweetheart, yes!" I said and she hugged me tightly again. I carried her downstairs so she could play in the sprinklers with her sister.

It had been a year since I remembered everything from that night in the summer of 2000 and Layla was growing up fast. I changed her into a bathing suit and watched her waddle up to her sister, her little toddler legs trying to keep up. Lillian scooped her up and they both erupted in laughter as the water sprayed them and I laughed too. It is at times like this that I can't believe I am present, alive and laughing with pure joy. That day, crying outside of her nursery was the closest I had ever come to ending my life. Seeing my girls laughing and loving life only reminds me of the power of love when we allow ourselves to just be. The beauty that is present every single day, every single minute, comes through no matter what is happening, if we open our eyes and our hearts and surrender. It is a choice, but when we do, what we find is only love. Does that mean our grief and pain goes away? No, it doesn't and it isn't supposed to.

Grief weaves through the souls of anyone who has lost something precious. The loss could be of a loved one, pet, relationship, career, health or even your own self. The list of what we can lose goes on and on, and no one is exempt from it. Grief rips through all our facades with no mercy exposing everything we try to hide from. Sometimes we get stuck in parts of grief. Sometimes we can actually believe we are grief, but while grief is real, we must not become it. What I failed to see before, was that I was already stuck in grief, even before I lost my son. I spent years silently mourning the young girl who vanished at sixteen in one single act of violence, by a monster who tried to kill me. In one hour, I had been robbed of my youth and my innocence and it seemed easier to just deny that night ever happened. This was what kept feeding my anxiety for so many years.

I didn't recognize that my anxiety was simply grief trying to talk to me. Anxiety was pointing me to move through the full circle of grief, so that I could experience it, but not become it. The pain of losing my innocence had shaken me so hard that my sense of who I was had been buried and frozen all these years. I was afraid to let go of my anger for many years because a part of me wasn't sure I could embrace the girl inside of me, who was screaming to be free. It was easier just to be angry, or sad, or guilty or in denial than to let grief guide me. Grief begs us to heal us and sets us free to be more fully alive. I never knew this was even possible. Grief is *not* the enemy. I didn't learn until I lost Joseph, that grief could set me free to become who I was meant to be.

Has it been easier since the full memory of the rape? No. It hasn't. However, it *has* been joyful. The memories of that night haven't gone away and neither has the day Joseph passed. Both of those traumas are still very clear in my mind. How does one move forward after being knocked down like that? One hour, one day at a time. Grief taught me how to allow these hard experiences to exist, while still choosing love, and that those experiences were *not* me. Standing back up after the ugliness of that night all came back, was like being in a boat in a raging storm in the ocean and suddenly falling off. Only to realize that I had a life jacket on and could see the peaceful shore just ahead. All I had to do was swim.

I chose to swim to shore after thirteen years of being tossed around on the boat of denial. Thirteen years of trying to control my life, holding on tight against angry waves of despair, hoping the boat would somehow take me back to safety. I was terrified to let go and let life unfold. Plunging into a stormy sea scared me beyond belief. Surrendering felt like a cop-out to me. I wasn't about to give up the safety of my boat, as it was the only place I knew to be.

Trauma inhibits us from our ability to choose life. It constantly reminds us of what happened, keeping us trapped in those parts of grief such as denial, fear, anger and guilt, making it almost impossible to feel true peace. For me, I didn't know that there was a way out of PTSD and that leaving my safe little boat would get me there. My heart was so blocked that I couldn't find the peace and joy that was *still* within. I was always so terrified to feel the pain of what happened to me. I didn't want to know what would happen if I reopened those wounds. I didn't want to show my daughters what would happen if I surrendered because, God forbid, what if I never got up again? But, to my surprise, when I finally let go, I didn't drown. Instead, I went safely to shore.

Once on dry land, my spirit soared high into the loving arms of divine love. Life supported me without judgment, or control or fear. It is all so new and exciting for me! Allowing my emotions to surface and fly free as they needed, began to heal me and even when triggers still come, I am able to find the ground again. The tears were simply the water that the soil of my heart needed, in order to cleanse my body and mind, so my spirit could continue to open like Mother Mary's signature rose. I was able to reach another part of me, not the just the damaged young girl, but my *true* self: An ever unfolding rose whose beauty has always been who she was created to be. The roses throughout my life had been clues, yet the despair and fear I tried desperately to control, kept me from listening to what those clues meant. Letting go allowed me to see that the beauty of the rose was, in fact, the same beauty within me, reaching for the light that it needed to unfold fully.

I can now tenderly, embrace the fragile young girl with the stronger, beautiful woman I have become. Love is beautiful and was all around me, softening my heart as I fell into the waves of the tossing seas of life. And love surrounds all of us, even as those tumultuous waves of life threaten to drown us on this glorious place called earth.

Love's power became stronger than I ever thought possible. It is unshakeable. Joy isn't the same as happiness. Happiness just happens. It is circumstantial. Joy is eternal and a deep inner resource given to all of us when we reach for it, in the quiet places of life. Its abiding presence is richer than anything I own or have, even my own children.

Joy is my *peace*.

Joy is my *stillness*.

Joy is my *power*.

Joy is the *quiet space* - between this moment and my past; this is where our true divine nature is found. Who we really are is not what happens to us, but who we are when *we just be*.

The crippling anxiety and flashbacks that kept me down all those years began to fade away against the backdrop of forgiveness and surrendering to what is present. Falling to my knees and surrendering my life to love gave me the strength to forgive the one person I thought I could never forgive: My rapist. I lived each day after the rape shackled to the chains of hatred and resentment. I hated him and hated myself, but I think the resentment was worse than the hate. Resentment held me down for too long, its bitterness locking in the horrors of what happened and not allowing me to be free.

Losing Joseph only intensified the resentment. Mother Mary showed me that love was present during his birth and while I briefly felt her peace, anger and guilt swallowed me again. For a long time after his loss, I refused to accept that my love for him was redirecting me to begin the steps of facing my truth. I was terrified of my feelings because I might have to open the pain again, but my heart burst wide open when Joseph died.

Though I didn't know it, the days I birthed him were the worst and best days of my life. The grief of losing my son and remembering the night of the attack, were the beginning of cleansing my soul of resentment, hatred, shame and guilt in the messy heartbreak of love.

For years, I never thought I was a capable woman. Love taught me that I am capable. I am capable of being a mother to my girls and to being Joseph's mother too. My child in heaven showed me that I am capable of loving deeper and wider than ever before. It is what supports all that I do at home and in helping others by offering what I've learned - to surrender and forgive. This is how to restore joy again after trauma. In this way, the love of Joseph perseveres, "mothering" the world, with his short and powerful legacy through me.

I began to view my attacker in a different light within the protection of my son's glorious, God-given love. For the first time, I saw him from where *he* stood in life and realized that was where the forgiveness was needed. I didn't forgive the act of rape and violence, but the person himself. Clearly, love was not present for him because violence is born from violence. Hate begets more hate. Perhaps, someone was violent toward him as a child. Who knows? But when I was finally able to see that, I could separate myself from the violence. I saw this man's own tortured soul and brokenness and I couldn't stay in hate any longer. Joseph's short mission on earth was accomplished. The Spirit of love, working through him, gave me the ability to find forgiveness, not only for the man who attacked me, but more importantly - *myself*. I forgave myself for choosing to stay in the destructive pain for so long. I was free.

The wind whipped across my face and the cardinal flew away. I watched him fly up and into the tall trees in our backyard. I stood up, reaching my arms over my head and filling my lungs with the clean, fresh air. Looking up at the blue sky, Oma's voice whispered in the clouds. I smiled at her.

"Oma, fly free with me now, let's dance!" I called. Warmth began radiating down my arms and legs, grounding me, filling me with light. Love had set us both free from decades of being in chains.

A gust of wind blew through my hair. *"Mommy,"* a voice whispered in the breeze. I knew that voice and my whole body tingled. My Joseph. I felt him near, just like in Layla's nursery only minutes before. I heard my girls laugh as they twirled and danced in the sun. Joseph was with them too, holding onto them in the bond of love, that has no beginning and no ending.

Somewhere in the distance, in a place where our souls unite after we leave this earth, my young, sixteen-year-old self was swaying along with their laughter. Dancing with my Oma, just like she taught us - only this time, not in secret. Instead, they danced like everyone is watching, soaking in love, where we are all free *to just be*.

Yes, he taught me a new kind of love. My son. My angel above.

Epilogue

"All that I had and all that I was is nothing, compared to all that I am through knowing love, which is everything." - Philippians 4:7-8

To the very end of writing this memoir, I realize that we are always receiving love. It's a continuous journey that keeps hope alive and joy present. Choosing to love is a moment by moment decision, in which we can tap into and release its potential - anytime. Joseph's love shows me each and every day, how to open and receive this eternal love that never ends.

Love – is *everything*.

In Loving Memory of:

Margot Ilse Bernhard-Cassity (Oma)
November 30, 1923 – March 5, 2010

Agnes O'Driscoll (Granny)
May 23, 1920 – December 10, 2013

Darcy Gibson (Our Beloved 'Fur-baby')
July 20, 2005 – March 14, 2016

Joseph Michael Gibson
Born into Heaven on November 12, 2013

A Special Thanks

My Jason – our love sings with passion and grows every day. I still get butterflies when I look at you. Thank you for your endless patience, support and always spoiling me – and knowing just when to close my computer so I can get to bed.

My Lillian – my fearless, first born daughter. You came into my life by surprise, gracing your daddy and me with your incredible charisma. You are one of the strongest people I know, as you never failed to reach for my hand through all of my tears. Thank you for always making me laugh, no matter what.

My Joseph – my angel above. Thank you for reminding me what love really means and opening my eyes to all that I was missing. You are my hero, my sweet boy.

My Layla – my incredibly strong, sassy and ever so loving second daughter. Thank you for showing me how to receive love again and providing me with you healing touch every day.

My Mother – for never giving up, even when I wanted to. For raising me to always know what love is, even when it became lost to me and showing me how to never be afraid to dig deeper.

My brother Matthew – for being the "big bro" in my life and being the first man to show me love and care.

My brother Derek – for being my best friend through all of the terror, the tears, and teaching me about life through your eyes.

Melissa Mirabilio – to my "sissy in law" whose creative eye has captured the essence of who I am and whose logical mind balances my creative mind, since I was a little girl.

To my family that are stateside -I love you all and thank you for always believing in me.

To my "family across the pond" - thank for your love and support and raising one heck of a man!

To my friends in this book – I would not be where I am today, if each of you did not play a part in my journey as you did. Each and every one of you pulled me through some of the darkest times in my life and never gave up on me. Time passes by, we grow older and distance may separate us, but nothing can take away the special bond that I have with you all. Thank you from the bottom of my heart for your friendship.

To those who have guided me, coached me and offered your gifts to help me heal: Reverend Dr. Rochelle Stackhouse, Kate Gorman, David Beatty, Victoria Jeter, Sandra Saren, JoAnn Livolsi, Mar De Carlo, Natural Health Associates, Women's Health Care of Trumbull, CT, Hope After Loss, HER Foundation and Healing in Harmony Center.

About the Author

Lindsay is an Author, Motivational Speaker, Birth Psychology and Maternity Health Specialist & Natural Mommy Blogger. She is the author of "Just Be Guide: Steps to Healing" – inspiring and empowering women to find inner healing after trauma through therapeutic writing and steps to forgiveness and restoring joy. When she isn't teaching, blogging and writing, Lindsay spends most of her day mothering her two young "blondie" daughters and her angel son above, whose love shines through in her every day. She is married to her husband, Jason, who still makes her blush, Irish brogue and all. www.lindsaymariegibson.com